M000119657

CiTY·SMaRT™
GUIDEBOOK

Kansas City

Michael J. Flynn
Linda Kephart Flynn

686-405-0377

John Muir Publications
Santa Fe, New Mexico

John Muir Publications, P. O. Box 613, Santa Fe, New Mexico 87504

Printed in the United States of America.
First edition. First printing April 1997.

ISBN 1-56261-348-0
ISSN 1092-0765

Editors: Kristin Shahane, Nancy Gillan, Dianna Delling
Design: Janine Lehmann
Graphics Coordinator: Tom Gaukel
Production: Janine Lehmann, Nikki Rooker
Cover Design: Suzanne Rush
Maps: Julie Felton
Typesetter: Diane Rigoli
Printer: Publishers Press
Front Cover Photo: Convention & Visitors Bureau of Greater Kansas City
Large Back Cover Photo: Country Club Plaza Merchants Association
Small Back Cover Photo: Convention & Visitors Bureau of Greater Kansas City

Distributed to the book trade by
Publishers Group West
Emeryville, California

CONTENTS

MAP CONTENTS

HOW TO USE THIS BOOK

Whether you're a visitor, a new resident, or a native of Kansas City, you'll find the *City•Smart Guidebook: Kansas City* indispensable. Authors Michael J. Flynn and Linda Kephart Flynn bring you an insider's view of the best Kansas City has to offer.

This book presents the city in six geographic zones. The zone divisions are listed at the bottom of this page and shown on the map on the following pages. Look for a zone designation in each listing and use it to help you locate the listing on one of the zone-specific maps included in each chapter.

Example:
THOMAS HART BENTON HOME
3616 Belleview, Kansas City
816/931-5722   CS

Zone abbreviation = CS
The museum location will be shown on the Central/South Kansas City map unless otherwise noted.

Kansas City Zones

DA–Downtown Kansas City Area
Bounded on the north by the Missouri River, on the east by I-435 to Independence Avenue, then west to Hardesty, south to 31st, west to the MO-KS state line.

CS–Central/South Kansas City
Bounded on the north by 31st St., south on Van Brunt Boulevard to Blue Parkway to I-45 to Hwy. 71; bordered on the south by 135th St., on the west by the state line.

JO–Johnson County
This area covers the entire area of Johnson County, Kansas.

NR–North of the River
This area covers the entire region north of the Missouri River, including Kansas City North, North Kansas City (a separately incorporated town) and KC International Airport.

EM–East Metro
This area covers KCMO east of Prospect Street plus towns east of the incorporated city such as Independence, Raytown, and Lee's Summit.

KCK–Kansas City, Kansas/West
This area covers Kansas City, Kansas, and other points in Wyandotte County.

GREATER KANSAS CITY

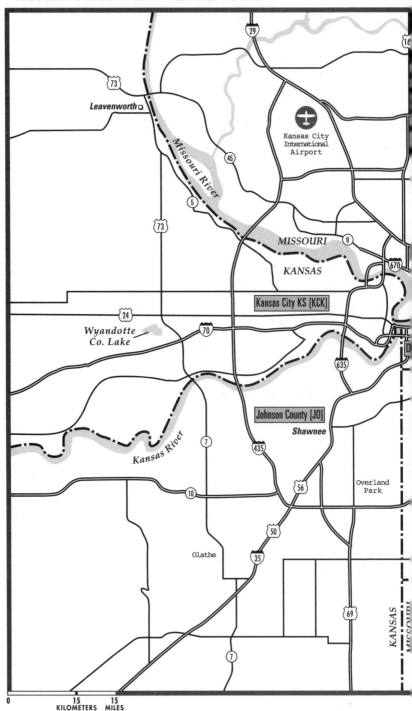

Leavenworth

Missouri River

Kansas City International Airport

MISSOURI

KANSAS

Kansas City KS [KCK]

Wyandotte Co. Lake

Kansas River

Johnson County [JO]

Shawnee

Overland Park

Olathe

KANSAS

0   15   15
KILOMETERS   MILES

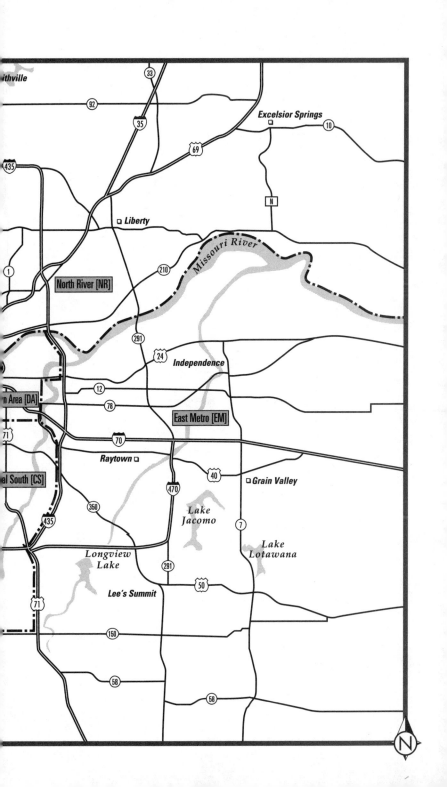

1

WELCOME TO KANSAS CITY

The swift current rushes a cottonwood branch downstream, hinting that the river merely passes this bend on its hurried way to other places. But no, the surging, swirling, roiling stream has hugged this precipitous bank as long as humans can remember. It's what made Kansas City. It will remain forever entwined in the city's history and future.

From the Missouri River, downtown Kansas City rises to the south. Brick and block, stone and stucco, the modern skyline sits atop upright bluffs that poke and prod as though reaching for a better view of the mighty tide that gave it life. From the river, the city and its sisters spread in all directions, crisscrossing two states in geographical abandon.

Since its waterborne beginnings, the Kansas City metro area has become a sensory delight: boulevards lined with majestic oaks and sweet-smelling sycamores, fountains that sound a welcoming gurgle, and architecture that evokes a sturdy foundation for the ebbs and flows of life. A place that's entertained everyone from Hurons to hoodlums, today's Kansas City beckons with a powerful combination of spontaneity and stability, amusement and aplomb.

"Kansas City is one of the best American cities of all," says author David McCullough, who spent ten years visiting the area to research his Pulitzer Prize–winning book *Truman.* "It has its own characteristic spirit that's open and friendly and energetic and unpretentious and lively."

It's also awash in color. In the spring, Kansas Citians emerge to tend their tulips, plant their peonies, and transform their city into a veritable garden. Throughout the seasons, the city's famous boulevards and parks come alive with new floral displays, leaves changing hue, and colorful decorations that highlight the natural beauty that's endemic to the area.

Ten Best Things about Kansas City, Missouri
by Mayor Emanuel Cleaver II

1. The **People**: the friendliest and kindest you'll ever meet.
2. The **Landscape**: rolling hills, tree-shaded parks and boulevards, interesting architecture.
3. The **Fountains**: more fountains than any city in the world (except Rome).
4. The **Neighborhoods**: vibrant neighborhoods and neighborhood organizations from the Hispanic West Side, the Italian/Asian North End, Hyde Park, Brookside, Blue Hills, Armour Hills, and more.
5. The **Jazz**: America's classic music form grew up in Kansas City and still thrives.
6. The **Food**: more than just the steaks and barbecue for which the city is famous.
7. The **Art**: with the Nelson Gallery, Kemper Museum, Art Institute, and a vigorous 1-percent-for-public-art program.
8. The **History**: Harry Truman, Tom Pendergast, Francois Chouteau, Charlie Parker, Count Basie, Jesse and Frank James, Jackie Robinson, Jean Harlow, Buck O'Neal . . .
9. The **Economy**: vibrant and growing, with new corporations like Harley Davidson and Gateway 2000 locating here.
10. The **Future**: a city growing and on the move.

First-time visitors to Kansas City often wonder what happened to the flat prairie, the lowing cattle herded through vast stockyards, the dusty roads filled with gangsters they somehow expected. Instead, they're greeted by an unexpectedly craggy topography, a singularly congenial citizenry, and a destination that's filled with surprises aplenty. Welcome to Kansas City: one of America's best-kept secrets.

Kansas City History

Long before pioneers arrived with their wagons, dreams, and supplies, the Kansas City area was home to several Native American tribes. The Hopewell Indians occupied a village on what is today called Line Creek in Platte County until climatic changes forced them to move in about A.D. 400. Later, between around A.D. 800 and 1300, the Mississippian Period Indians built pole houses overlooking the Missouri River in what is now Northeast Kansas City. The region's famous Indian tribes—the Kansa, Iowa, Omaha, Osage, and Missouri—all descended from this group.

French explorers were the first Europeans to visit the Kansas City area in the early 1700s. Etienne Veniard de Bourgmont, a French soldier of fortune, returned several years after his first visit to establish Fort Orleans in what is now Carroll County. French trappers loved the area; St. Louis' Chouteau family, in particular, was influential in settling the area by setting up a post for its American Fur Company.

In 1821, William Becknell launched a trading expedition to Santa Fe, New Mexico. The journey proved so successful that the Santa Fe Trail became a commercial superhighway. Traders would stock up in Independence, the trail's outfitting headquarters, then embark on the 40- to 80-wagon selling ventures. By 1849, Westport, a town founded by John McCoy 10 miles to the west, had become the chief post for equipping Santa Fe Trail expeditions.

Indeed, Westport was initially the area's most desirable development site. But in 1838, 14 businessmen led by McCoy formed The Kansas Town Company to bid on riverfront land that encompassed what is now downtown. Taming the limestone cliffs and canyons that carved this area just south of the Missouri River presented massive challenges, leading many to call the settlement "Gully Town."

During the 1860s, Kansas City welcomed countless travelers who arrived by water. In fact, the Missouri River was so popular that some 60 boats regularly made the journey between Kansas City and St. Louis, landing at the Town of Kansas. Passengers then traveled 5 miles to the bustling hub at Westport.

Shortly after the Civil War, cattlemen in the Southwest realized they needed to move their herds closer to the Chicago market for slaughter. Centrally located, Kansas City seemed the logical choice. Businessmen opened the area's stockyards to accommodate the herds. In 1869, town fathers wrested railroad attention from their surrounding competitors by christening the first span across the Missouri River. The Hannibal Bridge cemented Kansas City's importance as a transportation hub.

By 1900, visionaries had transformed Kansas City into a civilized society. Parks and boulevards had been planned and built, and a convention hall opened to host the 1900 Democratic Convention. After the hall burned in April of that year, Kansas Citians determined they could rebuild it in three months. Their success mobilized the city for future projects and launched what everyone called the "Kansas City Spirit."

Throughout the Twenties and Thirties, Kansas City was home to gangsters and speakeasies, art deco architecture and jazz. With World War II came economic diversification, as manufacturing companies poured into the area. By 1945, Jackson, Wyandotte, and Clay Counties had received 1 percent of every U.S. war dollar.

Through the next two decades, Kansas City began to sprawl in every

Missouri River flood of 1903

direction. An ambitious growth plan brought the area north of the river within the city limits. Infrastructure and architectural improvements continued throughout the Sixties and Seventies—and well beyond.

Always proud of their willingness to tear down, build up, and charge ahead, Kansas Citians continue to look for inventive ways to make their town more livable. An expanded convention center that promises to bring new groups to the area, a renewed appreciation for what a vibrant downtown could mean to the city, and a concerted effort throughout the area to attract new corporate citizens all hold promise for Kansas City's future. Still,

A.K.A. Possumtrot, Missouri

Although the first European settlers arrived in Kansas City in the 1820s, the town wouldn't officially bear the name it uses today for another 50 years. Abraham Fonda, a member of The Kansas Town Company—a group of merchants who purchased what is now downtown Kansas City, Missouri, from the Prudhomme family— wanted to name the place "Port Fonda." Others opted for "Possumtrot." Finally, they decided to adapt the name of the Kansa Indians, calling their home the Town of Kansas. Until 1889, however, the town was also referred to as "West Port Landing," "Chouteau's Town," and "Kawsmouth."

Kansas City Time Line

Etienne Veniard de Bourgmont, the first European to see the Kansas City area, passes it while mapping the Missouri River, believed to be an inland route to the Pacific Ocean.	**1713**
Meriwether Lewis and William Clark spend three days in the area on their way up the Missouri River to Oregon; they return two years later.	**1804**
Frenchman Francois Chouteau establishes his American Fur Company trading post on the waterfront.	**1821**
President Andrew Jackson signs the Indian Removal Bill, opening Missouri to mass migration by white settlers.	**1830**
The Kansas Town Company bids $4,220 for 257 riverfront acres owned by Gabriel Prudhomme, a Canadian killed in a barroom brawl.	**1838**
Missouri grants a charter to the City of Kansas.	**1853**
The Hannibal Bridge is completed, providing the first railroad link to Chicago.	**1869**
The Kansas City Stockyards open in the West Bottoms.	**1871**
Newspaper publisher William Rockhill Nelson begins his campaign to revitalize Kansas City.	**1880**
Kansas City's comprehensive parks-and-boulevard plan is introduced.	**1893**
The American Royal Livestock Show is founded, furthering Kansas City's growing reputation as an agricultural capital.	**1899**
The Missouri River floods, leaving more than 20,000 homeless.	**1903**
Union Station opens to adoring crowds.	**1914**
Liberty Memorial is dedicated to World War I veterans.	**1921**
J.C. Nichols opens his shopping area, dubbed the Country Club Plaza.	**1922**
City charter amendments launch the corrupt Pendergast era.	**1925**
Fifty all-night clubs line 12th Street offering bootleg whiskey and the beginnings of Kansas City jazz.	**1930**
The Nelson-Atkins Museum of Art opens.	**1933**
Boss Tom Pendergast lands in prison on tax-evasion charges.	**1939**

Aggressive annexation allows the metropolitan area to begin the march outward.	**1940**
Kansas City–based Trans World Airlines shifts from wartime cargo loads to transatlantic passenger service.	**1946**
Harry Truman wins an upset victory for president and announces it at downtown's Hotel Muehlebach.	**1948**
Chicago businessman Arnold Johnson brings the major league Philadelphia Athletics to Kansas City.	**1955**
Based in the area since 1963, the Kansas City Chiefs win the Super Bowl.	**1970**
Both the Kansas City International Airport and the Harry S. Truman Sports Complex open.	**1972**
The Kansas City Royals win the World Series.	**1985**
The last of Kansas City's stockyards are dismantled.	**1991**
New exhibits at the Kansas City Zoo expand its size and significance; the city expands Bartle Hall Convention Center, making it the world's largest contiguous column-free exhibit space.	**1993**
Water cascades, fountains, and landscaped walkways become part of the Brush Creek Flood Control and Beautification Project near the Plaza.	**1995**

the area must resolve its identity confusion, the riverfront remains largely ignored, and the various independent entities will have to forge a unified whole if the city's full potential is to be realized.

Kansas City is well-equipped to journey into the twenty-first century. The only question is how far will it go?

Getting to Know the Kansas City Metro Area

Like Kansas City's early settlers, today's visitors most readily decipher the area by starting at the water. The metro area rests at the confluence of the Missouri and Kansas Rivers, a joining of turbulent and muddy currents. Shortly after the rivers unite near downtown, the Kansas/Missouri state line detours southward while the Mighty Mo continues its journey across the state to St. Louis.

In truth, one of the Kansas City metro area's greatest challenges comes from the state line that divides it. Many American municipalities have experienced urban sprawl as young families have moved to newly developing suburbs farther beyond the central core. In Kansas City, that

TRIVIA

Locals usually refer to the Kansas River as the "Kaw" as did the
Kansa, the Native Americans who lived in the area before them.

growth has often occurred across the Kansas state line, creating competitive groups that argue about lifestyle and municipal priorities—with the
ability to keep their tax dollars separate.

As if to highlight their stalwart independence, many area neighborhoods in the past also decided they needed to incorporate. Now, in the
Kansas City area, you can cross the state line by crossing the street and
travel unaware between 11 counties and more than 140 municipalities.
North of the Missouri River, the city's rolling, tree-covered landscape eventually settles into prairie, as neighborhood pockets provide residents a
somewhat more rural way of life. To the west across the Kansas River,
modest Kansas City, Kansas, juts from the bluffs, providing the best—and
most underused—views of the grander Kansas City, Missouri, skyline.

Kansas City Landmarks and Layout

Late in the last century, civic leaders in Kansas City, Missouri, decided to
set their city apart for posterity. A rough and mud-splashed place, Kansas
City in its early days was home to dirt streets, boardwalks, and shanty
neighborhoods. In the 1890s, visionaries secured more than 2,000 acres
throughout the city and set about creating an interlocking parks-and-
boulevard system.

The planners were so successful that writers often called the area
"Paris on the Plains." In addition, the City Beautiful movement earlier in this
century took hold across the nation partly because of Kansas City's efforts.
Long after the push had weakened, real estate financier J.C. Nichols kept
the philosophy alive by developing additional parkways, importing European fountains, and adding genteel outdoor sculpture.

Today, Kansas City is often called the City of Boulevards. It's also become famous as the City of Fountains, since more than 200 geysers now
decorate the area. There are so many fountains, in fact, that many people
say Kansas City has more spouts than any metropolis besides Rome (some
local boosters claim the Kansas City tally has now surpassed the Italian
capital's). Kansas Citians' fondness for sculpture has added to the local
scenery countless other pieces that aren't water-related, from modern
shuttlecocks to majestic lions to martyred saints in battle. No doubt such
affinity for public ornamentation caused André Maurois, the French biog-
rapher, to write, "Who in Europe, or in America for that matter, knows that
Kansas City is one of the loveliest cities on earth?"

The Biggest Cities

The largest cities in the Kansas City metro area are Kansas City, Missouri, with approximately 450,000 residents; Kansas City, Kansas, 146,000; and Overland Park, 120,000. All together, some 1.6 million people live in the greater Kansas City area.

Neighborhoods

In Missouri

Downtown Kansas City is experiencing a rebirth of sorts, as newly renovated lofts and townhouses attract young professionals and others thirsting for the urban scene. In particular, the River Market and Quality Hill have seen a resurgence of interest. In Northeast Kansas City, urban pioneers restoring some of the area's Victorian "painted ladies" mingle with residents who arrived long ago from Italy and more recently from Vietnam. And in the area's West Side neighborhood, Hispanic culture comes alive in restaurants, shops, and fiestas.

Midtown Kansas City combines a happening night club scene with quaint shops and bistros and some of the area's oldest neighborhoods. New developments on either side of Main Street between 35th and 41st Streets have regenerated excitement in the area. Midtown residents range from writers and artists to African Americans who've created a renewal east of Troost.

The Country Club Plaza area, the nation's first shopping district planned for the automobile, was modeled after Seville, Spain. Built in 1922, the Plaza boasts 12 towers and numerous fountains, statues, and mosaics. Several distinct neighborhoods lie near the Plaza, including Brookside, Armour Hills, and those adjacent to the Nelson-Atkins Museum of Art. Residents of these vintage 1910–1920 homes range from young families to older professionals, from corporate executives to the self-employed. The nearby University of Missouri at Kansas City adds students to the mix as well.

South Kansas City homes are generally newer than their counterparts to the north. Neighborhoods such as Waldo have melded into close communities as residents often hold festivals and gather at the local shops and restaurants. Farther south, yards and homes grow larger in neighborhoods such as Red Bridge and Verona Hills. South Kansas City residents include families who want to be closer to nearby lakes and shopping malls.

North of the River encompasses several smaller towns, such as Parkville, Riverside, and Gladstone, as well as North Kansas City (a separately incorporated municipality) and Kansas City North (the designation for Kansas City, Missouri, north of the Missouri River). Homes here vary from older dwellings in tree-lined neighborhoods to contemporary designs in upscale developments. Many people who live north of the river do so be-

Best Views in Kansas City

Lewis & Clark Point (8th and Jefferson). Views of the Missouri and Kansas Rivers; Kansas City Downtown Airport; Kansas City, Kansas; and North Kansas City.

City Hall Observation Deck (414 E. 12th St.). Thirty-story views of downtown in all directions from this 1930s-era art deco building.

Liberty Memorial (Penn Valley Park). Although the World War I tower is closed for renovation, the lookout nearby provides encompassing downtown views.

Skies Restaurant (Hyatt Regency Crown Center). Downtown views from the 42nd floor's revolving restaurant.

Ritz-Carlton Kansas City elevator (401 Ward Pkwy.). A glass-enclosed elevator ride provides views of the Country Club Plaza.

cause they want or need to travel: Kansas City International Airport serves the area from its location 15 miles north of downtown.

Independence, a town filled with history, is most widely recognized as the home of President Harry S. Truman. A century earlier, Independence was the "jumping off" point for the Santa Fe Trail and the destination for Joseph Smith Jr., and his Latter Day Saints movement. Neighborhoods range from the historic to the modern. Residents vary from sixth-generation to newly arrived followers of the Reorganized Church of Jesus Christ of Latter Day Saints, whose world headquarters remains in Independence.

Neptune Fountain, one of over 200 in Kansas City

A Time for Crime

One of Kansas City's most notorious figures, Tom Pendergast parlayed five years on the City Council into a well-oiled machine that controlled local politicians and businesses. For nearly 30 years, Boss Tom reigned over graft, prostitution, gambling, rigged elections, and kickbacks. Pendergast's Riverside Racetrack pulled in millions, his Jefferson Hotel was a den of iniquity, and his Ready-Mix Concrete Company paved the Country Club Plaza's Brush Creek. Some even credit Pendergast with Harry Truman's early political success. Boss Tom was eventually indicted on tax evasion charges; he died days before his probation ended in 1945.

In Kansas

Johnson County comprises at least 15 distinct cities, from Overland Park to Fairway. Mission Hills, one of the oldest, is a neighborhood whose vast yards and lavish homes adorn the area's wooded hills and ravines. Old-money families and corporate chief executives live in this elite environment. Next door, Prairie Village's more modest homes appeal to younger families who want to enroll their children in Shawnee Mission schools. South Johnson County, notably Overland Park, Leawood, and Olathe, has experienced building booms as those cities' farms have quickly given way to tony shopping malls and two-story homes.

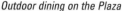

Outdoor dining on the Plaza

Joe Martin/Country Club Plaza Merchants Association

Kansas City, Kansas (KCK), suffers from an unfortunate reputation within the metropolitan area. Aside from the countrified neighborhoods near The Woodlands horse- and dog-racing tracks, much of the city faces lower household incomes and higher crime rates, on average. Near downtown KCK, the Strawberry Hill neighborhood was settled by Croatian immigrants, whose dedication to church and family has manifested itself in an orderly, if modest, community. Discount stores and salvage resellers abound within KCK's boundaries, evidence of a thriving entrepreneurial spirit.

The People of Kansas City

As a group, the residents of Kansas City are extraordinarily philanthropic. Volunteering their time, energy, and money ranks high on their lists of priorities. This may stem from an inherently friendly Midwestern ethic, but it could also signal residents' long-term commitment to their hometown. Although Kansas Citians heartily welcome newcomers, much of the population was born and remains in the area.

The Kansas City area's population totals about 1.6 million people. Ethnic groups include nearly every race. Kansas City's Latino community, for example, originated during the opening of the Santa Fe Trail. A large Irish contingent got its start when laborers came in 1857 to build a Catholic church. Croatians, Serbians, Russians, Greeks, and Slovakians followed in the late 1800s to work in the growing meat-packing industry. Today, females account for 51.6 percent of the population.

African Americans represent the area's largest minority. The *Kansas City Call*, a weekly newspaper, is produced for the black community, and KPRS-FM and KPRT-AM are two highly respected black-owned radio stations. African Americans live throughout greater Kansas City, although a large percentage reside east of Troost Avenue and in Kansas City, Kansas.

The Hispanic population also has its own newspaper, *Dos Mundos*, and a community that's growing increasingly active in restoring neighborhoods and supporting small businesses. Many Latino residents live in the West Side community near downtown and in Kansas City,

Kansas City skyline

Kansas. Businesses owned by Hispanics and African Americans often belong to their respective chambers of commerce.

In addition, the metro area comprises a sizable Jewish population. The *Kansas City Jewish Chronicle* delivers weekly news to the community, and the Jewish Community Center actively promotes metrowide programs, festivals, and civic awards. Like other ethnic groups, Jews reside throughout the metro area. A majority, however, live in Johnson County.

Metrowide: White 82.7 percent; Black 12.4 percent; Hispanic 3.1 percent; Asian/Pacific Islander 1.3 percent

In Jackson County, Missouri (DA, CS, EM): White 73.3 percent; Black 21.6 percent; Hispanic 3.3 percent; Asian/Pacific Islander 1.2 percent

In Johnson County, Kansas (JO): White 93.4 percent; Black 2.1 percent; Hispanic 2.2 percent; Asian/Pacific Islander 2.0 percent

In Wyandotte County, Kansas (KCK): White 62.7 percent; Black 28.1 percent; Hispanic 7.1 percent; Asian/Pacific Islander 1.3 percent

Business and Economy

People sometimes call Kansas City a cowtown, in part because of its prolific beef-producing past. Throughout its history, however, the region has been buffered from economic swings by a fairly diverse industrial base. Manufacturers, transportation companies, banks, health care, and service providers call Kansas City home. Greater Kansas City is the second-largest rail center in the country, the first inland foreign-trade-zone space, and the largest frozen-food storage and distribution location. And Kansas City hasn't forgotten its agricultural heritage: The area remains the headquarters for the nation's largest farm cooperative, Farmland Industries.

In addition, the Kansas City area has initiated an aggressive strategy for doing business electronically. Perhaps inspired by hometown Sprint Corp., the city has installed state-of-the-art communication systems downtown and north of the river. The efforts have lured high-profile companies that include Gateway 2000, Citicorp Credit Services, and EDS Global Travel Services.

Sprint also represents one of Kansas City's largest employers. Others include Ford Motor Company, Trans World Airlines, Health Midwest, Hallmark Cards, University of Kansas Medical Center, Southwestern Bell Telephone, and the federal and state governments.

As Johnson County's resident population has grown, so have its corporate players multiplied. Overland Park, in particular, has launched energetic efforts to attract companies. Organizations such as La Petite Academy, Winning Ways, and International Tours are headquartered in Johnson County.

Homes

Because the Kansas City area is so diverse, home prices range from $25,000 for a ragged-but-livable two-story house near downtown to $4 million or more for a Mission Hills mansion with acreage and a swimming pool.

Median price for the area in 1995, however, was $91,700, according to the National Association of Realtors. This compares with a national median of $113,800. In fact, the area is consistently rated among the most affordable large metro-area housing markets.

Kansas City Schools

New residents often target neighborhoods according to available schools. But it's daunting research considering that the Kansas City area contains 72 school districts, with more than 20,000 faculty members in 600 schools serving nearly 300,000 students.

In Johnson County, the Shawnee Mission and Blue Valley school districts represent a move-in magnet for many inbound. Others prefer the districts in small-town communities such as Parkville or Independence.

Until recently, the metro area's largest district was involved in one of the country's greatest desegregation endeavors, which began in 1986.

During the next decade, the Kansas City, Missouri, school district spent $1.7 billion trying to improve urban education, including the construction of 15 new schools. Now relieved of the massive federal spending that supported desegregation, the KCMO district is carving out a new future with a newly hired superintendent.

Some children elect to attend one of the many private schools available. Many are affiliated with religious institutions; others are nonsectarian. Among the most prestigious secondary schools are Pembroke Hill School, Rockhurst High School (for boys), and St. Theresa's Academy (for girls).

Higher-education options abound. The University of Missouri at Kansas City and the University of Kansas Medical Center; four-year colleges such as Avila College, the Kansas City Art Institute, and the Keller Graduate School of Management; and five community colleges provide a range of degrees. In addition, professional schools in chiropractic, osteopathy, and dentistry give students further choices.

Taxes

Comparing taxes from town to city and state to state can be a confusing proposition. In general terms, Kansas residents pay a maximum individual income tax rate of 6.45 percent, while Missouri residents pay 6 percent maximum. The city of Kansas City, Missouri, however, imposes a 1 percent tax on salaries, wages, and commissions earned by anyone who lives or works within its limits. Kansas residential real estate is taxed at 11.5 percent of appraised market value, while Missouri assesses real estate at 19 percent of true value.

Cost of Living

Kansas City is an affordable place to live. Homes are priced well below the national average, while staples such as bread and milk cost less, too. In a survey of 18 comparably sized cities, conducted by the American Chamber of Commerce Researchers Association, Kansas City's costs ranked lowest in groceries and health care. Prices for housing, utilities, transportation, and miscellaneous goods and services were also all below the national average. For comparison, here's a random selection of what you might pay in the Kansas City area:

Five-mile taxi ride: $7.50
Average dinner for two: $20
Daily newspaper: 50 cents
Hotel, double room: $65
Movie admission: $5.75; twilight shows range from $3 to $3.75; discount theaters from 99 cents to $1.50
Gallon of gas: about $1.05
Gallon of milk: $2.25

Calendar of Events

JANUARY
Kansas City Blades Professional Ice Hockey, Kemper Arena

FEBRUARY
Flower, Lawn & Garden Show, Bartle Hall, downtown Kansas City; Ice Carving Competition, Country Club Plaza

MARCH
St. Patrick's Day Parade, downtown Kansas City, Missouri; Annual Gem & Mineral Show, North Kansas City

APRIL
Spring Prairie Festival, Olathe; Michael Forbes Trolley Run, Country Club Plaza

MAY
Plaza Live! music series opens on Country Club Plaza; Kansas City Symphony's Memorial Day Concert, Crown Center Square

JUNE
Vaile Mansion Strawberry Festival, Independence; Heart of America Shakespeare Festival, Southmoreland Park

JULY
Kansas City Blues & Jazz Festival, Penn Valley Park; Wyandotte County Fair

AUGUST
Taste the World Ethnic Enrichment Festival, Swope Park; Kansas City Spirit Fest, Penn Valley Park; Santa-Cali-Gon Days Festival, Independence

SEPTEMBER

Renaissance Festival, Bonner Springs; Plaza Art Fair, Country Club Plaza; the NFL's Kansas City Chiefs season begins, Arrowhead Stadium

OCTOBER

American Royal Barbecue Contest, Parade, and Rodeo; Octoberfest, Lee's Summit; Kansas City Marathon, Country Club Plaza

NOVEMBER

Plaza Lighting Ceremony, Thanksgiving night; Annual Presentation of Handel's *Messiah,* RLDS Auditorium, Independence

DECEMBER

Annual Presentation of *A Christmas Carol,* Missouri Repertory Theatre

When to Visit

Like many other places that boast four distinct seasons, Kansas City attracts more attention during the year's warmer months. Spring through fall, a host of events tempt people outdoors to celebrate together.

Every municipality and community group devises its own methods of revelry. The Lenexa Spinach Festival, for example, culminates in building the world's largest spinach salad; the 18th & Vine Heritage Festival features a weekend of free concerts; Fiesta Hispaña celebrates Kansas City's Latino culture. Even neighborhoods get into the act; "historic homes" tours and

Neither Sleet Nor Snow . . .

In 1860, Alexander Majors, William Waddell, and William Russell, already partners in a successful Santa Fe Trail freight company, launched a new service called the Pony Express. They promised to deliver mail from St. Joseph, Missouri, to Sacramento, California, in only ten days. To do it, the trio built more than 150 relay stations across nearly 1,900 miles and hired 80 riders, including Buffalo Bill Cody (then only 15) and young James "Wild Bill" Hickok. After only 18 months, the expansion of both the telegraph and railroad systems ended the Pony Express. Today Majors' home, which once served as headquarters for his freighting operation, is open to the public at 83rd and State Line Road.

Kansas City Weather

Average annual Kansas City temperature: 53.6°F

	Average Highs	Average Lows
January	34.7°F	16.7°F
July	88.7°F	68.2°F

Average annual precipitation: 38.1 inches
Average annual snowfall: 21 inches
Average annual days of snow, ice, or hail in excess of 1 inch: 6.5
Average annual relative humidity at noon: 60 percent

subdivision open houses welcome the town. Weekends are packed with options throughout the greater metro area.

Spring is particularly enchanting in Kansas City. Trees and flowers begin waking from their winter's nap, in a surprisingly ample eruption. Fountains gurgle to life. It's a time when walkers stroll their favorite parks, runners gear up for weekly races, and spring showers prepare the city for summer.

Anyone with the good fortune to be in Kansas City during autumn will find a resplendent scene at every turn. The area's oaks, maples, and elms put on a foliage show that rivals those to the east. Before the air turns crisp, the Kansas City Chiefs kick off their National Football League season, while Major League Baseball's Kansas City Royals wrap theirs up. In fall, the area's two sports stadiums become a metrowide magnet, luring crowds of 80,000 to the games. Kansas City's other sports teams—playing soccer, hockey, and team tennis—also draw sizable crowds throughout their respective seasons.

Winter arrives in December—or is it November or January? In Kansas City, it's sometimes difficult to determine. Many residents consider the Plaza Lighting Ceremony the official transition, since the Thanksgiving-night event heralds the holiday season. Throughout December, historic homes welcome visitors for candlelight tours, tree-lighting rituals lure thousands, and musical oratories entertain. Winter also offers opportunities to enjoy opera, chamber music, ballet, and repertory theater.

About the Weather

Weather is a constant topic of conversation in the Kansas City area, partly because of its mercurial nature. A day might bring sunshine, rain, snow, or all three. Weeks of sweltering heat convince residents it's going to be a long, hot summer, until the morning they awake to a 60-degree rain. Winters bring piles of snow or mild temperatures perfect for prolonged walks outdoors.

Kansas City gets windy. A jacket or sweater is often necessary, and in the winter, bring something to cover hands and ears.

Dressing in Kansas City

Overall, Kansas City is a fairly casual town with plenty of leeway for individual expression. While men might feel more comfortable wearing suits and ties to evening functions—and women cocktail dresses—no one would look askance if the outfit varied. In fact, jeans are becoming increasingly common even at once-dressy functions such as the opera and the symphony. Business attire generally means coats and ties for men, except on Fridays, when most companies embrace casual days.

Winter visitors should plan on bringing coats and boots; even spring and fall can sometimes turn chilly. In the summer, plan on short sleeves and sandals.

Convention and Visitors Bureau of Greater Kansas City

2

GETTING AROUND KANSAS CITY

When calculating the size of Kansas City's metropolitan area, city officials differ on just how much to include. Some claim the territory covers more than 6,000 square miles in 13 counties. Others say it's closer to 4,500 square miles in 11 counties. Still others focus on much narrower parameters, considering cities isolated by significant stretches of countryside as distant suburbs or neighboring towns, not part of the metropolitan whole.

It's little wonder: On maps, the Kansas City area resembles Swiss cheese. Raytown, for example, lies surrounded by Kansas City, Missouri. Above the Missouri River, Gladstone cuts a similar doughnut hole in the Northland. Bits and pieces of municipal management pop up throughout the area, creating a hodgepodge of "local" civic pride.

Practically speaking, the sheer size of the greater metropolitan area makes it a challenge to travel extensively in anything other than an automobile. No bus system covers the entire region, for example, which means that riders who want to travel from one side of the metropolis to the other often must negotiate transfers both in routes and transportation companies. Discussions about adding a light-rail system have progressed apace during the past decade, but funding and route considerations promise long-term delays.

City Layout

Kansas City Streets

In Kansas City, Missouri, and much of Johnson County, streets follow a fairly predictable grid system. Numbered streets, which travel east to west,

What's in a Name?

Kansas City residents often find it frustrating to live in a city divided by a state line. Occasionally, they even discuss changing the boundary name—State Line Road—in an attempt to make the division less noticeable. Among the "most creative" ideas:

> Interstate Avenue
> MoKan Road
> Harmony Lane
> Our Road
> Date Line Road
> United Cities Road
> Hands Across the Border Street
> Rancor Road
> Bitterness Boulevard
> Eat Dirt Street

start at the Missouri River and are numbered successively both north and south, going as high as about 100th Street to the north and 175th Street to the south. Often, numbered streets are followed by the same-numbered terrace immediately to the south. For example, 55th Terrace is one street south of 55th Street.

Main Street is the major east-west divider south of the Missouri River; addresses begin with 0 at Main and ascend in both easterly and westerly directions (1400 E. 44th St., for example, lies 14 blocks east of Main). Blocks for north-south streets correspond to the numbered cross streets. For example, 5806 Main lies between 58th and 59th Streets. North of the Missouri River, streets follow the same basic format, with the addition of an "N." following the number. Therefore, 5800 N.W. 86th St. indicates the address is north of the river and west of Main Street.

Of course, there are exceptions throughout the area. Starting with J.C. Nichols, many local developers have favored street systems that follow the irregular contours of the land more closely. Streets in Mission Hills, for example, wander in conspicuous abandon. Many areas throughout Johnson County and the Northland, in particular, were developed as cul-de-sac havens to promote neighborliness and to reduce pass-through traffic. Additionally, Independence streets tend to follow a pattern of their own, although several numbered east-west Kansas City streets extend through the area and can provide reference points.

Major Arteries

A booming development era took place in the decades following World War II, creating an explosive expansion of Kansas City's borders. At the

That's Heartland, Not Heart Attack

Built in the late 1870s, Kansas City's original train station, Union Depot, was situated at the foot of steep cliffs below downtown. There, the West Bottoms were notorious for gambling halls, pawnshops, tacky hotels, and saloons.

In addition, passengers had to exit the area on the 9th Street Incline, a transportation device built in 1885 by streetcar owner Robert Gillham, who wanted to bring a piece of San Francisco to the heartland. Gillham's ride was breathtaking, both because the supports looked so rattletrap and because the trip occurred at a rapid, near-90-degree angle. In addition, the cable car brakes were none too reliable, sometimes causing the cars to jump off the cables.

same time, city fathers lobbied for—and received—massive federal funds to build the highways that would support a growing population and the region's increasing role as a transportation hub. Today, Kansas City has more highway miles per capita than any other major city in America.

Three interstate freeways serve the area: I-70, traveling east-west; I-35, northeast-southwest; and I-29, which heads north from Kansas City. Interstate 435 circles the metropolitan area then connects with I-470 and Highway 291 to pass through Lee's Summit and Independence. In addition,

The Annie Cade *steamboat, 1879*

TIP

When telephoning the Kansas side of Kansas City's metro area—including Kansas City, Kansas, and all Johnson County communities—the area code is 913. On the Missouri side—including north of the Missouri River and Independence—it's 816. When you're in the region, don't use either area code.

two more interstate linkages serve the area, and ten federal highways provide easy access around greater Kansas City.

Public Transportation

Bus Systems
Kansas City, Missouri's bus service, the Metro, serves Jackson County and parts of Kansas City, Kansas, with a fleet of full-size buses. Several routes start as early as 4 a.m., with the last scheduled route completed soon after midnight. The Metro offers an array of route maps and service information, obtainable aboard buses, in public libraries, within hotels, and from the Metro's main terminal at 1200 E. 18th St.

Fares depend on the routes and zones traveled. Generally, routes within Jackson County cost 90 cents. Travel in Kansas City, Kansas, costs $1 and Independence routes, $1.20. Seniors 65 and older, children to age 18, and disabled riders pay 50 cents. Monthly passes are available. Bus patrons can request free transfers within a zone; intraroute transfers require payment of the fare balance. For example, those traveling in Jackson County initially pay 90 cents upon boarding, then another 30 cents to complete a ride that ends in Independence. Exact change is required.

Call the Metro Information Center for routes, map, and service details, Monday through Friday 6 a.m. to 6 p.m., at 816/221-0660.

Johnson County Transit offers a Monday-through-Friday commuter service between Johnson County and downtown Kansas City, Missouri. Hours are from 6 to 9 a.m. and 2:30 to 7 p.m. Riders may get off the buses at intermediate stops along the route. Short, feeder-route fares within the system cost $1, regular routes are $1.25, and the full trip to downtown, $1.75. Discounts are available for seniors, students, and those with disabilities. Call Johnson County Transit at 913/541-8450 for information. Johnson Country Transit offers bicycle racks on its buses—the only metropolitan bus service to do so.

Kansas City, Kansas, and other portions of Wyandotte County are served Monday through Friday by The Bus. This regular service travels nine routes starting intermittently from 5:30 to 6:30 a.m. and ending by 7:30 p.m. The flat fare is $1; seniors, youths 12 to 18, and those with disabilities ride for 50 cents. The Metro's monthly passes and transfers are accepted; bus tokens are not. Route information is available on buses; at The Bus' main office in the Kansas City, Kansas, City Hall, 701 N. 7th St., Room 504; or by calling 913/551-0480.

Taxicab Service

Taking a taxi in the greater Kansas City area is simple—if you call in advance. Only a few select areas, such as downtown (on occasion), busy hotel entrances, and the airport, offer cab service within hailing distance. Telephone requests, however, provide fast, efficient driver response from a large number of competing transportation companies, which drive everything from standard cabs to limousines.

Because of an escalating fare problem, Kansas City now regulates fares by city ordinance. Flat fees between Kansas City International Airport (KCI) and downtown are set at $26. From KCI to the Country Club Plaza, the fare is $32. A typical driver starts off with $1.50 on the meter and charges $1.20 for each mile thereafter. Up to five passengers ride for the same price; luggage is free.

Among the area's largest taxicab services are Yellow Cab Company, 816/471-5000; Kaycee Cab Inc., 913/677-0444; and KCI Airport Limousine & Livery, 816/454-1500.

Kansas City Trolley

Anyone who believes the fun of arriving is getting there in style will want to try the Kansas City Trolley. This fleet of turn-of-the-century-styled trolleys provides one of the area's unique conveyances. The 35-passenger, open-side trolleys, with brass hand rails and varnished woodwork, travel a 14-mile loop between the River Market and the Country Club Plaza, stopping at 16 locations including Crown Center, Westport, major hotels, and cultural attractions. Removable rain curtains keep the colorful carriages running in inclement weather. Drivers narrate the trip, pointing out historic sites and mentioning local events of interest.

Trolley tickets are $4 for adults, $3 for seniors 65 and older, and $3 for children 6 to 12. Up to two toddlers 5 and younger ride free with each fare-paying adult; on Sundays and Mondays, all children 12 and under ride free with an accompanying adult. Fares include the option to reboard the trolleys up to three times on the day of purchase. Trolleys pick up at major

Because of its many one-way streets, walking through downtown Kansas City, Missouri, can provide one of the easiest ways to enjoy the area's sights and architecture—but the hills occasionally make it a rugged adventure. In particular, the blocks from 8th to 10th Streets, between Oak and Main, will raise aerobic levels. Slow down and enjoy the view.

stops about every 30 minutes, Mondays through Saturdays from 10 a.m. to 6 p.m. and Sundays from noon to 6 p.m. Route brochures and tickets are available at most hotels, attractions, and merchant associations. Call 816/221-3399 for information.

Plaza Carriages

In New York, travelers ride horse-drawn carriages around Central Park. In Kansas City, they can take similar equestrian-powered spins through the Country Club Plaza. Two carriage services treat passengers to views of passing pedestrians, Spanish architecture, public sculpture, and splashing fountains. The one-horsepower rigs provide a genteel pace that seems to stretch the 25-minute tour.

Surrey Ltd. on the Plaza has more than 250 wagons at its disposal, ranging from the sedate to the ornate. No one is sure just how many nervous suitors have proposed marriage from the rolling carriages, but romance seems hitched to this means of transport. Pride of Kansas City Carriages on the Plaza offers 20 vehicles, accommodating from two to 15 passengers per trip.

Both carriage companies follow a similar route, starting from the sidewalk on the south side of Seville Square. Hours vary with the season, but are generally between early evening and 10 or 11 p.m. Lap robes and narrated tours, if requested, are available from the drivers. Fares start at $25 for two adults, or $10 for adults and $5 for children younger than 10 in larger parties. Trips longer than 25 minutes may be arranged. Call Surrey Ltd. at 816/531-2673 and Pride of Kansas City at 816/531-1999.

Driving in Kansas City

Kansas Citians have a local reputation as notoriously bad drivers, although many would apply the designation to everyone in town but themselves. Residents forget to signal, speed up when approaching a yellow light, and honk indignantly when someone violates their space. Put them behind the wheel of a car and, most residents will admit, their generally friendly natures take a hike.

So here are some tips when driving in this otherwise pleasant hamlet: Always remain alert for drivers who may not be paying attention. When you're at an intersection, never punch the accelerator at the first sign of a green light. Never believe that an oncoming driver won't make a left turn in front of you just because his signal isn't on. Honking happens most often when you've decided to enter a street and an approaching driver thinks you've come too close. Don't take it personally.

Parking Tips

In downtown Kansas City, parking is at a premium, but it's reasonably priced compared to most large cities. Meters line the streets, and parking

The Trolley, By Golly

Trolleys once provided Kansas City with a unique public transportation. Patrons could travel to virtually any point in the city—as did freeloading adolescents, who often slipped aboard just out of the conductors' view. Although numerous trolley tracks still trace much of Kansas City, Missouri, the Kansas City Trolley Corp., a not-for-profit organization that uses rubber-tired, open-sided trolleys, now offers the only means of sampling this colorful transportation past.

garages charge about $2.75 a day. The largest lots are at the Municipal Auditorium and Bartle Hall. The River Market has several ample lots, which are most crowded on weekends.

The Country Club Plaza boasts free parking throughout the area. The only trick is to find the lots, which are often underground or rooftop. Look for signs. Street parking is also free.

Throughout the rest of the metro area, except for the free parking at major shopping malls and residential streets, meters rule. Be sure to carry quarters.

Biking in Kansas City

Kansas City is a wonderful biking town, with wide streets, plenty of traffic-free side streets, and a wealth of fellow cyclists from whom to seek advice. The problem is a distinct scarcity of designated bicycle lanes for a metropolitan area of its size. City planners and taxpayers, it seems, have yet to embrace two-wheel travel with the same enthusiasm as their counterparts in, say, Denver or Seattle.

Nevertheless, biking provides a satisfying way of seeing more of the region than can commonly be caught from a car seat. Kansas City drivers, despite the challenges they present to their fellow four-wheelers (see above), are generally friendly and accepting of those on bicycles. Exceptions, however, exist, and every local rider has a favorite near-miss story. Successful

Biking along Brush Creek

Joe Martin/Country Club Plaza Merchants Association

Ten Favorite Bike Rides
in the Kansas City Metro Area

by Steve Katz,
author of *Guide to Cycling Kansas City*, which includes
detailed maps and descriptions of these routes

1. **Prairie Village to Olathe** (40-plus miles). An easy ride through neighborhoods and over gently rolling hills.

2. **Prairie Village to Grandview** (35 miles). Includes a 10-mile loop of Longview Lake and a stretch of Blue River Road, one of the area's best cycling spots.

3. **The Colonel's Ride** (14 miles). An easy, flat ride from Loose Park to Overland Park starting at 2 every Sunday afternoon.

4. **75th Street Brewery Ride** (17 miles). Favored by brew-drinking cyclists, this ride starts at 6:30 every Tuesday night at 75th Street and Washington.

5. **Bill's Burrito Blast** (40 miles). Held the second Sunday of each month, this moderately hilly ride starts at Johnson County Community College and turns around in Gardner, Kansas.

6. **Corporate Woods to the Plaza** (27 miles). An easy ride that starts in Corporate Woods North and heads to the Country Club Plaza.

7. **Boardwalk to Platte City** (35-plus miles). Starting at the Boardwalk Shopping Center, this ride travels past KCI then on to Platte City.

8. **Mr. Mac's Annual St. Pat's Ride** (44 miles). Bicyclists in town on March 17 will want to join Mac McCallister's annual ride from the Ramada Inn at KCI.

9. **Parkville to Leavenworth** (40 miles). This scenic Northland ride follows the Missouri River from Parkville's English Landing.

10. **American Diabetes' Wheel to Weston** (35 miles one way). This annual ride is held every year on Father's Day, giving riders a view of historic Weston.

city cyclists, veterans say, follow all motor traffic rules and precautions, give way when prudent, and ride as though they're invisible to drivers.

Biking advice and companionship abound in Kansas City. The staffs of numerous bike shops, such as Turners Cycling & Fitness, 913/381-5298, and Midwest Cyclery, 816/931-4653, can prove helpful. Additionally, the area sports several cycling clubs and organizations. New riders are welcomed

Bus service from the Kansas City International Airport

by the Kansas City Bicycle Club, 816/436-5641, and the Johnson County Bike Club, 913/492-2600, among others.

Kansas City International Airport

It seemed like folly back in the Sixties, when civic leaders chose a 4,700-acre site in Platte County—miles north of downtown—to build a new international airport. But the Municipal Airport, just across the river from the central business district, had simply outgrown its space; airport backers believed a large, modern facility would carry them into the next century. At the time, the area's population seemed to be growing northward, and promoters promised that one day the airport would again be close to town.

Although it's still a fair distance from the major population centers, Kansas City International Airport has stood the test of time. When it opened in 1972, its innovative design was called a "drive to your gate" system, a classification that still holds true. Leaving and arriving at an airport doesn't get any simpler than this.

At KCI, three circular terminals are set some distance apart with each airline assigned to one terminal only. The scheme places check-in, gates, baggage retrieval, and parking areas within easy walking distance of each other.

Getting to KCI

About a 20-minute drive from downtown, KCI is easily reached via I-29 or I-435. From downtown, take I-35 or Highway 169 (over the Broadway Bridge), and get on I-29 north. Exit signs are well marked. From south Johnson County, I-435 north is often the fastest route—it has less traffic and higher speed limits than I-635. Again, airport exits are clearly noted.

Cruising the Muddy Mo

In the 1850s, the Missouri River was the Route 66 of the steamboat era. Waterborne traffic proved so frenetic that boats often lined up to unload at the local landing. Passengers on the first-class vessels spent $25 for accommodations, where they enjoyed the three-day trip from St. Louis.

Inside these luxurious paddle wheelers, travelers were treated to elegant dining rooms, ornate bars, and exquisite cuisine. Their cabins were richly furnished and carpeted, and they were entertained by the house orchestra. People in each port flocked to the docks when a luxury steamboat arrived, and greeting parties were a common occurrence.

The Mighty Missouri was a treacherous waterway, though, and many steamboats failed to reach their ports. Numerous vessels sank in the Missouri's dangerous bends, several near Kansas City. Although loss of life was minimal during ship disasters, cargo was rarely recovered.

The KCI Shuttle, among other competitors, offers round-the-clock service between the airport and hotels in the downtown, Crown Center, Plaza, Westport, Overland Park, Mission, and Lenexa areas. Tickets cost about $12 one way. Arriving passengers should look for KCI Shuttle ticket carts for assistance. To obtain a schedule with exact departure times, call 816/243-5000 or 800/243-6383.

Getting Around KCI
As travelers approach KCI, signs identify terminals that house the different departing airlines. If you want American Airlines, for example, head for Terminal A and park in the lot there. For Southwest, go to Terminal B. If you need to change terminals and don't want to move your car—or don't have a car—complimentary shuttles run between the terminals every few minutes or so.

Major Airlines Serving KCI
America West, Terminal A, 800/235-9292
American Airlines, Terminal A, 800/433-7300
Continental, Terminal C, 800/525-0280
Delta, Terminal B, 800/221-1212
Midwest Express, Terminal C, 800/452-2022
Northwest Airlines, Terminal C, 800/225-2525

Southwest Airlines, Terminal B, 800/435-9792
Trans World Airlines, Terminal B, 800/221-2000
United Airlines, Terminal C, 800/241-6522
USAir, Terminal A, 800/428-4322
Vanguard Airlines, Terminal B, 800/826-4827

Other Airports

Kansas City International handles all scheduled commercial flights in the area, but several smaller fields support private pilots flying through the region. Kansas City's old Municipal Airport, for example, is now called Kansas City Downtown Airport and serves arriving and departing corporate jets, celebrity charters, and cargo services. For more information, call 816/471-4946.

Other area airfields include the New Century AirCenter, 913/782-5335, Independence Memorial Airport, 816/795-8774, and Lee's Summit Municipal Airport, 816/251-2492.

A Station Left Waiting

When it opened in 1914, Union Station was one of the most modern railway terminals in the country. Already, Kansas City was making impressive strides in becoming a U.S. transportation hub, and the $5.8-million station ranked as the third-largest railroad facility in the world, second only to New York's Grand Central and Pennsylvania Stations.

By the end of the 1950s, however, airline and automobile travel had supplanted the rails, and fewer than two dozen trains passed through the station each day. Soon, Kansas City's enormous terminal was abandoned in favor of a tiny depot attached to one side.

In 1974, the city agreed to grant tax incentives to a developer who wanted to construct two new buildings on land east of the station in return for restoring the grande dame. The developer reneged, unfortunately, and two more decades were spent filing and settling expensive lawsuits. An independent group now owns Union Station and is raising funds to renovate the building and create a science museum inside.

Today, Kansas City ranks second only to Chicago in rail traffic volume, but little of it consists of passengers.

Train Services

Although Kansas City's reputation as a passenger-rail mecca has dwindled with the popularity of train service in general, Amtrak's *Southwest Chief* continues to roll through the area on its regular Chicago–Los Angeles run. Residents of Kansas City and St. Louis also are fond of the daily rail service running between their cities. A round-trip, unreserved ticket from Kansas City to St. Louis costs $52. Call Amtrak at 800/872-7245.

Kansas City's current Amtrak station sits directly northeast of the old Union Station, jutting from the modern office building called Two Pershing Square. The actual address is 2200 Main St., and a drive-through area allows passengers to pull in and drop off baggage. Parking is available beneath Union Station, entered via Pershing Road.

Interstate and Regional Bus Service

Both Greyhound and Jefferson bus lines serve the greater Kansas City area, with routes throughout the country. These two major lines share terminals at 1101 Troost Ave. in Kansas City, Missouri, and at 730 State St. in Kansas City, Kansas. In addition, a small terminal in Grandview serves passengers of the two major bus lines. Call 800/231-2222 for fare and schedule information.

3

WHERE TO STAY

Kansas City lodges visitors in style. Whether it's world-class suites and uniformed doormen or a handmade quilt and a relaxed morning sipping coffee, travelers can find it here.

It's possible to stay in one-of-a-kind accommodations throughout the metropolitan area. These unique properties are complemented by a host of regional and national hotel and motel chains. Such selection ensures that everyone can find a home-away-from-home at a range of affordable room rates.

Thanks to Kansas City's miles of urban highways and major thoroughfares, and light traffic compared to similarly sized cities, travelers can stay virtually anywhere and still easily reach what they came for. Reservations, however, are always recommended. When a large convention (drawing 35,000 Future Farmers of America, for example) or combined weekend events (such as a Chiefs game and the Plaza Art Fair) roll into town, the area's nearly 17,000 rooms quickly fire up their "No Vacancy" signs.

Beyond the lodgings suggested here, consider contacting your favorite national hotel management chain. Nearly all are represented in Kansas City or, given the local hotel-building boom underway, soon will be. Wheelchair accessibility is indicated by the ♿ symbol.

Price rating symbols:
$	**Under $50**
$$	**$50 to $75**
$$$	**$75 to $125**
$$$$	**$125 and up**

DOWNTOWN KANSAS CITY AREA

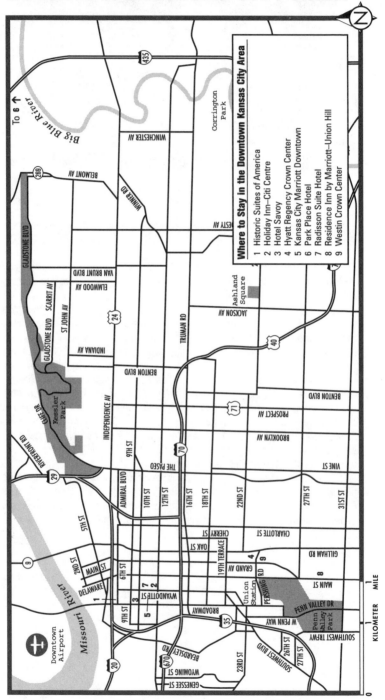

Where to Stay in the Downtown Kansas City Area

1 Historic Suites of America
2 Holiday Inn–Citi Centre
3 Hotel Savoy
4 Hyatt Regency Crown Center
5 Kansas City Marriott Downtown
6 Park Place Hotel
7 Radisson Suite Hotel
8 Residence Inn by Marriott–Union Hill
9 Westin Crown Center

DOWNTOWN KANSAS CITY AREA

Hotels and Motels

HISTORIC SUITES OF AMERICA
612 Central
Kansas City, MO 64105
816/842-6544
$$$–$$$$ DA

The former Builders and Traders Exchange building and Barton Brothers Shoe Factory have been transformed into the beautifully appointed Historic Suites. Within walking distance of the River Market, downtown, restaurants, and clubs, the all-suite hotel features a complimentary breakfast buffet and evening reception, exercise rooms, whirlpool tub, and an outdoor pool. Historic Suites' offers 100 kitchen-equipped suites that are configured in 32 different floor plans. &

HOLIDAY INN–CITI CENTRE
1215 Wyandotte
Kansas City, MO 64105
816/471-1333
$$$ DA

Built in 1925, the Holiday Inn–Citi Centre lies just across the street from Kansas City's Municipal Auditorium and Barney Allis Plaza. Inside, Italian marble, mahogany, and bronze highlight the public spaces, while the hotel's 192 rooms are decorated in florals. The Holiday Inn's mezzanine lounge, Gargoyles, was named for the stone carvings on the building's façade. Ashley's Restaurant is an on-site fine-dining option. &

HYATT REGENCY CROWN CENTER
2345 McGee
Kansas City, MO 64108
816/421-1234
$$$–$$$$ DA

Steps from Crown Center, the Hyatt sports sweeping views of the downtown skyline, especially from its revolving rooftop restaurant, Skies. The Hyatt's 731 rooms and suites reflect the company's customary attention to detail and come with 24-hour room service, minibars, and movie channels. Hotel amenities also include a complimentary health club, an all-weather pool, tennis courts, and two other restaurants. &

KANSAS CITY MARRIOTT DOWNTOWN
200 W. 12th St.
Kansas City, MO 64105
816/421-6800
$$$$ DA

The Marriott is a prime convention facility, its 573 rooms and suites within steps of Bartle Hall. The hotel also has 23 meeting rooms of its own. The Marriott's lobby, bars, and restaurants attract many downtown workers, who duck in for a meal or after-work cocktail. In 1997, the Marriott is set to open an additional 400 rooms in the renovated Muehlebach Hotel. Special weekend rates. &

PARK PLACE HOTEL
1601 N. Universal
Kansas City, MO 64120
816/483-9900
$$–$$$ DA

"Industrial/Office" could precede this hotel name and accurately describe its setting just off I-435 at Front Street. Nevertheless, this 327-room lodging offers quality accommodations and amenities such as an indoor swimming pool and health club. The location—2 miles from Worlds of Fun, minutes from Sam's Town casino, and 5 miles from Truman Sports Complex—is hard to beat, too. &

RADISSON SUITE HOTEL
106 W. 12th St.
Kansas City, MO 64105
816/221-7000
$$$–$$$$ **DA**

The Radisson opened in 1931 as the Phillips House, on the original site of the Haberdashery, a men's clothing store co-owned by Harry Truman. The hotel set a standard for European-style elegance with its art deco decor, grand dining room, and classic suites. Today, the hotel attracts business travelers and those looking for a historic setting in a central location.

Rooms come with computer hook-ups, HBO, and a complimentary breakfast buffet. &

WESTIN CROWN CENTER
One Pershing Rd.
Kansas City, MO 64108
816/474-4400
$$$$ **DA**

Like much of Kansas City, Crown Center's site was a hill of limestone that had to be excavated for development. The five-story waterfall in the Westin's lobby cascades over some of that remaining outcropping. Con-

---

Lodged in the Past

Downtown's coffee smell comes from the Folger Coffee Company at 7th and Broadway as it pumps the roasted beans through its plant. But coffee has long been a feature in Kansas City.

In 1888, the owners of the Arbuckle Coffee Company built the opulent Hotel Savoy on the corner of 9th and Central. Conveniently located, the hotel was the first lodging travelers saw as they came up the slope from the old Union Depot. The Savoy was an architectural wonder, featuring a rooftop garden, Italian tile floors, and a lavish ballroom. In its early years, the property welcomed guests such as Teddy Roosevelt, W.C. Fields, and Lillian Russell.

By 1903, hotel owners opened the Savoy Grill, exclusively for men although women were soon admitted. After dinner, guests would push aside their tables to dance.

When the nation's post–World War II suburban boom began, downtown started to wane—as did the fortunes of the Hotel Savoy. In 1960, restaurateur Don Lee bought the Grill, then purchased the hotel five years later. For 20 years, Lee operated the hotel as a residential property, even after it was placed on the National Register of Historic Places. In 1985 he renovated the Hotel Savoy and now operates it as an all-suite bed and breakfast.

---

nected to Crown Center's shops, theaters, and restaurants, the hotel is a
popular spot for travelers. Guests in
the hotel's 725 rooms can further
enjoy the skyline view from Benton's
rooftop steakhouse. &

Bed and Breakfast

HOTEL SAVOY
219 W. 9th St.
Kansas City, MO 64105
816/842-3575
$$$ **DA**
Nearly a dozen years ago, Don Lee
renovated the Hotel Savoy, changing
it from a residential hotel into a luxu-
rious B&B. He furnished each room
or suite in a turn-of-the-century
style, enhancing the original stained-
glass windows and Corinthian
columns. Now Lee markets the lodg-
ing with his Savoy Grill. Both are
near downtown's Garment District
and within walking distance of major
businesses.

Extended Stay

RESIDENCE INN BY
MARRIOTT–UNION HILL
2975 Main St.
Kansas City, MO 64108
816/561-3000
$$$–$$$$ **DA**
The Residence Inn resembles a
cozy enclave of brick and gray-
clapboard townhouses. Set in the
gentrifying Union Hill neighborhood,
overlooking Crown Center, the inn
provides equipped kitchens with
grocery service, complimentary
breakfast, fireplaces, and man-
ager's hospitality hours. Outdoors,
guests find a barbecue area, swim-
ming pool, and hot tub. Discounts
available for stays longer than a
week. &

© Hallmark Cards, Inc.

Hyatt Regency Crown Center, page 33

CENTRAL/SOUTH KANSAS CITY

Hotels and Motels

BEST WESTERN SEVILLE
PLAZA HOTEL
4309 Main St.
Kansas City, MO 64111
816/561-9600
$$$ **CS**
Although it's located right on busy
Main Street, the Best Western Seville
is only four blocks from the Country
Club Plaza and three blocks from
Westport. The Spanish-style hotel
features 77 spacious rooms with
complimentary continental breakfast,
local phone calls, and movie chan-
nels. In addition, an indoor whirlpool
spa gives guests a way to rest after
exploring the area. &

BUDGETEL INN
8601 Hillcrest Rd.
Kansas City, MO 64138
816/822-7000
$$ **CS**
This is the only hotel in the Central/

CENTRAL/SOUTH KANSAS CITY

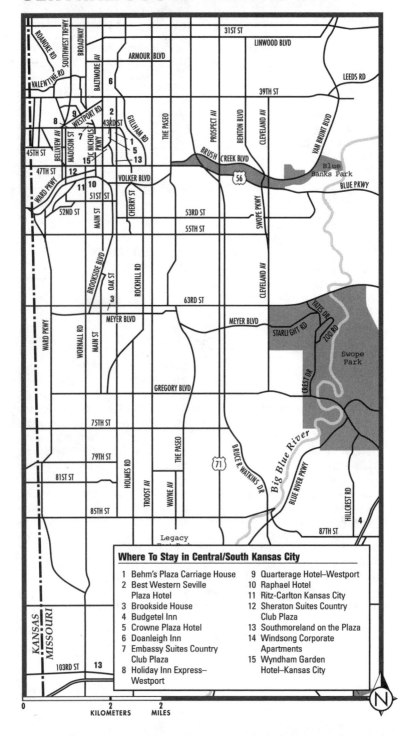

Where To Stay in Central/South Kansas City

1 Behm's Plaza Carriage House
2 Best Western Seville Plaza Hotel
3 Brookside House
4 Budgetel Inn
5 Crowne Plaza Hotel
6 Doanleigh Inn
7 Embassy Suites Country Club Plaza
8 Holiday Inn Express–Westport
9 Quarterage Hotel–Westport
10 Raphael Hotel
11 Ritz-Carlton Kansas City
12 Sheraton Suites Country Club Plaza
13 Southmoreland on the Plaza
14 Windsong Corporate Apartments
15 Wyndham Garden Hotel–Kansas City

South zone that is technically closer to the East Metro zone; that's because it sits just off I-435 at 86th Street. The Budgetel looks toward Benjamin Ranch, its beige-and-green exterior blending well with the surrounding landscape. Nearby Bannister Mall offers a variety of restaurants, from Luby's to the Olive Garden. &

CROWNE PLAZA HOTEL
4445 Main St.
Kansas City, MO 64111
816/531-3000
$$$–$$$$ CS

From this hotel, the Country Club Plaza, Westport, and the Nelson-Atkins Museum of Art are just minutes away. All 296 rooms feature two telephones with voice mail, individual climate control, and cable television. A health club and indoor swimming pool also are available. Additionally, the hotel serves lunch and dinner in the Main Street Grill and drinks in its Lobby Bar. &

EMBASSY SUITES COUNTRY CLUB PLAZA
220 W. 43rd St.
Kansas City, MO 64111
816/756-1720
$$$–$$$$ CS

It's hard to miss the hotel north of the Country Club Plaza. The salmon-and-teal color scheme—used both inside and out—put the hotel on the map. The Spanish-style property features suites with living rooms and bed-

149/night

rooms, as well as microwave ovens, coffeemakers, refrigerators, and wet bars. Rates include a complimentary breakfast each morning and beverages at the manager's reception each evening. &

HOLIDAY INN EXPRESS–WESTPORT
801 Westport Rd.
Kansas City, MO 64111
816/931-1000
$$ CS

The Holiday Inn celebrates its historic location on the original Santa Fe Trail with a plaque above the door. Inside, a trail map details the importance of the roads heading westward. The hotel's decor also plays up a western focus, with Southwest fabrics and a Frederic Remington sculpture. A complimentary continental breakfast comes with the room; other Westport restaurants and nightclubs lie nearby. &

THE QUARTERAGE HOTEL–WESTPORT
560 Westport Rd.
Kansas City, MO 64111
816/931-0001
$$$ CS

From the outside, The Quarterage seems contemporary. Inside, however, the oak, brass, and marble lobby—with its roaring wintertime fireplace—looks downright nineteenth-century. Still, the Quarterage Hotel provides modern courtesies, such as a health club, complimentary breakfast, and an evening cocktail hour. The Quarterage also gives free local calls and complimentary HBO. Nearby Westport's nightlife and shopping beckon. &

RAPHAEL HOTEL
325 Ward Pkwy.
Kansas City, MO 64112
816/756-3800
$$$–$$$$ **CS**
Built in 1927, the Raphael once was an apartment building with a commanding view of the Country Club Plaza. It was converted into 123 hotel rooms—72 of which are spacious suites—and opened as the Raphael in 1975. The lobby is intimate, with two Raphael paintings lending a European flair. The hotel operates a fine-dining restaurant, which also provides in-room continental breakfasts daily. &

THE RITZ-CARLTON KANSAS CITY
401 Ward Pkwy.
Kansas City, MO 64112
816/756-1500
$$$$ **CS**
The Ritz-Carlton, an AAA Four Diamond and Mobil Four Star property, lies just across an arching bridge from the Country Club Plaza. Between Thanksgiving and Christmas, rooms facing the shops usually are sold out months in advance for Plaza Lights aficionados. European art, crystal chandeliers, and rich fabrics create an Old World feel. Rooms include amenities such as bathroom telephones, hair dryers, and terry robes. &

SHERATON SUITES COUNTRY CLUB PLAZA
770 W. 47th St.

© Hallmark Cards, Inc.

Westin Crown Center, page 34

$140

Kansas City, MO 64112
816/931-4400
$$$–$$$$ **CS**
This hotel is right in the thick of the Plaza. Starting with its marble-decked lobby, the lodging provides an oasis within an oasis. Each of the hotel's 259 suites come with living room, bedroom, refrigerator, and coffeemaker, among other amenities. There's an indoor-outdoor swimming pool, whirlpool, and exercise room in the hotel, as well as The Gallery Art Restaurant & Bar. &

WYNDHAM GARDEN HOTEL–KANSAS CITY
1 E. 45th St.
Kansas City, MO 64111
816/753-7400
$$$ **CS**
After a $9-million overhaul, the former Hilton Plaza Inn reopened in late 1996 as the Wyndham Garden. This 240-room property perches on a hill just east of the Country Club Plaza. Inside, marble floors, antiques, and murals grace the public areas, while a restaurant, lounge, and library offer

chances for relaxation. An outdoor swimming pool and health club round out the lodging. ♿

Bed and Breakfasts

BEHM'S PLAZA CARRIAGE HOUSE
4320 Oak
Kansas City, MO 64111
816/753-4434
$$$ CS

This 1910 Georgian Colonial home, listed on Missouri's Register of Historic Places, sits on a quiet street between the Nelson-Atkins Museum of Art, the Country Club Plaza, and Westport. The stately brick residence, owned by innkeepers Shirley and Del Behm, has five bedrooms, each with private bath; guests enjoy a full breakfast and complimentary wine and hors d'oeuvres. No wheelchair access.

BROOKSIDE HOUSE
6315 Walnut
Kansas City, MO 64113
816/361-4111
$$$ CS

Industrial trainer Brenda Otte and veterinarian Vern Otte own this no-host bed and breakfast in residential Brookside, but they make certain the occupants of their Dutch Colonial are well cared for. Singles, couples, families, or groups—one party at a time—can rent the three-bedroom, no-smoking home and have full run of its living, dining, and family rooms and fireplace. Continental breakfast items are stocked daily. No wheelchair access.

DOANLEIGH INN
217 E. 37th St.
Kansas City, MO 64111
816/753-2667

$$$–$$$$ CS

This 1907 home features five luxuriously decorated guest rooms (two include fireplaces and four have jetted tubs) that come with their own direct telephone, bath, and cable TV. The Doanleigh offers a full breakfast and homemade cookies. The antique-filled mansion, owned by Cynthia Brogdon and Terry Maturo, provides a convenient setting between downtown and the Country Club Plaza. No wheelchair access.

SOUTHMORELAND ON THE PLAZA
116 E. 46th St.
Kansas City, MO 64112
816/531-7979
$$$–$$$$ CS

Susan Moehl and Penni Johnson make certain their guests find time to relax on the veranda, enjoy a roaring fire, or get to know each other. The Southmoreland's 12 rooms are named after prominent Kansas Citians, such as artist Thomas Hart Benton and candy barons Clara and

Southmoreland on the Plaza

Southmoreland on the Plaza

Russell Stover, and come decorated with a nod to their namesakes. Each room has a special touch such as a private deck, fireplace, or jetted tub. &

Extended Stay

WINDSONG CORPORATE APARTMENTS
114 W. 103rd St.
Kansas City, MO 64114
816/942-5997
$ CS
Formerly an apartment building, the Windsong offers guest lodgings for 30 days or more at an affordable price. Apartments come with one, two, or three bedrooms, as well as separate living rooms, dining rooms, kitchens, and baths. Guests can enjoy an outdoor swimming pool, HBO, wake-up calls, and 24-hour message service are standard; maid service, however, comes but once a week. &

JOHNSON COUNTY

Hotels and Motels

DAYS INN–LENEXA
9630 Rosehill Rd.
Lenexa, KS 66215
913/492-7200
$–$$ JO
"Follow the Sun" says the Days Inn logo, and this south Kansas City motel provides the cheery and relaxing setting, especially for those traveling along adjacent I-35 just west of this property. The three-story lodging underwent an extensive renovation in late 1996, providing guests with improved facilities and services ranging from guest rooms to swimming pool to its continental breakfast. &

Country Club Plaza Merchants Association

Sheraton Suites, Country Club Plaza, page 38

DOUBLETREE HOTEL KANSAS CITY, CORPORATE WOODS
10100 College Blvd.
Overland Park, KS 66210
913/451-6100
$$$ JO
A pillar of the College Boulevard business and residential corridor, the Doubletree provides convenient access to the offices within adjacent Corporate Woods. Walking and running trails of 1.5 to nearly 4 miles thread from the hotel through the office-park-within-a-park. The hotel's 370-plus rooms and suites also provide access to racquetball, indoor swimming, saunas, whirlpool, and the Rotisserie Restaurant. &

DRURY INN–MERRIAM
9009 Shawnee Mission Pkwy.
Merriam, KS 66202
913/236-9200
$$ JO
From this Drury Inn, near the intersection of I-35 and Shawnee Mission Parkway, travelers can drive to nearly any metropolitan area point

JOHNSON COUNTY

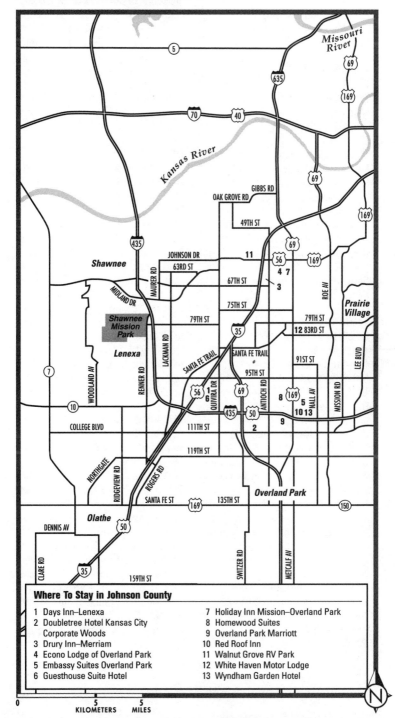

Where To Stay in Johnson County

1 Days Inn–Lenexa
2 Doubletree Hotel Kansas City Corporate Woods
3 Drury Inn–Merriam
4 Econo Lodge of Overland Park
5 Embassy Suites Overland Park
6 Guesthouse Suite Hotel
7 Holiday Inn Mission–Overland Park
8 Homewood Suites
9 Overland Park Marriott
10 Red Roof Inn
11 Walnut Grove RV Park
12 White Haven Motor Lodge
13 Wyndham Garden Hotel

speedily and easily. The motel itself offers comfortable rooms, swimming pool, continental breakfast, free local telephone calls, and complimentary passes to a nearby Gold's Gym. &

ECONO LODGE OF OVERLAND PARK
7508 Shawnee Mission Pkwy.
Shawnee Mission, KS 66202
913/262-9600
$ **JO**

This centrally located, 86-room motel lies only 5 miles west of the Country Club Plaza and even closer to Johnson County's malls, restaurants, and attractions. Free airport bus service provides access from Kansas City International; doughnuts and coffee are free each morning; and a Budget Rent-A-Car facility sits directly across Shawnee Mission Parkway from the motel. &

EMBASSY SUITES OVERLAND PARK
10601 Metcalf
Overland Park, KS 66212
913/649-7060
$$$ **JO**

East of Metcalf, near I-435, this property includes an atrium rising through the hotel's seven levels. Terraces overlook a bar, floral-print market umbrellas, and tropical vegetation. All rooms include a breakfast buffet and evening manager's reception. From the hotel, the NCAA Hall of Champions is a half-mile away; dinner theater's within a mile; and two malls are within 3 miles. &

HOLIDAY INN MISSION–OVERLAND PARK
7240 Shawnee Mission Pkwy.
Overland Park, KS 66202
913/262-3010
$$–$$$ **JO**

The most prominent amenity at this hotel, one of three Holidome lodgings in the metro area, is a swimming pool beneath a large atrium. Kids also thrill to the video arcade, table tennis, and indoor Nerf tennis court. While kids play, mom, dad, and other guests at this 194-room hotel can enjoy the whirlpool, exercise area, and in-house restaurant and lounge. &

OVERLAND PARK MARRIOTT
10800 Metcalf
Overland Park, KS 66210
913/451-8000
$$–$$$ **JO**

The College Boulevard corridor has become a southern-central business district, and the Marriott sits at dead center of the action. This 397-room property has myriad roles, providing meeting space, a number of restaurant venues, and amenities ranging from indoor/outdoor swimming pools to in-room movies. Such offerings mean the Marriott stays busy, hosting everything from visiting softball teams to ballroom-based purebred cattle auctions. &

RED ROOF INN
6800 W. 108th St.
Overland Park, KS 66211
913/341-0100
$–$$ **JO**

This hotel, one of three Red Roofs in the metropolitan area, provides some of the least-expensive accommodations near College Boulevard. Offering function, not frills, the inn allows easy access to nearby businesses, shops, and restaurants such as Dick Clark's American Bandstand Grill. The lodging's guest rooms include ESPN, Showtime, and CNN on remote-control televisions, morning coffee, and *USA Today*. &

Southmoreland: Inventing the Urban Inn

In 1989, two corporate executives decided to bag their jobs to open an upscale B&B catering to traveling businesspeople. Penni Johnson, a lawyer, and Susan Moehl, a Hallmark Cards marketing manager, laid out detailed plans to revive a 1913 Colonial Revival mansion near the Country Club Plaza. Then they watched as 19 banks turned down their loan applications.

Undaunted, the team finally found a lender and then, using the original blueprints, they renovated the 4,200-square-foot home, adding another 6,000 square feet. From their extensive research, the pair discovered what would appeal to typical B&B guests; from their own corporate trips, they knew what business travelers wanted. That combined knowledge spawned one of the country's first "urban inns."

During the week, Southmoreland guests tend to be executives. The business travelers enjoy atypical B&B amenities: fax, photocopier, 24-hour switchboard, audiovisual equipment, and sports/dining privileges at the Rockhill Tennis Club. On weekends, leisure visitors fill the lodging. In fact, many weekday business guests return with friends and spouses for weekends of fun and the full breakfasts Moehl creates in the professionally equipped kitchen.

The Southmoreland claims numerous awards, including INNovations' "Standing Ovation" award, recognizing the B&B as one of the ten best inns in the country; the Association of American Historic Inns' Outstanding Achievement Award for preservation; and Mobil's Four-Star Award, the only bed and breakfast so designated in the 20-state Midwest and South-Central regions.

WHITE HAVEN MOTOR LODGE
8039 Metcalf
Overland Park, KS 66204
913/649-8200
$–$$ **JO**
Operated by the White family since 1957, the cozy White Haven is one of Johnson County's oldest lodgings—

and one of its most respected. "Value and comfort" remain the driving forces behind its success. Guests park outside the rooms of the two-story building, which wraps around a statuary-bedecked swimming pool. The helpful staff provides new and faithful customers with everything from microwave ovens to morning doughnuts. &

WYNDHAM GARDEN HOTEL
7000 W. 108th St.
Overland Park, KS 66211
913/383-2550
$$$ JO
This former Best Western Hallmark Inn recently underwent a $7-million renovation, making it one of Johnson County's premier hotel properties. Marbled entryways lead to The Garden Cafe restaurant, full health club, ample on-site meeting space, and tastefully appointed guest rooms. Near the intersection of I-435 and Metcalf, the Wyndham provides easy access to Overland Park and attractions throughout the metropolitan area. &

Extended Stay

HOMEWOOD SUITES
10556 Marty Ave.
Overland Park, KS 66212
913/341-5576

The Quarterage Hotel–Westport, page 37

The Quarterage Hotel

$$–$$$ JO
All-suite hotel customers look for more than a single room, and this property delivers. From apartment-style accommodations, some with fireplaces, to full kitchens to an executive business center, Homewood lets both overnight and long-term guests settle in comfort. The lodging even offers an on-site, 24-hour convenience store with video rentals. &

GUESTHOUSE SUITE HOTEL
9775 Lenexa Dr.
Lenexa, KS 66215
913/541-4000
$$ JO
Living room, full kitchen, oversized bed, health club membership—you could be at home. That's exactly the idea behind this all-suite property directed at extended-stay business travelers and others who will appreciate its location near I-35, Oak Park Mall, and numerous restaurants. Guests can even access a library of books and family games. It's home—except for your pets, which are not welcome. &

Campgrounds

WALNUT GROVE RV PARK
10218 Johnson Dr.
Merriam, KS 66203
913/262-3023
$ JO
Pull up and plug in. What could be simpler? This RV park, nestled into a residential area with convenient access to I-35, could be just the place for those tired of unpacking, hauling luggage, and eating coffee-shop meals. The facility offers showers, coin laundry service, pay telephone, and long-term rates for those who wish to stay a while. Reservations are highly recommended. &

NORTH OF THE RIVER

Hotels and Motels

BEST WESTERN COUNTRY INN–KCI AIRPORT
11900 Plaza Circle
Kansas City, MO 64153
816/464-2002
$$ NR
Whether you're staying in Kansas City or leaving for a while, this 43-room hotel could be your ticket. The park-and-fly program allows those who stay at least one night to leave their cars for up to seven days. The convenient service includes free airport shuttle, complimentary continental breakfast, and air-conditioned rooms. &

BEST WESTERN COUNTRY INN WORLDS OF FUN
7100 N.E. Parvin Rd.
Kansas City, MO 64117
816/453-3355
$$–$$$ NR
For families intent on getting maximum roller-coaster time at Worlds of Fun or a full wash of waves at Oceans of Fun, this motel couldn't be more convenient. Handy to I-435 travelers and casino buffs as well, the Country Inn's 86 rooms come with daily continental breakfast service and summertime use of the outdoor swimming pool. &

COURTYARD BY MARRIOTT/KANSAS CITY AIRPORT
7901 N.W. Tiffany Springs Pkwy.
Kansas City, MO 64153
816/891-7500
$$–$$$ NR
It's a free shuttle ride from the airport to the Courtyard, with only 3.5 miles to cover. That leaves plenty of time to enjoy this 149-room hotel's amenities, ranging from an indoor swimming pool and exercise room to the Courtyard restaurant, serving breakfast and dinner. All rooms feature telephones, televisions, and in-room coffee. &

KANSAS CITY AIRPORT HILTON HOTEL
8801 N.W. 112th St.
Kansas City, MO 64153
816/891-8900
$$–$$$$ NR
Known until recently as the Doubletree Hotel, this lodging's 347 rooms lie less than a mile from KCI's runways. Rest assured, however, that all is calm within the Hilton confines, where indoor and outdoor swimming pools, whirlpool, saunas, and a lobby bar keep your jet-age cares at bay. Weatherby's restaurant, on the lobby level floor also serves up some memorable cafe-style meals. &

EMBASSY SUITES KCI AIRPORT
7640 N.W. Tiffany Springs Pkwy.
Kansas City, MO 64153
816/891-7788
$$$–$$$$ NR
An 8-foot waterfall highlights the atrium courtyard of this airport hotel. The tropical setting could place you nearly anywhere, but you'd probably never think you were 4 short miles from KCI. Like all Embassy Suites, this one includes a full breakfast buffet, and the manager throws in nightly cocktails to boot. &

FAIRFIELD INN BY MARRIOTT– LIBERTY
8101 N. Church Rd.
Kansas City, MO 64158
816/792-4000
$$ NR
Located five minutes from Liberty's town center and 15 minutes north of

NORTH OF THE RIVER

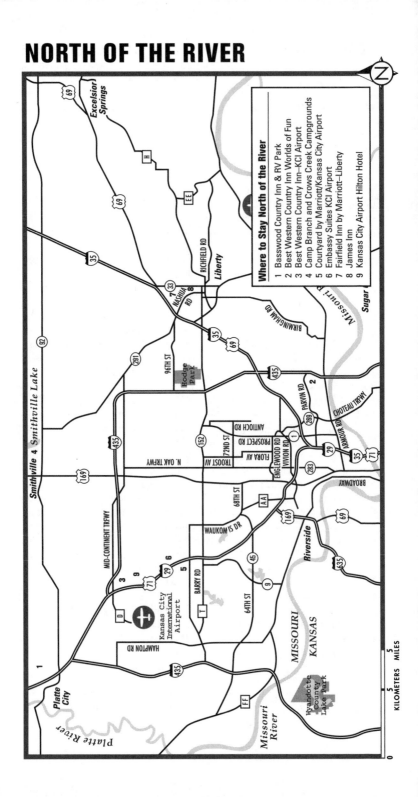

Where to Stay North of the River

1 Basswood Country Inn & RV Park
2 Best Western Country Inn Worlds of Fun
3 Best Western Country Inn–KCI Airport
4 Camp Branch and Crows Creek Campgrounds
5 Courtyard by Marriott/Kansas City Airport
6 Embassy Suites KCI Airport
7 Fairfield Inn by Marriott–Liberty
8 James Inn
9 Kansas City Airport Hilton Hotel

downtown Kansas City, Missouri, this 104-room hotel offers the budget end of Marriott's accommodation spectrum. That's not to say guests are given short shrift on amenities and services, though; they include an outdoor swimming pool, free local phone calls, and daily continental breakfast. &

Bed and Breakfast

JAMES INN
342 N. Water
Liberty, MO 64068
816/781-3677
$$$ NR
Lodged in a former church, this B&B maintains its peaceful atmosphere. The check-in area, once the sanctuary, lies beneath a St. James crucifixion mural painted by a German artist in 1918. Guest rooms off the lobby boast queen beds and unusual bathrooms, placed in overhead lofts in the old choir station. The basement serves as an exercise room with an outdoor deck and hot tub. Full breakfast served. &

Campgrounds

BASSWOOD COUNTRY INN
& RV PARK
15875 Interurban
Platte City, MO 64079
816/858-5556
$–$$$ NR
This former fish hatchery offers something for everyone. The owners spent eight years converting the lakes and surrounding 73 acres into a resort that combines bed and breakfast suites, RV and tent sites, a country store, activities, and four spring-fed fishing lakes. Although the park lies 25 miles from downtown Kansas City, visitors looking for a

summertime getaway from the city often opt for Basswood. &

CAMP BRANCH AND CROWS CREEK CAMPGROUNDS
2619 N.E. 188th St.
Smithville, MO 64089
816/532-0803
$ NR
Clay County Parks and Recreation maintains these camping areas, which rim Smithville's 7,200-acre lake. More than 750 camping spaces—many with electric, water, and sewer hookups—can be had year-round, although the water is shut off during winter. Both campgrounds include showers and laundry facilities, and are within a half-mile of boat ramps. No credit cards. &

EAST METRO

Hotels and Motels

ADAM'S MARK KANSAS CITY
9103 E. 39th St.
Kansas City, MO 64133
816/737-0200
$$–$$$ EM
The Adam's Mark overlooks I-70 toward the Truman Sports Complex, which makes it a great hotel for sports-minded visitors in town for a professional football or baseball game. The lodging features the well-regarded Remington's Steak & Seafood Grill and one of the best party nightclubs in the East Metro area, Quincy's. An indoor pool and exercise room round out the amenities. &

HOLIDAY INN SPORTS COMPLEX
4011 Blue Ridge Cut-off
Kansas City, MO 64133

EAST METRO

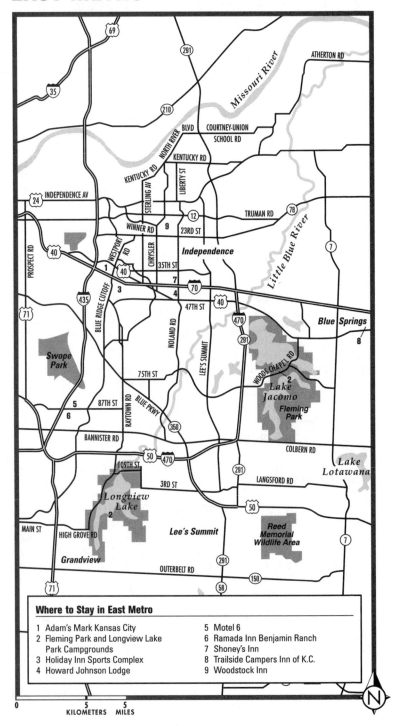

Where to Stay in East Metro

1 Adam's Mark Kansas City
2 Fleming Park and Longview Lake
  Park Campgrounds
3 Holiday Inn Sports Complex
4 Howard Johnson Lodge

5 Motel 6
6 Ramada Inn Benjamin Ranch
7 Shoney's Inn
8 Trailside Campers Inn of K.C.
9 Woodstock Inn

0   5   5
KILOMETERS MILES

816/353-5300
$$$ EM

The Holiday Inn is a prime spot for sports lovers: across the street from Kansas City's two professional stadiums. Newly renovated, the hotel features 163 guest rooms with private balconies, many of which face the impressive sports complex. There's an on-site restaurant and lounge, as well as a business center with a wide range of professional office equipment. An indoor pool, sauna, and whirlpool tempt the post-game crowd. &

HOWARD JOHNSON LODGE
4200 S. Noland Rd.
Independence, MO 64055
816/373-8856
$$ EM

Located on the southwest corner of I-70 and Noland Road, Howard Johnson's is about 3 miles from the Truman sites in Independence. A Country Kitchen next door serves meals 24 hours a day, although the lodge offers free coffee and doughnuts during the week. An indoor pool, hot tub, and miniature putting green appeal to families, while the 170 rooms and meeting space attract business travelers, too. &

MOTEL 6
6400 E. 87th St.
Kansas City, MO 64138
816/333-4468
$ EM

A modern, two-story building, this Motel 6 commands a hill a half-mile north of Bannister Mall and across the street from Benjamin Ranch. Rooms are simple and clean; coffee's available at the front desk until 10 a.m. Right next door, a Denny's restaurant is open 6 a.m. 'til midnight. &

RAMADA INN BENJAMIN RANCH
6101 E. 87th St.
Kansas City, MO 64138
816/765-4331
$$–$$$ EM

Yeeee-haw! This hotel property caters to folks interested in the adjacent Benjamin Ranch, a working spread that now rustles up barn parties, hayrides, and horseback rides. The Ramada resembles a Swiss chalet on the outside, but inside is an all-western motif. Within the hotel, the Benjamin Cattle Co. restaurant specializes in huge steaks and prime rib. &

SHONEY'S INN
4048 S. Lynn Court Dr.
Independence, MO 64055
816/254-0100
$–$$ EM

Anyone who's bellied up to one of Shoney's famous "all you can eat" breakfast bars can appreciate the proximity of this hotel to the company's restaurant. Shoney's Inn boasts a convenient I-70 location, a few miles from the attractions in Independence. The hotel has a pool, cable TV, and free local calls. &

Bed and Breakfast

WOODSTOCK INN
1212 W. Lexington
Independence, MO 64050
816/833-2233
$$ EM

Although it's in the Independence historic district, the Woodstock Inn has a decidedly more contemporary ambience. Set across the street from the RLDS Temple and Auditorium, this B&B features 11 rooms with TVs, telephones, and tasteful furnishings. Each morning, owners Todd and Patty Justice lay out a gourmet breakfast that includes delicacies ranging from thick Belgian waffles to crepes to quiche. &

Campgrounds

FLEMING PARK AND LONGVIEW LAKE PARK CAMPGROUNDS
22807 Woods Chapel Rd.
Blue Springs, MO 64105
816/229-8980, for information and free campground guide
$ EM
Together, Fleming Park and Longview Lake Park offer nearly 240 RV or tent-camping sites within easy driving distance of most area attractions. Many sites include electric, water, and sewer hookups, or a limited combination of the three. During high season, all campgrounds have attendants on duty. Only Lake Jacomo's campground remains open year-round; Blue Springs and Longview operate spring through fall. Boat ramps are within minutes of all camping areas. No credit cards. &

The Ritz-Carlton Kansas City, page 38

Ritz-Carlton Kansas City

TRAILSIDE CAMPERS INN OF K.C.
1000 R.D. Mize Rd.
Grain Valley, MO 64029
816/229-2267
$ EM
Open since 1969, Trailside provides 100 RV and 14 tent sites within 20 to 30 minutes of Independence and the Truman Sports Complex. Besides water, electric, and sewer hookups, the complex includes seasonal swimming pool and hot tub, and year-round shower and laundry facilities. Take Exit 24 from I-70. &

KANSAS CITY, KANSAS/WEST

Hotels and Motels

BEST WESTERN INN & CONFERENCE CENTER
I-35 and Highway 169
Kansas City, KS 66103
913/677-3060
$$ KCK
Two blocks from the University of Kansas Medical Center, the refined Best Western Inn & Conference Center also hosts small meetings and folks in town for the American Royal festivities each fall. Rooms come with refrigerators and coffeemakers, complimentary continental breakfast, and free local phone calls. There are also a heated outdoor pool, an indoor whirlpool, and restaurants on three sides. &

BEST WESTERN FLAMINGO MOTEL
4725 State Ave.
Kansas City, KS 66102
913/287-5511
$$ KCK
Bargain-shoppers love this hotel's view: the Dillard's (department store)

KANSAS CITY, KANSAS/WEST

Where to Stay in Kansas City, Kansas/West
1 Best Western Inn & Conference Center
2 Best Western Flamingo Motel
3 Gables Motel
4 Relax Inn
5 Travelodge Home & Hearth Inn
N
0
5 MILES
5 KILOMETERS
MISSOURI
KANSAS
Missouri River
Kansas River
Riverside
Riss Lake
Wyandotte Co. Lake Park
Wyandotte County Park
INDEPENDENCE AV
31ST ST
MINNESOTA AV
38TH ST
KANSAS AV
57TH ST
59TH ST
72ND ST
78TH ST
86TH ST
99TH ST
LEAVENWORTH RD
PARALLEL PKWY
STATE AV
RIVERVIEW AV
KAW DR
1
5
7
9
24
29
32
35
40
69
70
71
73
132
169
435
635
670
FF

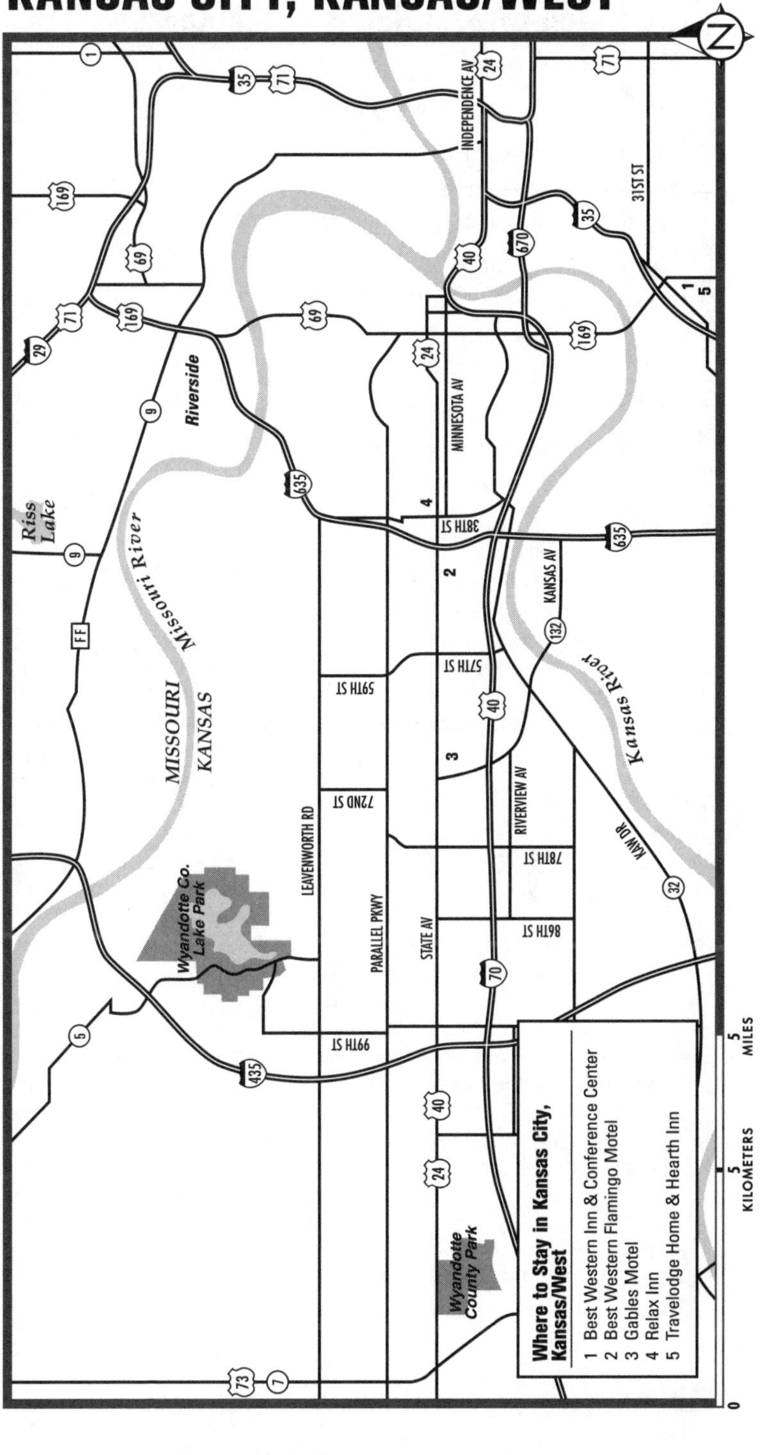

Ten Largest Hotels in the Kansas City Area

1. Hyatt Regency Crown Center, 731 rooms
2. The Westin Crown Center, 725 rooms
3. Kansas City Marriott Downtown, 573 rooms
4. Overland Park Marriott, 397 rooms
5. Omni Kansas City Hotel, 397 rooms
6. KCI Airport Marriott, 382 rooms
7. Adam's Mark, 374 rooms
8. The Ritz-Carlton Kansas City, 373 rooms
9. Doubletree Hotel at Corporate Woods, 357 rooms
10. Kansas City Airport Hilton Hotel, 348 rooms

Source: Convention and Visitors Bureau of Greater Kansas City

Clearance Center at Indian Springs. Staffed by a friendly bunch, this brick, two-story motel is, admittedly, not situated amidst a tourist mecca. But it's a less-expensive alternative—and comes with an outdoor pool and free continental breakfast. &

THE GABLES MOTEL
6831 State Ave.
Kansas City, KS 66102
913/299-8111
$ KCK
Reminiscent of a 1950s-style highway motel, the family-owned Gables Motel has 17 rooms in a one-story building set near the road. The rooms are clean and simple, and come with front-door parking and free ice. The location is inconvenient, however, if you're hoping to stay near Kansas City's major sites. No wheelchair access.

RELAX INN
3228 State Ave.
Kansas City, KS 66102
913/342-3333
$–$$ KCK
Since opening less than two years ago, the Relax Inn remains a fresh, clean, and serviceable option for budget travelers. The 27 rooms feature basic amenities, including telephone, TV, and air conditioning. No swimming pool. &

TRAVELODGE HOME & HEARTH INN
3930 Rainbow Blvd.
Kansas City, KS 66103
913/236-6880
$$ KCK
This 80-room Travelodge is not a fancy motel, but you can count on a clean room here in a location convenient to Kansas City, Kansas, destinations. Set across the street from KU Medical Center, the two-story brick property offers an outdoor swimming pool (open only during summer months) and complimentary coffee and doughnuts each morning. &

Convention and Visitors Bureau of Greater Kansas City

4

WHERE TO EAT

In the early days, Kansas City cuisine gained acclaim largely for its beef. From sirloins to strips, steak in all its incarnations was usually the heartland's meal du jour. And why not? The stockyards that bustled down at the West Bottoms gave local restaurateurs a tailor-made way to develop their gastronomical talent.

But times have changed in Kansas City. Latinos have introduced chile rellenos and chalupas; Japanese their soba noodles and shark fin. Vegetarians have opened restaurants featuring meatless delicacies. Fresh fish flown in daily—from albacore to mahimahi—now appears regularly on Kansas City menus.

Still, in all fairness, many people visit here hankering for barbecue. One of the nation's great barbecue capitals, Kansas City boasts nearly 100 different barbecue restaurants, from hole-in-the-wall joints to renovated roadhouses to cloth-napkin-and-silver cafes. You could make it your mission to sample every barbecue bistro in the area and spend a pleasant year in the effort, hitting one every third day.

Whether you want a baby-back rib or a baby artichoke heart, you can find it in this Midwestern enclave. Although trends hit Kansas City a little later than on the coasts, the metro area catches on quickly. From coffeehouses to brew pubs, the greater Kansas City area offers stylish options to diners of all ages.

This chapter begins with a list of restaurants organized by the type of food each offers. For details about each restaurant, see the following listings. Dining spots are listed alphabetically within each geographic zone.

Price rating symbols:
$ Under $10 per person
$$ $11 to $20
$$$ $21 and up

Dollar-sign symbols indicate how much you can expect to spend per person for a meal (one appetizer, one entree, and dessert) at each restaurant. Wheelchair accessibility is indicated by the &. symbol.

Barbecue

Allen's Bar-B-Que (KCK)
Arthur Bryant's Barbeque (DA)
BB's Lawnside Barbecue (CS)
Gates Bar-B-Q (DA, CS, JO, EM, KCK)
Hayward's Pit Bar-B-Que (JO)
K.C. Masterpiece Barbeque
    & Grill (CS, JO)
L.C.'s Bar-B-Q (EM)
Lil' Jake's Eat It and Beat It (DA)
Marty's Bar-B-Q (NR)
Ricky's Pit Bar-B-Que (KCK)
Rosedale Barbeque (KCK)
Smokehouse Bar-B-Que (NR)
Smoke Stack Bar-B-Q (CS)
Winslow's City Market
    Smokehouse (DA)

Breakfast

Anthony's Restaurant (DA)
Cascone's Grill (DA)
Corner Restaurant (CS)

Brew Pubs

River Market Brewing Company (DA)
75th Street Brewery (CS)

Burgers and More

Chappell's Restaurant & Lounge (NR)
Dick Clark's American Bandstand
    Grill (JO)
Otto's Malt Shop (CS)
Paradise Grill (NR)

Chinese

Bo Ling's Chinese Restaurant (CS, JO)

Genghis Khan Mongolian Grill (CS)

Contemporary

Cafe Allegro (CS)
Club 427 (DA)
Grand Street Cafe (CS)
Harold's (NR)
Harry's Bar & Tables (CS)
Yia Yia's Eurobistro (JO)
Zola (CS)

Delis

Bagel & Bagel (DA, CS, JO)
d'Bronx on Bell Street (CS)
New York Bakery
    & Delicatessen (CS)
Wild Oats Market (JO)

Down Home

Main Street Inn (EM)
Maxine's Fine Foods (CS)
Mrs. Peter's Chicken Dinners (KCK)
Stroud's (CS, NR)

Fine Dining

The American Restaurant (DA)
EBT Restaurant (CS)
Jasper's Italian Restaurant (CS)
JJ's (CS)
Peppercorn Duck Club (CS)
Rembrandt's Restaurant (NR)
Rooftop Restaurant at the
    Ritz-Carlton (CS)
Savoy Grill (DA)

French

La Méditerranée (JO)
Tatsu's French Restaurant (JO)

German

Berliner Bear (CS)
Emile's (CS)

Greek

Mr. Gyro's Greek Food
   & Pastries (JO)
Tasso's Greek Restaurant (CS)

Italian

Cafe Itàlia (JO)
Cascone's Restaurant
   & Lounge (NR)
Garozzo's Ristorante (DA, EM)
Il Trullo (JO)
V's Italian Ristorante (EM)

Japanese

Hibachi Japanese Steak House (CS)
Jun's Authentic Japanese
   Restaurant (JO)
Kabuki Japanese Restaurant (DA)

Light Lunch

Andre's Confiserie Suisse (CS)
Rozelle Court Restaurant (CS)

Mediterranean

Blvd Cafe (DA)
Cafe Barcelona (DA)
Cafe Nile (CS)
Jerusalem Cafe (CS, JO)
Papagallo (CS)
Pyramids Cafe (CS)
Shiraz Restaurant (DA)

Mexican

Acapulco Mexican Restaurant (NR)
California Taqueria (DA)
Guadalajara Café (JO)
La Fonda El Taquito (DA)
Los Amigos Mexican
   Restaurant (KCK)
Manny's Restaurante Mexicano (DA)
Margarita's (DA)
Panzon's (JO)

Outdoor dining at Crown Center

© Hallmark Cards, Inc.

Pizza

Minsky's (CS)
Wood Roasted Pizza (EM)

Seafood

The Bristol Bar & Grill (JO)
Mad Jack's Fresh Fish (KCK)
Marina Grog & Galley (EM)

Steak

Golden Ox (DA)
Hereford House (DA)
J. Gilbert's Wood-Fired
   Steaks (JO)
Plaza III–The Steakhouse (CS)

Vegetarian

Bluebird Cafe (DA)
Eden Alley (CS)

Vietnamese

May Vietnamese Restaurant (JO)
Saigon 39 (CS)

DOWNTOWN KANSAS CITY AREA

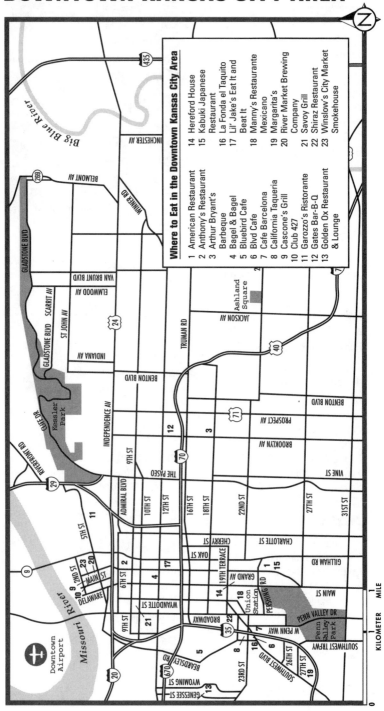

Where to Eat in the Downtown Kansas City Area

1 American Restaurant
2 Anthony's Restaurant
3 Arthur Bryant's Barbeque
4 Bagel & Bagel
5 Bluebird Cafe
6 Blvd Cafe
7 Cafe Barcelona
8 California Taqueria
9 Cascone's Grill
10 Club 427
11 Garozzo's Ristorante
12 Gates Bar-B-Q
13 Golden Ox Restaurant & Lounge
14 Hereford House
15 Kabuki Japanese Restaurant
16 La Fonda el Taquito
17 Lil' Jake's Eat It and Beat It
18 Manny's Restaurante Mexicano
19 Margarita's
20 River Market Brewing Company
21 Savoy Grill
22 Shiraz Restaurant
23 Winslow's City Market Smokehouse

DOWNTOWN KANSAS CITY AREA

THE AMERICAN RESTAURANT
Crown Center, Kansas City
816/426-1133
$$$ DA

One of Kansas City's most revered fine-dining restaurants, The American boasts a generous view of downtown. The cuisine, designed by husband-and-wife chef team Michael Smith and Debbie Gold, features locally grown meats and produce blended into artistically created dishes comprising seafood, game, and veal. An elegant spot for a quiet dinner, and the place to be seen power lunching. Reservations recommended for lunch, required at dinner. Closed Sun. &

ANTHONY'S RESTAURANT
701 Grand, Kansas City
816/221-4088
$ DA

Anyone lucky enough to be downtown at the breakfast hour should try Anthony's. An unassuming spot just south of I-35 and the River Market, Anthony's serves up hearty early-morning eye-openers that include eggs, homemade biscuits and gravy, and hand-cut potatoes. Lunch and dinner can be just as memorable. No breakfast Sun. &

ARTHUR BRYANT'S BARBEQUE
1727 Brooklyn, Kansas City
816/231-1123
$-$$ DA

More than any other Kansas City restaurant, Arthur Bryant's is a legend. Despite its seedy neighborhood, the restaurant packs in everyone from downtown executives to K.C. visitors. Eager diners line up at the counter, while a sweaty crew labors

Arthur Bryant's Barbeque

before the blackened oven to load plates with beef brisket or ribs and unpeeled fries that will be sure to shoot cholesterol-counters into the stratosphere. Lunch and dinner. No credit cards. &

BAGEL & BAGEL
111 Main St., Kansas City
816/221-2080
$ DA

For a description, see listing in the Central/South Kansas City section.

BLUEBIRD CAFE
1700 Summit, Kansas City
816/221-7559
$ DA

One of the area's few vegetarian restaurants, the Bluebird Cafe provides tasty lunch specials in a cozy spot near downtown. Highlights include daily soup and pizza specials, salads, bruschetta, and desserts—not to mention a garden across the street, from which owner Kathy Marchant harvests the restaurant's fresh produce. The restaurant's attached to City Garden health food store. Lunch Tue–Fri; brunch is served Sat and Sun. ♿

BLVD CAFE
703 Southwest Blvd., Kansas City
816/842-6984
$$ **DA**
Local art and oriental rugs adorn the walls, while chairs and tables are mixed and matched. Bohemian ambience aside, it's the food that keeps folks coming back here. The Blvd serves an eclectic menu combining foods from around the Mediterranean. Diners can order their own baba ganoush, hummus, or quiche—or request a variety to share family-style. Live music on weekends. Lunch and dinner Mon–Fri; dinner only Sat; Sun brunch. ♿

CAFE BARCELONA
520 Southwest Blvd., Kansas City
816/471-4944
$$ **DA**
Created in a former gas station, Cafe Barcelona was one of K.C.'s first restaurants to feature tapas. The Spanish-style way to sample a variety of dishes, tapas have proven big winners here. White tablecloths add an upscale feel to the space, while an outdoor deck expands the cafe during warm weather months. Lunch Mon–Fri; dinners nightly. Closed Sun.

CALIFORNIA TAQUERIA
700 Southwest Blvd., Kansas City
816/474-5571
$ **DA**
Skip trying to figure out CT's cafeteria line: it's simply a feeding frenzy of Mexican-food fans trying to get a dose of authentic south-of-the-border food. Variety reigns at this cantina, with shredded-beef tamales, chicken tacos, and the cheesiest enchiladas this side of *con queso*. Cali-

fornia Taqueria also features a full-service bar and an outdoor patio. Lunch and dinner. Closed Sun. ♿

CASCONE'S GRILL
20 E. 5th St., Kansas City
816/471-1018
$ **DA**
Eating breakfast here on a Saturday morning is like dining in a Brooklyn boxcar. A counter; two long rows of booths set next to sweaty, griddle-flipping cooks; and a line snaking out the door create a memorable atmosphere. The Italian omelet stuffed with peppers and onions, served with fried potatoes and Italian toast, start a morning off with decadence. Lunch, Cascone's other meal service, is also good and less hectic. No credit cards; no reservations. Closed Sun. ♿

CLUB 427
427 Main St., Kansas City
816/421-2582
$$ **DA**
You'd never know this nightly jazz venue was created by Dave Winslow, the owner of Winslow's City Market Smokehouse next door. Club 427 is strictly uptown, with balcony tables overlooking the main floor and a tasteful gray-and-mauve decor. Dishes are innovative, ranging from fresh pasta to steak, but the live talent and sophisticated environment often steal the show. Reservations recommended. Lunch, dinner, and Sun brunch. Closed Mon. ♿

GAROZZO'S RISTORANTE
526 Harrison, Kansas City
816/221-2455
$$ **DA**
Sinatra tunes provide the backdrop at this cozy bistro, a gem of a restaurant in an erstwhile Italian neighborhood. Old World specialties range

Ten Best Places to Drink Wine
by Doug Frost,
author of *Uncorking Wine* and one of only two people in the world to hold both the Master of Wine and Master Sommelier designations

Kansas City is a happy accident of very good restaurants and excellent wine lists. There is surprising seriousness to the wine offerings at many establishments. Best of all, food is just as serious at the places listed below:

1. **Classic Cup Cafe** (4130 Pennsylvania). This multi-personalitied Plaza eatery boasts a massive list and the best prices in the city.

2. **The American Restaurant** (Crown Center). I work here, but I'm compelled to talk about it anyway. This wine list is a wine-lover's dream.

3. **JJ's** (910 W. 48th St.). A Plaza bistro that owns a *Wine Spectator* Grand Award for its bigger-than-massive list, excellent pricing, and enough champagne and port to drown yourself in.

4. **Starker's Private Reserve** (200 Nichols Rd.). Once a private club, this elegant room is open to the public, has an even longer list than before, and sports its own *Wine Spectator* Grand Award.

5. **Joe D's Winebar** (6227 Brookside Plaza). The friendliest waitresses in town serving from a wine-by-the-glass selection of more than 50 offerings. The list is revamped every few months.

6. **Cafe Allegro** (1815 W. 39th St.). This restaurant's great food is complemented by a rich, selective, and exciting list and by equally serious wine-by-the-glass offerings.

7. **Il Trullo** (9056 Metcalf, Overland Park). It's fun to drink wine here because the food's so straightforward and delightful, just like the proprietor.

8. **The Vineyards** (505 Spring, Weston). This tasty bistro is worth a drive to nearby Weston. There's good wine to slurp and even better food.

9. **Plaza III—The Steakhouse** (4749 Pennsylvania). A long list of reds and some great rarities.

10. **Blvd Cafe** (703 Southwest Blvd.). Mediterranean-eclectic food paired with a wine and beer list that's long on food and short in its pricing. You can afford a second bottle.

from veal to chicken to pasta, from most regions of Italy. Tables are set close in this intimate spot, while old family photos look down from the walls. Every dish on Mike Garozzo's menu is *molto bene*. Dinner reservations recommended. Lunch Mon–Fri; dinner Mon–Sat. Closed Sun. ♿ Additional location: EM.

GATES BAR-B-Q
1221 Brooklyn, Kansas City
816/483-3880
$ **DA**
For a description, see listing in the Central/South Kansas City section.

GOLDEN OX RESTAURANT & LOUNGE
1600 Genessee, Kansas City
816/842-2866
$$ **DA**
K.C.'s stockyards have vanished, but the Golden Ox carries on the tradition within grilling distance of the one-time cattle confab. Dark paneling and a 1950s Western motif provide a nostalgic background to the hearty steak-and-potatoes menu. Any of the hickory-grilled steaks—including the Kansas City Strip—will be paradise for any beef-eater. Reservations recommended. Lunch Mon–Fri; dinner nightly. ♿

HEREFORD HOUSE
20th and Main, Kansas City
816/842-1080
$$$ **DA**
A local institution since 1957, the Hereford House cooks its T-bone, prime rib, and K.C. Strip dinners over a hickory-fueled fire. Diners enjoy the clubby atmosphere, filled with dark woods and soft lighting. Desserts, especially peach cobbler, top off many meals. In 1996, *Wine Spectator* gave the restaurant an "Award of Excel-

lence" for having one of the world's outstanding restaurant wine lists. Reservations recommended. Lunch Mon–Fri; dinner nightly. ♿

KABUKI JAPANESE RESTAURANT
2450 Grand Ave., Kansas City
816/472-1717
$$$ **DA**
Lending an Asian flair to Crown Center, the Kabuki serves Japanese specialties such as tempura and sukiyaki. An authentic sushi bar gives diners a chance to try everything from onaga to tako to the venerable California roll. Sit at one of the Kabuki's tables or right at the sushi bar, where you can watch the edible works of art unfold. Lunch Mon–Sat; dinner nightly. Reservations are recommended. ♿

LA FONDA EL TAQUITO
800 Southwest Blvd., Kansas City
816/471-1675
$ **DA**
This neighborhood restaurant has a real family feel to it—especially when dark-eyed children trundle the tortilla chips to your table. Hearty portions with an authentic Mexican bite, homemade salsa and chips, and an unpretentious decor make La Fonda a relaxing and casual place to dine. You know it's good when the place is filled with Hispanic American diners. Reservations recommended Fri and Sat. Closed Mon. ♿

LIL' JAKE'S EAT IT AND BEAT IT
1227 Grand Ave., Kansas City
816/283-0880
$–$$ **DA**
Danny Edwards, dubbed "Lil' Jake" after his father, opened this tiny, low-key lunch spot in the shadow of downtown skyscrapers in 1983. Ever since, his 18 seats have remained

Cocktail lounge at the Hereford House

filled, and carry-out traffic from surrounding businesses runs strong. Fans come for everything from the Lil' Jake's beef sandwich to the burnt ends and full slabs. Lunch only, Mon–Fri. No reservations. &

MANNY'S RESTAURANTE MEXICANO
207 Southwest Blvd., Kansas City
816/474-7696
$ **DA**

You can't miss Manny's: Its Southwest-style building has an impressive gold-topped tower. Inside, the restaurant features two kinds of salsa, generous portions at reasonable prices, and an ongoing fiesta atmosphere. Dining rooms flow from one to the next, some at different levels. A popular spot for Mexican-food aficionados. Lunch and dinner. Closed Sun. &

MARGARITA'S
2829 Southwest Blvd., Kansas City
816/931-4849
$ **DA**

Voted Kansas City's best Mexican restaurant for nine years, Margarita's boasts a loud and fun *ambiente,* especially during Friday happy hours. Expect a wait at Margarita's, but the abundant portions and tasty namesake concoctions make the delay worthwhile. Margarita's also serves at three other locations (in Gladstone, Shawnee Mission, and Martin City). Lunch and dinner. &

RIVER MARKET BREWING COMPANY
500 Walnut, Kansas City
816/471-6300
$$ **DA**

Before the River Market Brewing Company moved in, every restaurant in recent memory had failed at 500 Walnut. But this brew pub packs them in, serving pizzas, sandwiches, and American-style specialties—in addition to its own signature brews. A billiard parlor and live music on weekends round out the entertainment. Lunch and dinner. &

SAVOY GRILL
9th and Central, Kansas City
816/842-3890

$$$ **DA**

Open since 1903, the Savoy is a K.C. classic. In the movie *Mr. and Mrs. Bridge,* the characters played by Paul Newman and Joanne Woodward favored the elegant restaurant for its timeless appeal. From the revolving glass doors to the white-jacketed waiters to the steak-and-seafood menu, the Savoy remains a traditional fine-dining favorite. Reservations required. Lunch Mon–Sat; dinner nightly. &

SHIRAZ RESTAURANT
320 Southwest Blvd., Kansas City
816/472-0015
$$ **DA**

The chef/owner at Shiraz blends some of his favorite flavors into an eclectic menu that combines Asian with American, Middle Eastern with continental. The result is a tasty ensemble of innovative dishes. A courtyard provides pleasant seating in warmer weather, while monthly exhibits featuring local artists create a decorative dining experience. Reser-

Rozelle Court Restaurant, page 70

vations recommended. Lunch Mon–Fri, dinner Mon–Sat. Closed Sun. &

WINSLOW'S CITY MARKET SMOKEHOUSE
20 E. 5th St., Kansas City
816/471-7427
$–$$ **DA**

Those in the River Market can follow the fragrant fumes to Winslow's City Market Smokehouse. Inside they'll discover the Famous Smokie, a chopped burnt-ends sandwich that's a patrons' favorite, while a trio of rib platters tempts the big eaters. Everything's fresh, bought right from the farmer's market. Dave Winslow regularly offers live Kansas City blues and owns a pub called Slow's City Market Bar next door. Lunch seven days a week; dinner Tue–Sat. &

CENTRAL/SOUTH KANSAS CITY

ANDRE'S CONFISERIE SUISSE
5018 Main St., Kansas City
816/561-3440
$ **CS**

They make it simple at Andre's. Each day, the chef prepares three lunch entrees; at least one is always the most delicious quiche you've ever tasted. A crispy vegetable and a dressed salad accompany the main course, followed by dessert—either one of several from the cart or anything from the amply stocked cases up front. Diners appreciate the Swiss-chalet atmosphere, the appetizingly simple fare, and the one-price-gets-all format. Lunch only. No reservations. Open Tue–Sat. &

BAGEL & BAGEL
556 Westport Rd., Kansas City
816/561-2080

CENTRAL/SOUTH KANSAS CITY

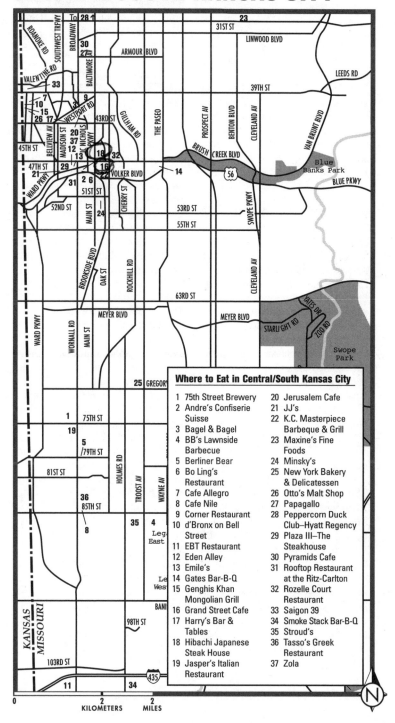

Where to Eat in Central/South Kansas City

1 75th Street Brewery
2 Andre's Confiserie Suisse
3 Bagel & Bagel
4 BB's Lawnside Barbecue
5 Berliner Bear
6 Bo Ling's Restaurant
7 Cafe Allegro
8 Cafe Nile
9 Corner Restaurant
10 d'Bronx on Bell Street
11 EBT Restaurant
12 Eden Alley
13 Emile's
14 Gates Bar-B-Q
15 Genghis Khan Mongolian Grill
16 Grand Street Cafe
17 Harry's Bar & Tables
18 Hibachi Japanese Steak House
19 Jasper's Italian Restaurant
20 Jerusalem Cafe
21 JJ's
22 K.C. Masterpiece Barbeque & Grill
23 Maxine's Fine Foods
24 Minsky's
25 New York Bakery & Delicatessen
26 Otto's Malt Shop
27 Papagallo
28 Peppercorn Duck Club–Hyatt Regency
29 Plaza III–The Steakhouse
30 Pyramids Cafe
31 Rooftop Restaurant at the Ritz-Carlton
32 Rozelle Court Restaurant
33 Saigon 39
34 Smoke Stack Bar-B-Q
35 Stroud's
36 Tasso's Greek Restaurant
37 Zola

$ **CS**

Bagel & Bagel's Brookside location (6322 Brookside Plaza) was the first in Kansas City to take the round rolls mainstream, but the company's Westport spot is its largest and most accessible. Bagel & Bagel features all kinds of bagel sandwiches as well as salads, soups, and beverages. Bagels, flavored with onion, cinnamon raisin, and a whole lot more, are available to go, too. Breakfast, lunch, and dinner daily. Closes at 5 p.m. on Sun. ♿ Additional locations: DA, CS, JO.

BB'S LAWNSIDE BARBECUE
1205 E. 85th St., Kansas City
816/822-7427
$–$$ **CS**

Set in a ramshackle roadhouse, BB's Lawnside combines owner Lindsay Shannon's dual passions: barbecue and blues. BB's signature pork ribs come slathered in a sweet sauce slightly reminiscent of apples and cinnamon. Side dishes, such as batter fries and baked beans with green peppers, fill out the fare. Diners sit family-style at long tables covered with checkered tablecloths or in booths along the walls. Live blues lights up BB's Thur–Sun. Lunch and dinner. Closed Mon and Tue. No reservations; no credit cards. ♿

BERLINER BEAR
7815 Wornall Rd., Kansas City
816/444-2828
$–$$ **CS**

It's just a simple storefront along Wornall Road, but inside unfolds the world of Germany. This venerable restaurant/bar has delivered the tastes, sounds, and sights of Deutschland for close to a quarter-century. All the standards, from Wiener schnitzel to sauerbraten, can

be found, but the goose dinner is a house specialty, along with German beers, wines, and liqueurs. Lunch and dinner, Tue–Sat. ♿

BO LING'S RESTAURANT
4800 Main St., Kansas City
816/753-1718
$$ **CS**

Bo Ling's original location commands the Board of Trade building's first floor, serving as a refined gathering spot for local Chinese families. In addition to traditional Asian dishes, the menu includes delicacies such as steamed buns, four-happiness rolls, and dim sum. Two locations in Johnson County offer the same flavorful food, with a slightly different ambience. Reservations recommended. Lunch and dinner daily. ♿

CAFE ALLEGRO
1815 W. 39th St., Kansas City
816/561-3663
$$–$$$ **CS**

When founding chef/owner Steve Cole opened Cafe Allegro in the 1980s, it was the start of 39th Street's restaurant revival. Within this sophisticated cafe, Cole has devised an eclectic menu featuring veal, fish, and pasta, artfully combined with exceptional sauces and accompaniments. The restaurant specializes in seasonal produce, so you know everything's fresh. Reservations recommended. Lunch weekdays; dinner Mon–Sat. ♿

CAFE NILE
8433 Wornall Rd., Kansas City
816/361-9097
$$ **CS**

Tucked into a curb-hugging strip mall, Cafe Nile delivers Mediterranean cuisine at its most authentic. Dishes such as baba ganoush, hummus, and

Ten Favorite Kansas City Barbecue Joints

by Carolyn Wells,
publisher of *The K.C. Bullsheet*, the official
publication of the Kansas City Barbeque Society
(motto "Barbecue: It's not just for breakfast anymore.")

1. **Arthur Bryant's**. "Beef and fries" is the order of the day— brisket piled high between slices of white bread, complemented by fries, fresh cut and fried in pure lard. Be adventuresome: try the vinegar/paprika sauce for which Bryant's is famous.

2. **K.C. Masterpiece Barbeque & Grill**. Upscale "que" here, covered with the famous K.C. Masterpiece Barbecue Sauce. The only place in town to get a "Carolina" pork sandwich—my personal favorite.

3. **Lil' Jake's Eat It and Beat It**. This tiny, 18-seat establishment has a big following. Best bets are the brisket sandwich, followed closely by the grilled chicken breast.

4. **BB's Lawnside Bar-B-Q**. Blues and barbecue aficionado Lindsay Shannon serves up hickory-smoked ribs and rib tips. The fries are a house specialty.

5. **Grand Emporium**. "Amazing Grace" Harris, head pitmaster, rules her barbecue kingdom at this wildly eclectic blues, booze, and barbecue palace. She offers a full complement of barbecue meats, seasoned with her secret sauces and rubs.

6. **Gates Bar-B-Q**. Local "living legend" Ollie Gates has the closest thing to a chain of barbecue restaurants in K.C. Servers enthusiastically call, "HI! MAY I HELP YOU?" as you enter. Gates' regionally popular sauces complement the array of barbecued meats.

7. **Winslow's City Market Smokehouse**. The perfect ending to a morning of heavy-duty City Market shopping. The beef sandwich is the best bet.

8. **Marty's Bar-B-Q**. All the standard barbecued fare, and Memphis-style pork and Texas-style beef. Grilled chicken breast and great Italian sausage offer additional variety in this Northland eatery.

9. **Rosedale Barbeque**. From the oldest continually operated barbecue place in the Kansas City area, Anthony Riecke serves loyal rib aficionados. Offerings are topped with his signature sauce.

10. **L.C.'s Bar-B-Q**. With a smoker chained to a utility pole in front of this modest establishment, L.C.'s is the pit stop of choice for sports fans on the way to Arrowhead and Kauffman Stadiums.

falafel are expected, but the stuffed lobster filled with fresh vegetables, filet of sole, and rack of lamb may not be. Cafe Nile's white tablecloths, fresh-cut flowers, belly dancers, and live Greek music on weekends are pleasant touches. Weekend reservations are recommended. Dinner Mon–Sat. Closed Sun. &

CORNER RESTAURANT
4059 Broadway, Kansas City
816/931-6630
$ **CS**
The Corner is an authentic neighborhood coffee shop that serves up hearty omelets, pan-fried potatoes, pancakes, and sandwiches. Once a vegetarian hangout for Westport's hippie crowd, the Corner now attracts residents from all over town who value a good breakfast, lunch, or dinner at a reasonable price. Expect a weekend wait on the sidewalk. No reservations; no credit cards. Closed Sat and Sun evenings. &

D'BRONX ON BELL STREET
3904 Bell St., Kansas City
816/531-0550

$ **CS**
Here's a deli that will make you think you're in the heart of Manhattan. The food—ranging from piled-high pizzas to massive deli sandwiches—fills you up, while the intellectually hip atmosphere often prevalent in the 39th Street area feeds your "cool" quotient. Kansas Citians in the know head for this deli, which is also a hangout for baseball legend George Brett. No reservations. Lunch and dinner Mon–Sat. Closed Sun. &

EBT RESTAURANT
1310 Carondelet, Kansas City
816/942-8870
$$$ **CS**
EBT stands for Emery Bird Thayer, a long-time downtown department store. Today this restaurant features some of the store's architectural treasures, from gilded elevator cages to massive stone pillars. Diners descend on EBT for special occasions, from sealing a business deal to proposing a marriage. The American and French-style cuisine, served in a garden-like setting, is elegant and re-

The Savoy Grill, page 61

Convention and Visitors Bureau of Greater Kansas City

fined. Reservations recommended. Lunch weekdays; dinner nightly. &

EDEN ALLEY
707 W. 47th St., Kansas City
816/561-5415
$–$$ CS

The basement of Unity Temple on the Plaza provides an unconventional setting for Monica Jones' and Sandi Corder's unconventional restaurant, but the quirky combination works. Vegetarian victuals—from a veggie burger to a falafel platter, Moroccan pizza to quesadilla—prevail among the hand-painted tables and local artwork. Live music on Friday nights. Lunch and dinner Mon–Fri. Closed first Tue of each month. No credit cards. &

EMILE'S
302 Nichols Rd., Kansas City
816/753-2771
$ CS

Opa! Smack dab in the center of the Country Club Plaza, Emile's serves an authentic German menu that includes bratwurst, rouladen, schnitzel, and hot and cold potato salad—plus apple strudel for dessert. In the summer, Emile's tree-shaded outdoor patio provides one of the best spots to while away a warm afternoon. Weekend reservations are recommended. Lunch and dinner daily; closes at 5 p.m. Sun. No wheelchair access.

GATES BAR-B-Q
4707 Paseo, Kansas City
816/923-0900
$ CS

The first time you enter a Gates restaurant, the shouts of "HI! MAY I HELP YOU?" knock you back. Get used to it, though, because this is an important selling point proprietor

Ollie Gates instills in his staff at his legendary Rib Tech. Another important element at Kansas City's seven Gates locations is the barbecue itself: succulent, spicy beef and pork that keep 'em coming back. No reservations; no credit cards. Lunch and dinner. & Additional locations: DA, JO, EM, KCK.

GENGHIS KHAN MONGOLIAN GRILL
3906 Bell, Kansas City
816/753-3600
$$ CS

The novelty of dining at a Mongolian grill can often be as enjoyable as the food—and Genghis Khan proves it. This quiet Westport restaurant lays out a splendid buffet of raw meats, vegetables, and condiments that diners pile onto their plates, then take to the chef at the expansive grill. It's one price for all you can pack away. Weekend reservations recommended. Lunch and dinner; closed Sun. &

GRAND STREET CAFE
4740 Grand, Kansas City
816/561-8000
$$ CS

Across Main Street from the Country Club Plaza, the Grand Street Cafe offers a stylishly contemporary setting, including European-style bar, gigantic picture windows, and ivy-painted walls. The food's creative here, too, thanks to chef Michael Peterson, who constantly invents new specials to wow his diners. Count on dishes like double-thick pork chops, grilled tenderloin, and nightly fish specials, and an impressive wine list. Lunch and dinner. &

HARRY'S BAR & TABLES
501 Westport Rd., Kansas City
816/561-3950

$$ CS

Harry's occupies a prime corner in Westport, with large windows that look out on the passing crowd. Plenty of interest takes place inside, however, starting with Harry's 58 brands of single-malt Scotch and 30 cigar varieties. It's definitely a smoke-and-Scotch setting, but the place offers everything from tapas to a fixed-price menu to steak and seafood à la carte. In warm weather, Harry's opens its converted caboose patio. Lunch and dinner. Weekend dinner reservations recommended. Call ahead for wheelchair assistance.

HIBACHI JAPANESE STEAK HOUSE
4745 Wyandotte Rd., Kansas City
816/753-0707
$$ CS

Need a meal *and* entertainment? Head to Hibachi, where knife-wielding chefs command your attention at the teppanyaki grill. At Hibachi, more than a dozen grills invite diners to pull up a seat and watch the chefs work their cutting-edge magic. This team is ready to cook just about any Japanese-style grilled food imaginable. Lunch and dinner. Up one flight of stairs, Hibachi has limited wheelchair access.

JASPER'S ITALIAN RESTAURANT
405 W. 75th St., Kansas City
816/363-3003
$$$ CS

A Kansas City landmark since 1954, Jasper's creates memorable food from Italy's Tuscan, Sicilian, and Piedmont regions. The restaurant, owned by the venerable Mirable family, is now run by the second generation: Jasper Jr. in the kitchen with brother, Leonard, as president. Jasper's was recently voted one of

the eight best Italian restaurants in the U.S. and listed in the *Veronelli Guide,* the prestigious bible for native Italians traveling abroad. Reservations recommended. Dinner only; closed Sun. &

JERUSALEM CAFE
431 Westport Rd., Kansas City
816/756-2770
$ CS

Look for a blend of Greek, Middle Eastern, and other Mediterranean foods in this midtown favorite. Located in Westport, between the artsy Tivoli Theatre and Natural Wear's organic apparel, Jerusalem recently doubled its space to accommodate the crowds. The moussaka rates especially high, as do the falafel and hummus. A less-crowded location operates in Overland Park. Lunch and dinner. Limited wheelchair access.

JJ'S
910 W. 48th St., Kansas City
816/561-7136
$$$ CS

An intimate restaurant just west of the Country Club Plaza, JJ's boasts one of the city's most acclaimed international wine lists. The American/continental menu features specialties such as seafood, pasta, and steaks in a romantic, artistic setting. Waiters are attentive and the food is divine. Reservations recommended. Lunch weekdays; dinner nightly. &

K.C. MASTERPIECE BARBECUE & GRILL
4747 Wyandotte Rd., Kansas City
816/531-3332
$–$$ CS

The barbecue at K.C. Masterpiece will probably seem most familiar to visitors, since the signature sauce is sold nationwide. Kansas City's two Masterpiece locations (the other's in Overland Park) serve everything from burnt ends to baby back ribs to brisket; the K.C. Combo is a good way to sample several hickory-smoked favorites, while Ribs, Ribs, Ribs provides enough ribs for two. Onion straws—mounded on a platter—have become a popular pre-dinner warm-up. Lunch and dinner. ♿

MAXINE'S FINE FOODS
3041 Benton Blvd., Kansas City
816/924-2004
$–$$ **CS**

Maxine Byrd opened her place more than 35 years ago. Same restaurant, same place, same great soul-food menu. Breakfast here is big: consider link, Polish, beef, or Italian sausage for starters. Lunch always includes baked chicken and dressing and black-eyed peas, then runs to pig hocks, oxtails, and neck bones. Photographs of athletes, musicians, and other prominent African Americans line the walls. Breakfast and lunch Mon–Fri; breakfast only Sat and Sun. No credit cards. ♿

MINSKY'S
5105 Main St., Kansas City
816/561-5100
$ **CS**

A trusty neighborhood joint, Minsky's lures diners who love pizza. Especially noteworthy are Nature's Choice, a veggie pizza on a honey-whole wheat crust; and the Tostada Pizza, stacked high with chicken, beans, cheese, tomatoes, and salsa. Minsky's also serves pasta and sandwiches in its pubby setting just south of the Plaza. Six other locations. Lunch and dinner. ♿

NEW YORK BAKERY & DELICATESSEN
7016 Troost, Kansas City
816/523-0432
$ **CS**

Reminiscent of Manhattan's Lower East Side, the New York Bakery concocts a wonderfully versatile mix of kosher specialties, pastries, and party trays. Sandwiches here come piled high, and side dishes provide ample portions. Lunch and dinner; closed Sun. ♿

OTTO'S MALT SHOP
3903 Wyoming, Kansas City
816/756-1010
$ **CS**

Owners Dave Otto Miller and Kathleen Sweeny bring the Fifties-style diner back to life, complete with burgers, blue-plate specials, shakes, and malts. The big-eyed brave go for "bucket-size" malts—a whopping 32 ounces—and Fat Boys, a 6-ounce patty beneath four cheeses, bacon, and a fried egg. Lunch and dinner Sun–Thur; open 24 hours Fri and Sat. No credit cards. ♿

PAPAGALLO
3535 Broadway, Kansas City
816/756-3227
$$ **CS**

Chef/owner Ray Kattan often greets his guests at the door, usually wearing his signature fedora. Kattan's delectable cuisine ranges from artichoke-heart sauté to linguini with clams to tenderloin marsala—all with a Mediterranean flair. Kattan was a prize-winning chef from Caesar's Palace Properties, and his showmanship radiates. Local art adorns the walls at Papagallo, and jazz greats croon over a sound system. Lunch, dinner, and Sun brunch. Closed Mon. ♿

THE PEPPERCORN DUCK CLUB–HYATT REGENCY
2345 McGee, Kansas City
816/421-1234
$$$ CS

True to its name, this fine-dining restaurant features a variety of innovative duck dishes, from grilled to sautéed with several sauces. Other gourmet entrees, including beef, lamb, and seafood, round out an impressive selection, while the lavishly stocked Ultra-Chocolate Bar fulfills every chocoholic's fantasy. Dinner reservations recommended. Lunch weekdays; dinner nightly; Sun brunch. ♿

PLAZA III–THE STEAKHOUSE
4749 Pennsylvania, Kansas City
816/753-0000
$$$ CS

Resembling a dark-paneled men's club of the Forties, the Plaza III reigns as one of Kansas City's favorite upscale steak houses. Specialties include prime cuts of Midwestern beef, as well as fresh fish and lobster. At lunch, look for lighter fare, including sandwiches, salads, and the signature Steak Soup. Plaza III has been noted for its extensive wine list. Reservations recommended. Lunch Tue–Sat; dinner nightly. ♿

PYRAMIDS CAFE
3421 Broadway, Kansas City
816/561-5520
$$ CS

At this Midtown eatery, the cuisine stays true to its name: mostly Egyptian influences fill a menu of delicious dishes. Chicken Musaheb, for example, is a chicken breast marinated with garlic and sprinkled with a delicate yogurt sauce. Pyramids also features Mediterranean specialties such as gyros, kabobs, and falafel. Lunch and dinner; closed Sun. ♿

ROOFTOP RESTAURANT AT THE RITZ-CARLTON
401 Ward Pkwy., Kansas City
816/756-1500
$$$ CS

Executive chef Michael Fallacara offers a menu at the Rooftop that gives familiar items some unfamiliar twists. A Tuscan hunter-style strip steak with porcini mushrooms, for instance, has been delightfully popular with loyal patrons, as has sautéed veal tenderloin with pumpkin risotto. The Rooftop—with an outstanding view of the Plaza and awards for both food and wine—also features Cuisine Vitale and macrobiotic meals as healthful dining choices. Dinner nightly; Sun brunch. ♿

ROZELLE COURT RESTAURANT
4525 Oak, Kansas City
816/751-1ART
$–$$ CS

Dining at the Rozelle Court makes you think you're in Italy. Tucked within the Nelson-Atkins Museum of Art, this three-story, domed courtyard recalls a Tuscan villa. Food is served in an informal cafeteria style, but the restaurant's chefs create some ambrosial dishes and the artistic surroundings couldn't be more inspiring. Lunch Tue–Sat; dinner Fri only, featuring live music; desserts Sun. Restaurant closed Mon. ♿

SAIGON 39
1806 1/2 39th St., Kansas City
816/531-4447
$$ CS

Vietnamese specialties at this bustling Westport restaurant include all kinds of stir-fried meats, fish, and vegetables served over a variety of noodles and fried rice. You can choose mild or spicy; it's all flavorful and authentic. Occasionally, owner/

chef Mimi Perkins ventures into the dining area to make sure you're happy with what she's cooked. Lunch and dinner; closed Sun. &

75TH STREET BREWERY
520 W. 75th St., Kansas City
816/523-4677
$$ **CS**

Set on a busy street in the Waldo neighborhood, the 75th Street Brewery draws a yuppie crowd for happy hour. Handcrafted beer, made in a glass-walled room in the brew pub's center, varies from Cowtown Wheat Light to the very dark Muddy Mo Stout. The food at 75th Street shows a real artistry, too: pizzas, sandwiches, and grilled entrees are served in the terraza-like setting. Live music on weekends. Lunch and dinner. &

SMOKE STACK BAR-B-Q
13441 Holmes, Martin City
816/942-9141
$$ **CS**

Martin City is a long way from downtown, but the Smoke Stack is worth the trip. Ribs, pork sandwiches, and burnt ends, all cooked on a hickory-wood grill, will satisfy even the pickiest barbecue aficionado. Smoked fish is another house specialty, while the baked beans and coleslaw make the ideal accompaniment. Lunch and dinner. No reservations; expect at least an hour wait on weekend nights. &

STROUD'S
1015 E. 85th St., Kansas City
816/333-2132 or 454-9600
$$ **CS**

Stroud's is one of those Kansas City traditions that soundly deserves its reputation. This humble-looking joint features pan-fried chicken, mashed potatoes, green beans, and cinna-mon rolls that attract diners willing to wait as long as two hours for a table. Set in a sprawling, wood bungalow, Stroud's epitomizes the days when folks ate real food in real surroundings. No reservations. Lunch and dinner. & Additional location: NR.

TASSO'S GREEK RESTAURANT
8411 Wornall Rd., Kansas City
816/363-4776
$$ **CS**

Save room for the baklava at this fun-loving spot. On weekends, a tasty Hellenic meal of moussaka, spring lamb, or gyros comes with live Greek music and belly dancing. A small cafe with its own loyal following, Tasso's is the place to go for celebrating like the Athenians. Beware the owner, however, bearing countless glasses of the licorice-like ouzo. Lunch and dinner; closed Mon and Tue. Weekend dinner reservations recommended. &

ZOLA
4113 Pennsylvania, Kansas City
816/561-9191
$$–$$$ **CS**

A fairly new bistro in Westport, Zola combines classy comfort with inventive fare. Cuisine in this genteel restaurant—carved from a historic brick building—ranges from wasabi chicken to black-pepper pasta with pork tenderloin to littleneck clams stewed with garlic and pancetta. Lunch Mon–Sat; dinner nightly. Reservations suggested. &

JOHNSON COUNTY

BAGEL & BAGEL
8600 College Blvd., Overland Park
913/338-2084
$ **JO**

JOHNSON COUNTY

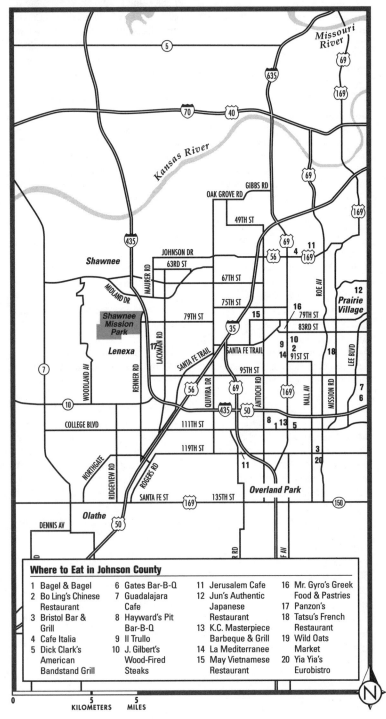

Where to Eat in Johnson County

1. Bagel & Bagel
2. Bo Ling's Chinese Restaurant
3. Bristol Bar & Grill
4. Cafe Italia
5. Dick Clark's American Bandstand Grill
6. Gates Bar-B-Q
7. Guadalajara Cafe
8. Hayward's Pit Bar-B-Q
9. Il Trullo
10. J. Gilbert's Wood-Fired Steaks
11. Jerusalem Cafe
12. Jun's Authentic Japanese Restaurant
13. K.C. Masterpiece Barbeque & Grill
14. La Mediterranee
15. May Vietnamese Restaurant
16. Mr. Gyro's Greek Food & Pastries
17. Panzon's
18. Tatsu's French Restaurant
19. Wild Oats Market
20. Yia Yia's Eurobistro

For a description, see listing in the Central/South Kansas City section.

BO LING'S CHINESE RESTAURANT
9055 Metcalf, Overland Park
913/341-1718
$$ **JO**
For a description, see listing in the Central/South Kansas City section.

THE BRISTOL BAR & GRILL
5400 W. 119th St., Leawood
913/663-5777
$$–$$$ **JO**
Long a staple on the Country Club Plaza, the Bristol was unceremoniously bounced a few years ago by Plaza owners who wanted some new blood. The Bristol rebounded in a south Johnson County location, boasting bigger crowds than ever. Known for its classy seafood dishes—from seared yellowfin tuna to mesquite-grilled mahimahi—the Bristol also offers nonstop buttermilk biscuits and an impressive wine list. Reservations recommended. Lunch, dinner, and Sun brunch. &

CAFE ITÀLIA
6524 Martway, Mission
913/262-9242
$$ **JO**
Perhaps a small Mission strip mall doesn't seem the typical spot for white tablecloths and attentive waiters. But this Italian restaurant blends stylish service with some of the best Italian food in Kansas City. One of the restaurants launched by Joe Avelluto, Cafe Itàlia and its pastas and desserts will simply knock your socks off. Lunch Mon–Fri; dinner Mon–Sat; closed Sun. &

DICK CLARK'S AMERICAN BANDSTAND GRILL

10975 Metcalf, Overland Park
913/451-1600
$$ **JO**
Dick Clark entertained millions with his weekly TV show. Now you can enjoy his restaurant and dance club, which serves everything from burgers, pasta, and seafood to chicken, steaks, and ribs. At Dick Clark's Walk of Fame, celebrity hounds can see mementos from stars such as Elton John, Madonna, and Michael Jackson. Dessert specials such as the "45 RPM Chocolate Orgy" (chocolate ice cream, chocolate chip cookie, dark chocolate sauce) continue the theme. Lunch and dinner. &

GATES BAR-B-Q
103rd St. and State Line Rd., Leawood
913/383-1752
$ **JO**
For a description, see listing in the Central/South Kansas City section.

GUADALAJARA CAFE
1144 W. 103rd St., Leawood
913/941-4471
$$ **JO**
Mexican food in a fine-dining setting: it doesn't get any better than this. Restaurateurs Victor Esqueda and Gilbert Gutierrez base their extensive menu on foods from their native Mexican city. Steak, chicken, and seafood specialties hold center stage, with the standard tacos, enchiladas, and burritos a happy sideline. Lunch and dinner. Dinner reservations recommended. &

HAYWARD'S PIT BAR-B-QUE
11051 Antioch, Overland Park
913/451-8080
$ **JO**
Barbecue master Hayward Spears dishes up succulent ribs, smoky

Ten Favorite Kansas City Restaurants
by Neil Smith,
6-foot 4-inch, 273-pound defensive end for the Kansas City Chiefs, who, at this printing, leads the National Football League in quarterback sacks

1. **Copeland's** (11920 Metcalf, Overland Park; Smith's own just-opened Cajun restaurant)
2. **The Bristol Bar & Grill** (5400 W. 119th St., Leawood)
3. **Houston's** (4640 Wornall Rd., Kansas City)
4. **Parkway 600** (600 Ward Pkwy., Kansas City)
5. **Gates Bar-B-Q** (several locations)
6. **Maxine's Fine Foods** (3041 Benton Blvd., Kansas City)
7. **Harry Starker's** (200 Nichols Rd., Kansas City)
8. **Los Corrals** (408 W. 9th St., Kansas City)
9. **Jules'** (4740 Jefferson, Kansas City)
10. **Plaza III–The Steakhouse** (4749 Pennsylvania, Kansas City)

brisket, and delicious sauces in his College Boulevard location. Johnson Countians naturally line up here for lunch, but the rest of the city heads over, too, for Hayward's chicken, smoked sausage, and beef sandwiches on plump buns. Lunch and dinner. &

IL TRULLO
9056 Metcalf, Overland Park
913/341-3773
$–$$ **JO**
Joe Avelluto's newest restaurant features food from the Adriatic coast's Apulia region, often described as the heel of Italy's boot. The cozy, candlelit atmosphere only enhances the food, which includes everything from pizza with homemade ingredients to *zuppa di mare* (soup of the sea). Lunch Mon–Fri; dinner nightly. Weekend reservations recommended. &

J. GILBERT'S WOOD-FIRED STEAKS
8901 Metcalf, Overland Park
913/642-8070
$$ **JO**
Hand-selected steaks cooked over a visible, wood-fired grill give J. Gilbert's an Old West feel. House specialties include some unusual side dishes, including homemade potato chips covered with melted bleu cheese, and poblano au gratin (a crusty baked chili pepper). The menu also features roasted chicken, barbecued salmon, and pasta. Reservations recommended. Dinner only. &

JERUSALEM CAFE
10136 W. 119th St., Overland Park
913/663-1743
$ **JO**
For a description, see listing in the Central/South Kansas City section.

JUN'S AUTHENTIC JAPANESE RESTAURANT
7660 State Line Rd., Prairie Village
913/341-4924
$$ JO

An unexpected discovery across the parking lot from Schnucks' grocery store, Jun's combines an expertly staffed sushi bar with knee-high tables, from which you can dine on Japanese specialties such as tempura, udon, and stir-fry. Light and simple, Jun's attracts a solid following from around the city. Try the sake. Reservations suggested. Lunch and dinner. Closed Sun. &

K.C. MASTERPIECE BARBEQUE & GRILL
10985 Metcalf, Overland Park
913/345-8646
$-$$ JO

For a description, see listing in the Central/South Kansas City section.

LA MÉDITERRANÉE
9058 Metcalf, Overland Park
913/341-9595
$$-$$$ JO

Once a Plaza institution, La Méditerranée has continued serving its classic French menu to adoring fans who followed it to Johnson County. The formal setting provides a stunning backdrop to dishes such as salmon with wasabi sauce, seasonal wild boar, and chateaubriand. Lunch Mon–Fri; dinner Mon–Sat; closed Sun. Reservations suggested. &

MAY VIETNAMESE RESTAURANT
8841 W. 75th St., Overland Park
913/648-1688
$-$$ JO

"May" is old-growth bamboo, and a symbol that to this family-run operation means flexibility for customers and the hope for a long business history. They're on the right track. Serving 80 percent Vietnamese dishes, from sautéed vegetables to meal-size soups, and 20 percent Vietnamese-influenced Chinese, the restaurant keeps patrons returning for more. A waterfall, pond, and fountain add to the serene surroundings. Weekend reservations recommended. Lunch and dinner; closed Sun. &

MR. GYRO'S GREEK FOOD & PASTRIES
8234 Metcalf, Overland Park
913/381-4218
$ JO

Mr. Gyro's is an auspicious amalgam of fast food and palate-pleasing Greek comestibles. As the name implies, the restaurant specializes in gyro sandwiches, but you can also find delicious souvlaki, moussaka, and tsatsiki with generous portions of pita bread. A great place to get a quick Athenian fix. Lunch and dinner; closed Sun. &

PANZON'S
8710 Lackman Rd., Lenexa
913/492-9555
$ JO

Widely regarded as the best place in town for guacamole, Panzon's also boasts a variety of vegetarian and black-bean Mexican specialties. While there's often a dinner wait, Panzon's makes it worth your while, delivering fresh and spicy enchiladas, tacos, and tamales in gigantic portions. Reservations for parties of eight or more. Lunch Mon–Sat; dinner nightly. &

TATSU'S FRENCH RESTAURANT
4603 W. 90th St., Prairie Village
913/383-9801

$$$ **JO**

Tatsu's Japanese owner/chef—who lent his own name to his exquisite restaurant—has created a nearly hidden gem in a tiny Johnson County commercial development. Combining elegant French cuisine with stylish surroundings, Tatsu serves fresh seafood, beef tenderloin, and veal among his specialties, all impeccably presented at your table. Fresh flowers and French decor await as well. Lunch Mon–Fri; dinner served Mon–Sat; closed Sun. Reservations are recommended. &

WILD OATS MARKET
5101 Johnson Dr., Mission
913/722-4069
$ **JO**

Although it's technically a health-food supermarket, Wild Oats' deli stacks up well with the best of them. A salad bar chock-full of organic veggies accompanies the day's specials—everything from sandwiches to sushi to lasagna. The juice bar mixes fresh fruits and vegetables into a dozen or so different concoctions. The market also offers cafe seating at the store's front and outdoors during warm weather. Lunch and dinner; no reservations. &

YIA YIA'S EUROBISTRO
4701 W. 119th St., Overland Park
913/345-1111
$$ **JO**

One of the best places to see and be seen in Johnson County, Yia Yia's features a diverse menu that ranges from innovative pasta dishes to a hearty pot-roast supper. Casual yet elegant, uptown yet relaxed, Yia Yia's also attracts an after-work crowd who come to wind down at its chic bar. Lunch and dinner. Reservations recommended. &

NORTH OF THE RIVER

ACAPULCO MEXICAN RESTAURANT
1041 Burlington,
North Kansas City
816/472-8689
$ **NR**

After 30 years downtown, restaurant owner Rafael Jimenez moved his Acapulco Mexican Restaurant to a larger location north of the river. The food, however—made from recipes the Guadalajara native learned from his mother—stayed the same, as did the trademark palm-tree sign out front. Spicy tamales, cheesy enchiladas, and bean tacos have their enthusiastic following. The Acapulco has a full bar, serving tasty margaritas. Lunch and dinner. Closed Sun. &

CASCONE'S RESTAURANT & LOUNGE
3733 N. Oak, Kansas City
816/454-7977
$$–$$$ **NR**

Italian food lovers head to Cascone's—both this one and the alternate location in Overland Park—for chicken, seafood, and *fantastico* pasta dishes such as baked lasagna and fettucini Alfredo. Cascone's covers Italy from north to south, in a friendly, family-owned setting. Lunch Mon–Sat; dinner nightly. &

CHAPPELL'S RESTAURANT & LOUNGE
323 Armour Rd., North Kansas City
816/421-0002
$$ **NR**

Owner Jim Chappell has amassed a championship collection of sports memorabilia, including World Series trophies, vintage uniforms, and thousands of photos. It's all on display at this all-American restaurant.

NORTH OF THE RIVER

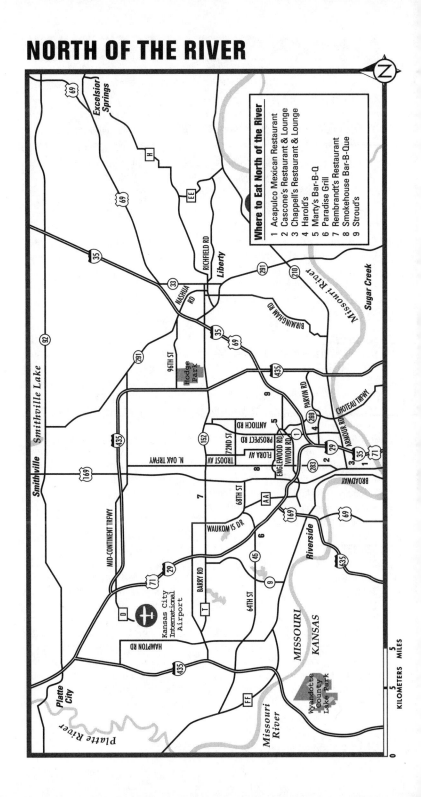

Where to Eat North of the River

1. Acapulco Mexican Restaurant
2. Cascone's Restaurant & Lounge
3. Chappell's Restaurant & Lounge
4. Harold's
5. Marty's Bar-B-Q
6. Paradise Grill
7. Rembrandt's Restaurant
8. Smokehouse Bar-B-Que
9. Stroud's

Kansas City and New York share many similarities, including having a beefsteak that bears their names. Actually, a Kansas City Strip and its New York cousin are the same cut of meat. The strip, cut from the loin section of a side of beef, is a porterhouse steak with the filet removed. The Kansas City moniker, a nod to the city's past as a leading livestock market, now adds to the local popularity. Steak lovers will find Kansas City Strip, most often flame broiled, in everything from 10-ounce to platter-plastering 16-ounce servings.

Specialties range from stuffed jalapeños to juicy burgers to succulent prime rib. Don't miss the football helmet collection hanging from the rafters. Lunch and dinner. Closed Sun. &

HAROLD'S
4071 N.E. Prather Rd., Kansas City
816/454-8500
$$ NR

This popular family-owned Northland restaurant has occupied the same location for nearly 40 years. Favorite dishes at Harold's range from prime rib, steaks, and fried chicken to chicken-fried steak, shrimp, and catfish. In addition, the restaurant features plenty of lunch and early dinner specials. Reservations for parties of four or more. Lunch and dinner. &

MARTY'S BAR-B-Q
2516 N.E. Vivion, Kansas City
816/453-2222
$–$$ NR

Hunkered on the northwest side of a very busy intersection, Marty's wafts its fragrant barbecue smoke for all to enjoy. Inside this family operation, a long bar and old-style chandelier provide the decoration for a hearty spread of barbecued ribs, chicken, and sandwiches.

Marty's cheese soup is especially popular in the fall and winter. Lunch and dinner. &

PARADISE GRILL
5225 N.W. 64th St., Kansas City
816/587-9888
$$ NR

"High-tech Fifties" is the way this restaurant explains its bright colors and local artwork design. "Fun" is the word most regular patrons use to describe the food and experience here. Consider the Squawking Nachos, Kickin' Chicken, or Vodka Chive Pasta, just a few of the wacky menu winners at this eatery 8 miles south of KCI airport, off I-29. Lunch and dinner. Reservations are recommended. &

REMBRANDT'S RESTAURANT
2820 N.W. Barry Rd., Kansas City
816/436-8700
$$–$$$ NR

A genteel restaurant set on a 15-acre estate, Rembrandt's features four dining rooms and a European-style menu. Entrees include prime rib, smoked Missouri ham, and leg of lamb. Every Sunday, Rembrandt's lays out an enormous brunch. The estate is also a favorite spot for weddings, receptions, and other parties. Lunch Tue–Sat; dinner nightly; closed Mon. Reservations recommended. &

SMOKEHOUSE BAR-B-QUE
6304 N. Oak Tfwy., Gladstone
816/454-4500
$–$$ **NR**
This is a full-service restaurant, but it's the hickory-smoked ribs, fish, and chicken that have earned its reputation. Burnt ends also continue to be a favorite. The not-so-barbecue-enamored can try steak, catfish, and trout for variety. The Smokehouse's stained glass and wood decor make everyone feel right at home. Lunch and dinner. &

STROUD'S
5410 N.E. Oak Ridge Dr.,
Kansas City
816/454-9600
$$ **NR**
For a description, see listing in the Central/South Kansas City section.

EAST METRO

GAROZZO'S RISTORANTE DUE
12801 E. Hwy. 40, Independence
816/737-2400
$$ **EM**
For a description, see listing in the Downtown Kansas City Area section.

GATES BAR-B-Q
10440 E. Hwy. 40, Independence
816/353-5880
$ **EM**
For a description, see listing in the Central/South Kansas City section.

L.C.'S BAR-B-Q
5800 Blue Pkwy., Kansas City
816/923-4484
$ **EM**
This ain't no fancy joint, but L.C.'s

smokes up some of the best barbecue in the city. Tucked into a minuscule building with cars speeding by, L.C.'s grabbed attention by smoking its Q outdoors in a homemade steel barrel. The aromatic advertising worked; now those in the know head to this great-smelling smoke hole for huge sandwiches and succulent ribs. Sides such as beans and 'slaw are equally tasty. Lunch and dinner; closed Sun. &

MAIN STREET INN
714 Main St., Grandview
816/761-9016
$ **EM**
When you need some real comfort food, head south to Grandview's Main Street Inn. There, crispy fried chicken, juicy filet mignon, and barbecued meats served with a mild sauce head the menu. Now a third-generation operation, the Main Street makes everyone feel like they've found family. Lunch Mon; lunch and dinner Tue–Sat; closed Sun. &

MARINA GROG & GALLEY
22A North Shore Dr.,
Lake Lotawana
816/578-5511
$$ **EM**
About a 30-minute drive east of town—on the shores of residential Lake Lotawana—Marina Grog & Galley provides one of the area's only first-class, waterfront dining opportunities. The shoreline views from this former boat shop are superior, and the cuisine ranges from seafood to steaks. A wall-size saltwater aquarium separating the bar and dining room enhances the shoreside theme. Lunch Wed–Sat; dinner nightly. Reservations recommended. &

EAST METRO

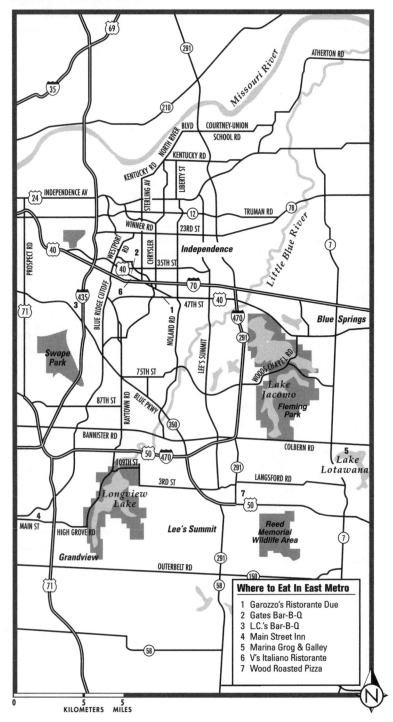

Where to Eat In East Metro

1 Garozzo's Ristorante Due
2 Gates Bar-B-Q
3 L.C.'s Bar-B-Q
4 Main Street Inn
5 Marina Grog & Galley
6 V's Italiano Ristorante
7 Wood Roasted Pizza

0   5   5
KILOMETERS   MILES

V'S ITALIANO RISTORANTE
10819 E. Hwy. 40, Independence
816/353-1241
$$ **EM**

Grapes are the theme at this beloved Italian eatery. Vine-covered arbors start curbside, then continue inside among the tables. House specialties here range from veal parmigiana to haddock lemonata to baked lasagna. Early dinner specials, from 4 to 6 p.m., provide a pleasing choice at a reduced rate—and include a house salad, bread, and Italian rum cake. Lunch, dinner, and Sun brunch. Reservations recommended for four or more. &

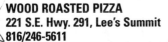

WOOD ROASTED PIZZA
221 S.E. Hwy. 291, Lee's Summit
816/246-5611
$ **EM**

Owner Len Ricci bases his pizza recipes on how the pies were made hundreds of years ago in Naples, Italy. The method has ensured him success; he's now opened another location in Overland Park. Pizzas here are indeed roasted over wood, topped with delicacies such as fresh vegetables and cheese. Other items include pastas, sandwiches, and salads. Lunch and dinner. Reservations are not accepted. &

KANSAS CITY, KANSAS/WEST

ALLEN'S BAR-B-QUE
3737 State Ave.,
Kansas City, Kansas
913/342-5200
$ **KCK**

This family-owned, cafeteria-style restaurant proudly proclaims itself "Kansas City's best barbecue." It's certainly up there. Three types of ribs reign, along with homemade potato

salad, coleslaw, and daily specials. A drive-through window makes it all so easy. Lunch and dinner. Closed Sun. &

GATES BAR-B-Q
10th and State Ave.,
Kansas City, Kansas
913/621-1134
$ **KCK**

For a description, see listing in the Central/South Kansas City section.

LOS AMIGOS MEXICAN RESTAURANT
2808 State Ave.,
Kansas City, Kansas
913/281-4547
$ **KCK**

Charlie Moretina guarantees you won't leave his casual, family-run restaurant hungry—that's because he serves feasts such as the Ultimate Burrito Spread, a beef, chicken, or pork wonder with chili, cheese, cheese sauce, and sour cream. Conservative weight estimate: 1.5 to 2 pounds of food. Lunch and dinner Mon–Sat. Closed Sun. Limited wheelchair access.

MAD JACK'S FRESH FISH
1318 State Ave.,
Kansas City, Kansas
913/371-8862
$ **KCK**

Proprietor John Reed renamed the long-time State Avenue Fish Market after its former owner, a commercial fisherman who hauled hoop nets from Missouri River backwaters. The fish no longer come from the Muddy Mo, but Reed serves some of the best fried fish in Kansas City, from catfish to shark to bluegill (no kidding). It's all delivered in a funky structure that still features a fresh-fish counter. Lunch and dinner; closed Sun. &

KANSAS CITY, KANSAS/WEST

N

Riss Lake

Missouri River

Riverside

MISSOURI

KANSAS

Wyandotte Co. Lake Park

Wyandotte County Park

Kansas River

INDEPENDENCE AV

MINNESOTA AV

38TH ST

KANSAS AV

57TH ST

59TH ST

72ND ST

78TH ST

84TH ST

98TH ST

166TH ST

165TH ST

31ST ST

LEAVENWORTH RD

PARALLEL PKWY

STATE AV

RIVERVIEW AV

KAW DR

Where to Eat in Kansas City/Kansas West

1 Allen's Bar-B-Que
2 Gates Bar-B-Q
3 Los Amigos Mexican Restaurant
4 Mad Jack's Fresh Fish
5 Mrs. Peter's Chicken Dinners
6 Ricky's Pit Bar-B-Que
7 Rosedale Barbeque

5 MILES

5 KILOMETERS

0

Barbecue Beginnings

Kansas City's barbecue fame was unassumingly launched in the late 1920s by Henry Perry, a black entrepreneur who dug a pit outside an abandoned streetcar barn to cook meat he sold wrapped in newspaper. In fact, barbecue was primarily the domain of Kansas City's African American community until the late 1940s.

Today, many of the area's barbecue restaurants remain African American–owned and –operated: Ollie Gates, who runs Gates Bar-B-Q, Kansas City's largest barbecue enterprise; Hayward Spears, who caters to the suburban lunchtime crowd; Ricky Smith, who claims a direct barbecue line to President Clinton with his Ricky's Pit Bar-B-Que; and Grace Harris, who owns H & M Bar-B-Que, which she opens in the wee hours of the weekend for spicy barbecue and 2 a.m. blues. All add their definitive touches to Kansas City's barbecue culture, combining their individualistic interpretations into a joyous local cuisine.

MRS. PETER'S CHICKEN DINNERS
4960 State Ave.,
Kansas City, Kansas
913/287-7711
$ **KCK**
The local newspaper calls Mrs. Peter's "an icon" and the publication's truly got it right. Fried chicken served family-style with all the fixings—mashed potatoes, vegetables, salads, and biscuits—keep both the faithful and new converts coming back for more. Pork chops and catfish also have their followings here. Lunch and dinner Tue–Sun; closed Mon. &

RICKY'S PIT BAR-B-QUE
5934 Leavenworth Rd.,
Kansas City, Kansas
913/334-7000
$ **KCK**
Set in a functional-not-flashy roadside building, Ricky's serves up traditional favorites. Crowds flock here for the restaurant's signature sandwiches: the RickBo, a triple-decker of beef, ham, and turkey; and Ricky's Melt, sliced meat with sauce and hot-pepper cheese, steamed on rye. Unlike his competitors, Ricky mixes cherry and hickory woods together for a unique smoking blend that comes out in the flavoring. Lunch and dinner. &

ROSEDALE BARBEQUE
600 Southwest Blvd.,
Kansas City, Kansas
913/262-0343
$ **KCK**
Down among the railroad tracks and

warehouses, Rosedale continues its long-standing tradition: dishing out high-quality barbecue. A modest setting that attracts a veritable cross-section of the population, Rosedale presents substantial servings of smoked ribs, sandwiches piled high, and tasty accompaniments. Some in town will let no other sauce touch their lips. Lunch and dinner. &

Convention and Visitors Bureau of Greater Kansas City

5

SIGHTS AND ATTRACTIONS

Every traveler stumbles onto those choice discoveries: a tiny perfect statue tucked beneath a garden's shady foliage; an off-the-beaten-path cafe where people-watching should be listed on the menu; a golden cathedral spire jutting between glass-and-steel towers. In Kansas City, treasures like these wait at every turn. From north to south, across two rivers and more, bits of history mingle with local scenery and culture, creating a lavish collection of sights and attractions.

Downtown Kansas City combines its river-town heritage with contemporary castles of commerce. From the waterfront—where nearby shabby storefronts are newly emerging as quaint shops and markets—you head south into the financial district and government center, also rebuilding and reshaping themselves. The hilly canyons between the under-construction civic mall and Bartle Hall yield a trove of sights old and new.

Walking the streets that compose the Country Club Plaza affords a picturesque look into an earlier place and time. An old Spanish mosaic under an eave, a winsome fountain spurting from a side-street wall, a bronze boar with its snout rubbed smooth: The Plaza delivers European style in America's heartland.

Throughout the area, evidence abounds of Kansas City's connection to the past: the place President Harry Truman called home in Independence; the Pony Express headquarters on State Line Road; the spread where Jesse James was born in Kearney. All offer insightful glimpses into a region that remains at the heart of the country.

In part, it's that geography that provides such a wealth of things to see and do in the Kansas City area. Whether you're exploring on foot or meandering the streets by car, get ready to make your own Kansas City discoveries.

DOWNTOWN KANSAS CITY AREA

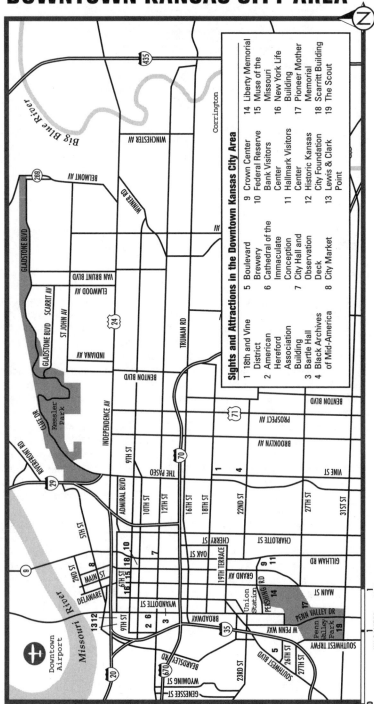

Sights and Attractions in the Downtown Kansas City Area

1 18th and Vine District
2 American Hereford Association Building
3 Bartle Hall
4 Black Archives of Mid-America
5 Boulevard Brewery
6 Cathedral of the Immaculate Conception
7 City Hall and Observation Deck
8 City Market
9 Crown Center
10 Federal Reserve Bank Visitors Center
11 Hallmark Visitors Center
12 Historic Kansas City Foundation
13 Lewis & Clark Point
14 Liberty Memorial
15 Muse of the Missouri
16 New York Life Building
17 Pioneer Mother Memorial
18 Scarritt Building
19 The Scout

DOWNTOWN KANSAS CITY AREA

18TH & VINE DISTRICT
18th Street and Vine, Kansas City
816/871-3016 **DA**
Famous worldwide for its role in the development of jazz, Kansas City's 18th & Vine District is undergoing a $22-million redevelopment set to enlarge the Negro Leagues Baseball Museum, add a Jazz Museum and 18th & Vine Visitors Center, and incorporate the renovated Gem Theatre. In this important historic district, sax player Charlie "Yardbird" Parker began his career in the Thirties, Count Basie played with his band, and Joe Turner developed his signature style. Museums are expected to open in late spring 1997.

THE AMERICAN HEREFORD ASSOCIATION BUILDING
715 Hereford Dr. (a.k.a. W. 11th St.), Kansas City **DA**
Built in 1951, this building is still guarded by the American Hereford Association's massive bovine statue, even though Argus Health Systems now occupies the facility. The building's not open to the public, but from the shadow of the heroic Hereford is a great view of the West Bottoms, the Kansas River valley, and downtown Kansas City, Kansas.

BARTLE HALL
13th St. between Baltimore and Broadway, Kansas City
816/871-3700 **DA**
When artist R.M. Fischer placed his Sky Stations/Pylon Caps atop the Kansas City Convention Center's expanded H. Roe Bartle Hall, locals ungraciously started referring to them as "hair curlers" and similar descriptive names. Kansas City's most popu-

Fountain of Bacchus on the Plaza, page 95

lar photographic skyline view, however, now includes these space-age creations. Bartle (named for a former mayor) offers the largest contiguous, column-free exhibit space in the country. Lobby open daily; free.

BLACK ARCHIVES OF MID-AMERICA
2033 Vine, Kansas City
816/483-1300 **DA**
Near the historic 18th & Vine district, the Black Archives is home to one of the country's largest collections of African American paintings, sculpture, and research material on famous black leaders of the Midwest. Mon–Fri 9–4:30. Adults $2.50; students 18 and under, 50 cents.

BOULEVARD BREWERY
2501 Southwest Blvd., Kansas City
816/474-7095 **DA**
The owners of this small brewery had a tough time finding financing for their venture—especially with beer powerhouse Anheuser-Busch headquartered on the other side of the Missouri. But the entrepreneurs

finally prevailed upon family members and opened in 1989, creating fine ales and lagers. Now a local favorite, Boulevard gives free tours at 1:30 every Saturday. Call for reservations.

CATHEDRAL OF THE IMMACULATE CONCEPTION
416 W. 12th St., Kansas City
816/842-0416   **DA**
Kansas City's first Catholic church was built in 1856 by Father Bernard Donnelly, often called the "builder priest" for his success at luring Irish immigrant laborers and expanding the church's influence. The architecture is commonly labeled neo-Baroque with a Romanesque style. In 1960, 23-karat gold leaf was added to the dome to protect the original copper sheathing. You can enter the building from 11th Street and Broadway. Mass daily.

CITY HALL AND OBSERVATION DECK
414 E. 12th St., Kansas City
816/274-2222   **DA**
Office to Kansas City's mayor and City Council, City Hall was built in the depths of the Depression. It remains a renowned example of stunning art deco architecture. From the building's 30th floor, you can look out in all directions, taking in an unmatched view of the Kansas City metro area. The building's open, with the elevator running, Mon–Fri 8:30–4:15. Free.

CITY MARKET
5th Street between Wyandotte and Grand, Kansas City
816/842-1271   **DA**
One of Kansas City's original business districts, this area has been revitalized and now plays host to 35 shops, groceries, and restaurants—and the largest farmer's market in the region. Kansas Citians flock to the Market—primarily on Saturdays—to browse through the fresh fruits, veggies, flowers, and crafts. The Arabia Steamboat Museum anchors one side of the square, while Winslow's City Market Smokehouse lures with its barbecue. A great family outing.

CROWN CENTER
Main to Gillham, Pershing to 24th Street, Kansas City
816/274-8444   **DA**
Once known as Signboard Hill, this area is now decorated with modern buildings, thanks to Hallmark Cards. The greeting-card giant—privately owned by the philanthropic Hall family—surrounds its world headquarters with retail shops, movie and live theaters, restaurants, an outdoor ice skating rink, and a hotel.

FEDERAL RESERVE BANK VISITORS CENTER
925 Grand, Kansas City
816/881-2200   **DA**
Money, money, money. That's the focus at the Federal Reserve Bank Visitors Center. Here, you can see some 30 educational displays that describe how the Federal Reserve system works, plus view traveling and regional exhibits in the Roger Fuggey Gallery. Mon–Fri 8–5. Free.

HALLMARK VISITORS CENTER
25th and Grand in Crown Center, Kansas City
816/274-3613   **DA**
More than just one company's story, the Hallmark Visitors Center touches something in everyone who's ever given or received a greeting card. Exhibits show visitors how Hallmark Cards has harnessed creativity and craftsmanship to become the largest card company in the world. Videos

Top Ten African American Sights in Kansas City

by Frances Hill,
president of CWT/Accent Travel, one of the area's largest minority-owned businesses

1. **Negro Leagues Baseball Museum** (1601 E. 18th St., Kansas City)
2. **The Black Archives of Mid-America** (2033 Vine, Kansas City, 816/483-1300)
3. **Bruce R. Watkins Cultural Heritage Center** (3700 Blue Pkwy., Kansas City, 816/923-6226)
4. **18th & Vine Historic District**
5. **Metropolitan Baptist Church** (2310 E. Linwood Blvd., Kansas City, 816/923-3689)
6. **St. Stephen Baptist Church** (1414 E. Truman Rd., Kansas City, 816/842-6311)
7. **Epicurean Lounge** (7502 Troost, Kansas City, 816/333-8383)
8. **Bodyworks Unlimited** (8625 Troost, Kansas City, 816/363-6910)
9. **Gates Bar-B-Q** (Several locations)
10. **The Hitching Post Restaurant** (3448 Prospect, Kansas City, 816/924-9579)

show clips from award-winning Hallmark Hall of Fame TV productions. Mon–Fri 9–5; Sat 9:30–4:30. Free.

HISTORIC KANSAS CITY FOUNDATION
712 Broadway, Suite 404, Kansas City
816/471-3391 **DA**
This ardent activist in the preservation of Kansas City's historic buildings and neighborhoods offers extensive knowledge about the area's past. At the foundation's downtown office, you can find brochures and slide programs on historic/preservation areas. The group also gives tours (by reser-

vation only) on topics ranging from art deco architecture to the River Market neighborhood, for a group donation of $25.

LEWIS & CLARK POINT
8th and Jefferson, Kansas City **DA**
In 1806, Meriwether Lewis and William Clark camped for three days on this bluff that overlooks the confluence of the Kansas (or Kaw) and Missouri Rivers. It was a well-deserved rest during their return trip from Oregon. From this Quality Hill point, you can read the marker that commemorates their stay and notes

Ten Favorite Historic Buildings
by Jane Fifield Flynn,
past president of the Jackson County Historical Society
and author of several historical books on the region

1. **Kansas City Power and Light Company Building** (1330 Baltimore Ave.). For more than 30 years, this building dominated Kansas City's skyline as the tallest building in the city and the state. A series of setbacks and stylized geometric architectural detailing characterize its art deco style. The building is most resplendent after dark when floodlights, concealed at each recessed step, are directed up toward the six-story crowning shaft with its multicolored light display.

2. **Pierce Street Houses** (48th Street, Locust Street to Rockhill Road). The adage of "power in numbers" is exemplified by this block of identical houses located in the historic Rockhill neighborhood. The design, using shingle siding and native limestone, is but one of several architectural styles within the neighborhood. All came from William Rockhill Nelson, who was the publisher of the *Kansas City Star.*

3. **Apartments** (East 43rd, Oak, and McGee Streets). Dignified, symmetrical, and massive describe these three-story apartments with their handsome columns and front porches. Once a part of many streetscapes, the apartments are a "dying" type of the city's residential structures. The stone wall defines the site where a 20-room mansion once stood. It was razed for the apartments' construction.

4. **Walter E. Bixby Residence** (6505 State Line Rd.). It was not until the completion of this residence in 1937 that the local citizenry received an opportunity to view a wonderful example of the International style of architecture. Horizontal lines and geometric forms complement the white stucco exterior. The original landscape, designed by Hare & Hare, greatly enhanced the appearance of this less-than-traditional home.

5. **Boley Clothing Company Building** (1124 Walnut St.). When it first became known that architect Louis Singleton Curtiss intended to "wrap" a building in a glass skin, skeptics and traditionalists must have had a field day. But in 1908, Curtiss did indeed wrap this building. Cited for his unique design and pioneering construction materials, Curtiss recessed the building's supporting columns several feet from the facades, which allowed the glass wrap. The columns were made of steel, the first ever rolled in the United States.

6. **Mutual Musicians Foundation** (1823 Highland Ave.). Originally a duplex when it was built in 1906, this building at first reveals little of its importance. Since 1928, it has been the home of the Black Musicians Union Local 627. Located in the 18th and Vine Historic District, jazz greats including Charlie "Yardbird" Parker, Count Basie, Bennie Moten, and Mary Lou Williams came here for jam sessions. The building was designated a National Historic Landmark—Kansas City's only one—in 1982.

7. **Pendergast Headquarters** (1908 Main St.). This unassuming building is unchallenged in its contribution to Kansas City history. For almost 30 years, this was the operational site of Thomas J. Pendergast, the city's all-time most influential political figure. For decades, Pendergast's Democratic machine controlled the activities of the city, dispensing favors for patronage. Ironically, income-tax evasion caused his downfall.

8. **New York Life Building** (20 W. 9th St.). It was the 1880s, the decade of one of Kansas City's greatest building booms. Eastern money poured into the city creating confidence and stylish architecture. Most obvious was the construction of the New York Life Building. Adorned with a magnificent bronze eagle, cast in the studio of Augustus Saint-Gaudens, the building was the city's tallest structure for many years.

9. **John B. Wornall House** (146 W. 61st Terr.). Originally surrounded by 500 acres of farmland, this antebellum Greek Revival–style house has become a rarity in Kansas City. John Bristow Wornall, who built the house in 1858 for his bride, Eliza, made a comfortable living selling agricultural products to the fortune-seekers heading west. During the Civil War Battle of Westport (in 1864), the brick mansion served as a hospital for Union and Confederate wounded. The house has been cited for both architectural and historical significance. Open to the public, it is owned by the Jackson County Historical Society.

10. **Union Station** (Pershing Road and Main Street). When the building opened to the public on October 30, 1914, crowds pushed their way into the massive 400-foot-by-800-foot Grand Hall and then into the north waiting room, which exceeds the length of a football field. Once the third-largest passenger station in the country (it has now risen to second), Union Station served for more than 30 years as the city's public square. On June 17, 1933, local newspaper headlines read, "Union Station Massacre!" That day, during an attempt to free a notorious federal prisoner, four people were killed in the crossfire. A stray machine-gun bullet is still lodged in a wall to the west of the east entrance.

NCAA Hall of Champions, page 98

the importance of French fur traders to the area, while enjoying a view of the rivers, the downtown airport, and Kansas City, Kansas.

LIBERTY MEMORIAL
Penn Valley Park, Kansas City
816/221-1918   DA
President Calvin Coolidge dedicated Liberty Memorial in 1926 to honor those who fought and died in World War I. Over the years, the memorial's museum amassed the only collection specializing in WWI artifacts, including weapons, uniforms, and other memorabilia. Although the 217-foot-high column, walkway, and museum are closed pending renovation, two satellite museums are open: in the Town Pavilion at 12th and Main Streets, and on the lower level of Ward Parkway Shopping Center. You can still stroll the lawn surrounding the Memorial. The Town Pavilion museum is open Mon–Fri 10–6; Ward Parkway Tue–Sun 10–6. Free.

MUSE OF THE MISSOURI
Main St. between 8th and 9th Sts.,

Kansas City   DA
She's hard to miss, casting her net from an attractive median on Main Street. Installed in 1961, the 30-foot bronze sculpture pays homage to the Missouri River's importance in the creation and history of Kansas City. Three pools surround the flowing female figure.

NEW YORK LIFE BUILDING
20 W. 9th St., Kansas City   DA
When it was completed in 1887, the brick New York Life Building was the largest in the city. Its striking bronze eagle was an awesome site along the street, which was the beneficiary of significant corporate investment at the time. Eventually, however, New York Life moved out and on, and the building sat empty, slowly deteriorating. In 1995, local company Utilicorp United spent more than $30 million transforming the building into its technologically "smart" headquarters.

PIONEER MOTHER MEMORIAL
Penn Valley Park, Kansas City DA
Located southwest of the Liberty

Memorial, this sculpture was dedicated in 1927 to honor the spirit of all pioneer women who crossed the Great Plains. The dramatic, multifigured bronze statue was designed in New York by Alexander Phimister Proctor and cast in Rome. It took four years to complete.

SCARRITT BUILDING
9th St. and Grand,
Kansas City DA

The magnificent Scarritt was built between 1906 and 1907, and was one of the city's first skyscrapers (even though it's only 11 stories high). Faced with terra cotta adornments characteristic of the famed Chicago School of Architecture, the building honors an early Kansas City pioneer, the Rev. Nathan Scarritt.

THE SCOUT
Penn Valley Park, off 31st St.
between Broadway and
Southwest Trafficway,
Kansas City DA

The Scout remains one of Kansas City's most beloved sculptures—in a city filled with sculptures—even though it was originally intended for another location. The memorial to Native Americans was created for San Francisco's 1915 Panama-Pacific Exposition, but during its journey back East, the Sioux brave mounted on horseback appeared temporarily in Penn Valley Park. Local residents were so fond of the sculpture that they raised $15,000 to purchase it.

CENTRAL/SOUTH KANSAS CITY

ALEXANDER MAJORS HOUSE
8201 State Line Rd., Kansas City
816/333-5556 CS

It's hard to imagine now, but Pony Express co-founder Alexander Majors lived out in the middle of nowhere. His home, just north of today's Ward Parkway Shopping Center, served as the headquarters for the Pony Express (during the 18 months it was in operation) and two other early freight operations. The 1856 farmhouse has been restored and offers tours and special events. Hours: Thur–Sun 1–4 from Mar 25–Dec 18. Adults $2.50, children under 12 $1.

BOARD OF TRADE
4800 Main St., Kansas City
816/753-7500 CS

Founded before the Civil War, the Board of Trade became a grain exchange in 1869 and now it tracks the region's agribusiness concerns. The world's largest futures market for hard red winter wheat trades just south of the Country Club Plaza, as do a variety of other commodities. From the third-floor observation deck you can also watch as traders deal in value line stock index futures. Mon–Fri 8:15–3:30. Free.

Liberty Memorial

Convention and Visitors Bureau of Greater Kansas City

CENTRAL/SOUTH KANSAS CITY

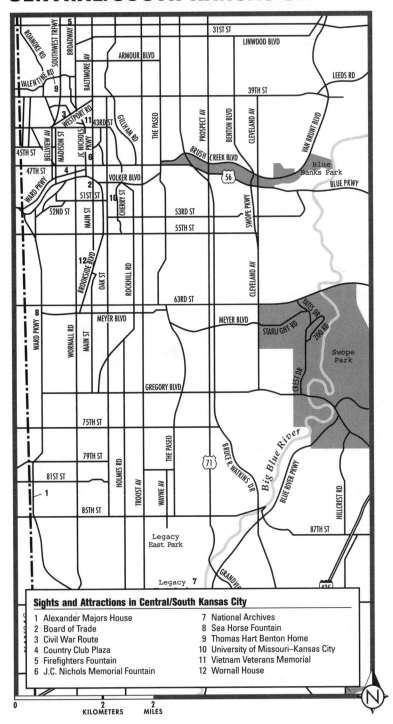

Sights and Attractions in Central/South Kansas City

1 Alexander Majors House
2 Board of Trade
3 Civil War Route
4 Country Club Plaza
5 Firefighters Fountain
6 J.C. Nichols Memorial Fountain
7 National Archives
8 Sea Horse Fountain
9 Thomas Hart Benton Home
10 University of Missouri–Kansas City
11 Vietnam Veterans Memorial
12 Wornall House

0   2   2
   KILOMETERS MILES

N

CIVIL WAR ROUTE   CS

The Battle of Westport was a bloody conflict that took place October 21–23, 1864, and marked the end of the Civil War in the West. The major battle occurred in what is now Loose Park, but more than 20 other sites also saw conflict. A self-guided driving tour takes you from Westport to the Big Blue River to the Santa Fe Trail and back, with markers describing the action at each spot. An explanatory brochure is available in hotel lobby racks or from the Civil War Round Table of Kansas City, 1130 Westport Rd., 816/931-6620.

COUNTRY CLUB PLAZA
46th St. to Ward Pkwy., Roanoke to Main, Kansas City   CS

Even if you don't shop or eat at any of the Plaza's boutiques or bistros, plan a walking tour through this area. Of special note: The Plaza's tallest tower, at 47th Street and J.C. Nichols Parkway, is a scaled-down replica of the famous Giralda in Seville, Spain. The Fountain of Bacchus in Chandler Court (northwest of the Cheesecake Factory) is a 1911 lead statuary acquired from a Worcestershire, England, estate. The Boy and Frog Fountain, corner of Central and Nichols Road, is an original by Raffaello Romanelli of Florence. The Spanish Bullfight Mural, handcrafted in Seville, is on the east side of Central, between 47th and Nichols Road. Free art brochures are available at the Plaza Merchants Association, 450 Ward Pkwy., 816/753-0100.

FIREFIGHTERS FOUNTAIN
31st St. and Broadway, Kansas City   CS

Located in Penn Valley Park, the Firefighters Fountain is among the largest fountains in Kansas City. Besides its Tom Corbin sculpture, the fountain features plenty of water: its 80-foot diameter basin holds 76,000 gallons. Dedicated to the city's firefighters in 1991, the fountain also features a memorial terrace area with fallen firefighters' names carved in granite.

J.C. NICHOLS MEMORIAL FOUNTAIN
47th and Main Sts., Kansas City   CS

Two years after legendary Plaza developer J.C. Nichols died in 1950, his family purchased a spirited group of heroic figures mounted on rearing horses. Originally sculpted in 1910 in Paris by Henri Greber, the statuary was designed for a fountain on a Long Island estate. It took another eight years before the fountain was finally functional. Missing parts of the grouping were created by local sculptor Herman Frederick Simon; architect Edward Tanner designed the fountain itself. One of Kansas City's best-known fonts, the circular pool is a gathering spot from the moment the city turns the water on in the spring until it's doused in early winter.

NATIONAL ARCHIVES
2312 E. Bannister, Kansas City
816/926-6272   CS

This is one of 12 field branches of the U.S. National Archives and Records Administration—and the branch specifically noted for its genealogy information, diplomatic dispatches, and war documents. A favorite place for people researching their family trees. Weekdays 8–4; every third Sat 9–4. Free.

SEA HORSE FOUNTAIN
Meyer Circle on Ward Pkwy., Kansas City   CS

When You Care Enough . . .

One of Kansas City's most notable companies is the nation's largest greeting-card manufacturer, Hallmark Cards. In fact, Hallmark's $3-billion-plus annual revenues make it the largest player in a $6-billion greeting-card industry.

Founder Joyce C. Hall, a cocky 18-year-old from Nebraska, started the business in 1910 by brazenly delivering postcard packs on spec to Midwestern merchants, while living in his room at the Kansas City YMCA. In the Thirties Hall decided his company needed more visibility, so he contacted a long list of advertising agencies, all of which laughed at the concept of selling greeting cards under a brand name. Hall prevailed, however, and finally found an agency that linked his company with a radio program, a precursor to the company's later introduction of television's award-showered Hallmark Hall of Fame.

Under Hall's leadership, Hallmark tapped the talents of artists such as Norman Rockwell, Georgia O'Keeffe, Salvador Dali, and Pablo Picasso. President Dwight Eisenhower commissioned Hallmark to produce the first official White House Christmas card in 1957, and every president until Bill Clinton followed the tradition.

Hallmark has also amassed the world's largest creative team— 665 painters, engravers, photographers, stitchery artists, calligraphers, and writers—who pour heart and soul into developing sentiments that speak to the human relationship.

Part of Hall's legacy is on display at the Hallmark Visitors Center in Crown Center.

For the past decade or so, Kansas City officials have tried various methods to straighten the curves that circle Ward Parkway's Sea Horse Fountain. Nothing satisfies residents who, frankly, don't mind the traffic obstruction. One of the best examples of developer J.C. Nichols' blend of water and statuary, the fountain was fashioned from a seventeenth-century Venetian cherubim and sea-horse figures he had purchased during a trip to Italy earlier in the decade.

THOMAS HART BENTON HOME
3616 Belleview, Kansas City
816/931-5722   CS

Missouri's most famous twentieth-century artist lived in this home from 1939 until he died in 1975, creating many of his colorful depictions of American history and folkways in the converted carriage house out back. Benton's late-Victorian-style home was a center of creative activity; his studio still holds many of his tools and equipment, as though he walked out yesterday. Guided tours last about an hour. Mon–Sat 10–4; winter Sun 11–4; summer Sun noon–5. Admission: 13 and over $2; 6–13 $1.25.

UNIVERSITY OF MISSOURI–KANSAS CITY
50th to 55th Sts. between Oak and Troost, Kansas City
816/235-1000 **CS**

This educational institution was founded in 1933 as the University of Kansas City. Thirty years later, in 1963, it joined the University of Missouri system, and now offers 53 bachelor's, 47 master's, and 28 doctoral degree programs. Specialty areas include nationally recognized programs in health sciences, urban affairs, and performing arts. On campus, though not officially part of the college, the Linda Hall Library is the largest privately funded library of science, engineering, and technology in the United States. The nonlending facility sports more than 1 million volumes, the oldest dating from 1472. Library open Mon 9–8:30; Tue–Fri 9–5; Sat 10–4. No charge.

VIETNAM VETERANS MEMORIAL
43rd St. and Broadway,
Kansas City **CS**

The Vietnam Veterans Memorial, between the Plaza and Westport on the northeast corner of Broadway and 43rd Street, was dedicated in 1986 to

One of the many towers on the Plaza, page 95

all Vietnam War veterans. Resembling the larger memorial in Washington, D.C., the stone wall pays special tribute to the 336 Kansas City–area Vietnam veterans killed or missing in action. The memorial includes restful reflecting pools and fountains.

WORNALL HOUSE
61st Terrace and Wornall Rd.,
Kansas City
816/444-1858 **CS**

Although the Wornall House is now surrounded by residential neighborhoods, it was located on 500 acres of farmland when it was built in 1858. The Greek Revival house was originally owned by John Bristow Wornall and his wife, Eliza, and was considered the most pretentious house in the region. During the 1864 Battle of Westport, the house was used as a hospital for both Confederate and Union soldiers. Open for tours Tue–Sat 10–4; Sun 1–4 (the house is closed in Jan and has shortened hours in Feb). Adults $3; groups and seniors $2.50; children $1.

JOHNSON COUNTY

LANESFIELD SCHOOL
HISTORIC SITE
18745 S. Dillie Rd., Edgerton
913/893-6645   JO
This one-room school, now on the National Register of Historic Places, dates from 1869 when kids came from miles around to attend the little school on the prairie. Today's visitors can see what it was like back then, and even learn lessons from a costumed schoolteacher who gives tours of the restored schoolhouse. Tue–Sun 1–5. Free.

MAHAFFIE FARMSTEAD & STAGE
COACH STOP
1100 Kansas City Rd., Olathe
913/782-6972   JO
The Santa Fe Trail was one of the highways of its day. Along the way west, farms became rest stops for weary stagecoach passengers. The Mahaffie farm, established in 1858, was one such spot, serving dinner to travelers between 1863 and 1869. Restoration is ongoing at the three-story limestone home; it's also the last remaining stagecoach stop of its kind. Tours available Mon–Fri 8–5; Sat 10–4; Sun 12:30–4:30. Adults $2.50; under 12 $1.50; under 3 free. Closed Jan.

MISSION HILLS, KANSAS
West of State Line, between 55th
and 71st Sts.   JO
This neighborhood features rolling hills, winding roads, and multimillion-dollar homes. The tony Kansas City Country Club and Mission Hills Country Club provide the area's northern boundary; to the south, you can drive past notable mansions. Candy magnates Russell and Clara Stover, for example, built the enormous hilltop home at Mission Drive and Overhill. The late Ewing Kauffman, former owner of the Kansas City Royals and founder of Marion Merrell Dow, lived on Mission Drive as well. Other current movers and shakers reside throughout the area.

NCAA HALL OF CHAMPIONS
6201 College Blvd., Overland Park
913/339-0000   JO
Go, team! The NCAA Hall of Champions pays homage to intercollegiate athletes in a moving collection of photographs, video, and sports memorabilia. One exhibit lets you experience the thrill of center court during a rousing Final Four championship; another recreates a college football game kickoff. The 12,000-square-foot facility also acts as the NCAA's national headquarters. Mon–Sat 10–5; Sun noon–4. Adults $2; students $1; children under 6 free. Free admission on Sun.

OVERLAND PARK
FARMERS MARKET
Downtown Overland Park
between 79th and 80th Sts. and
Marty   JO
On Wednesdays and Saturdays from early May through October, residents crowd Overland Park's quaint downtown area to purchase homegrown fruits and vegetables, flowers, honey, and crafts. It's the Farmers Market, smaller than the one in the River Market but often less crowded. The major action occurs in the Farmers Market pavilion, starting at about 7 a.m.

SHAWNEE INDIAN MISSION
STATE HISTORIC SITE
53rd St. and Mission Rd., Fairway
913/262-0867   JO
In the 1820s and 1830s, westward expansion forced the Shawnee and

JOHNSON COUNTY

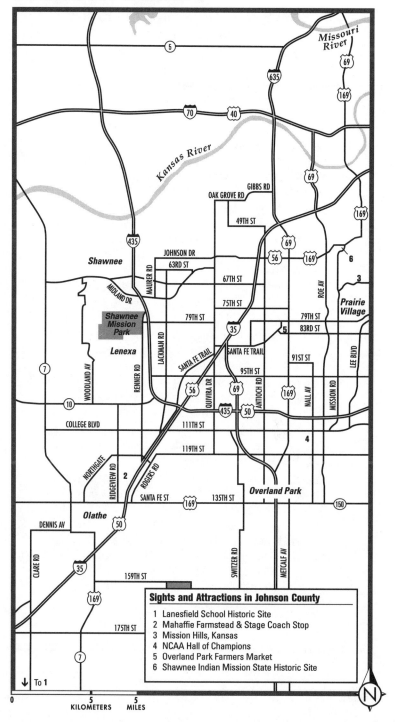

Missouri River

Kansas River

Shawnee

Shawnee Mission Park

Lenexa

Prairie Village

Overland Park

Olathe

OAK GROVE RD
GIBBS RD
49TH ST
JOHNSON DR
63RD ST
67TH ST
75TH ST
79TH ST
83RD ST
SANTA FE TRAIL
95TH ST
91ST ST
111TH ST
119TH ST
SANTA FE ST
135TH ST
DENNIS AV
159TH ST
175TH ST
COLLEGE BLVD
MIDLAND DR
MAURER RD
LACKMAN RD
RENNER RD
WOODLAND AV
QUIVIRA DR
ANTIOCH RD
NALL AV
MISSION RD
ROE AV
LEE BLVD
NORTHGATE
RIDGEVIEW RD
ROGERS RD
CLARE RD
SWITZER RD
METCALF AV

Sights and Attractions in Johnson County

1 Lanesfield School Historic Site
2 Mahaffie Farmstead & Stage Coach Stop
3 Mission Hills, Kansas
4 NCAA Hall of Champions
5 Overland Park Farmers Market
6 Shawnee Indian Mission State Historic Site

To 1

0   5   5
    KILOMETERS MILES

N

Ten Must-Do Things in Overland Park
by Mary Birch,
president of the Overland Park Chamber of Commerce

1. **Deanna Rose Children's Farmstead** (138th St. and Switzer Rd., 913/897-2360). This popular family experience attracts more than 250,000 visitors a year. The ultimate in interactive fun.

2. **The New Theatre Restaurant** (9229 Foster St., 913/649-7469). Known as the best dinner-theater in the country, its 600 seats offer food, fun, and excellent theater entertainment to both residents and visitors.

3. **Johnson County Community College Cultural Education Center** (12345 College Blvd., 913/469-4445). A variety of high quality cultural and community events in 1,400-seat Yardley Hall and the 400-seat theater complement the educational and tourist-related aspects of this facility.

4. **NCAA Hall of Champions** (6201 College Blvd., 913/339-0000). A perfect stop for a tour through the history of collegiate athletic excellence and achievement.

5. **Shopping/dining**. It's the best in the Midwest, with two regional malls and more than 1,600 retail stores complemented by a variety of 250-plus restaurant choices.

6. **Arboretum Botanical Gardens** (17940 Antioch, 913/685-4582). Although only an infant in its development, this 300-acre park is already popular for its trails and water-park areas.

7. **Fall Parade and Craft Show**. For more than 20 years and more than 10,000 people, this event delights visitors and residents and showcases downtown Overland Park.

8. **Festivals.** The four-day Jazz Festival in June and the annual Fourth of July festival and fireworks in Corporate Woods Park bring out the best of Overland Park for more than 30,000 attendees.

9. **Farmers Market.** Located near the Clock Tower in downtown Overland Park, this Wednesday and Saturday gathering offers the freshest to everyone, with a concert series for atmosphere.

10. **Art in the Woods**. A classy, two-week display of beauty in art in Corporate Woods every May.

Missouri River Queen, page 110

other tribes to move from the eastern United States to present-day Kansas. To help the relocated Indian children, the Reverend Thomas Johnson established this mission school in 1839. Later, it became a stopping point on the Santa Fe Trail for figures such as John Fremont and Francis Parkman. Today, guided group tours are given by appointment, and family events are held throughout the year. Tue–Sat 10–5; Sun 1–5. Free.

NORTH OF THE RIVER

CLAYBROOK HOUSE HISTORIC SITE
Opposite the Jesse James Farm, Kearney
816/635-6065   NR
This restored pre–Civil War mansion is best known as the home of Jesse James' daughter, Mary James Barr. But Virginian George Claybrook originally developed it as a Southern-style plantation in 1858, although the architecture is more indicative of mid-1800s rural Missouri. Spring and

Christmas events are held each year. Memorial Day–Labor Day daily 9–4; months of May and Sept Sat–Sun 9–4; closed Oct–Apr. Adults $2; 6–12 $1; seniors $1.80.

GLADSTONE TEACHERS MEMORIAL
70th and North Holmes, Gladstone
816/436-2200   NR
Christa McAuliffe, the teacher-crew member who died in the 1986 space shuttle *Challenger* disaster, is honored in this special memorial. Located near Gladstone's City Hall and Central Park, the monument is dedicated to the heroic efforts of all teachers.

JESSE JAMES FARM AND VISITORS CENTER
21216 James Farm Rd., Kearney
816/635-6065   NR
In 1847, Jesse James was born at this Kearney, Missouri, farm. At age 16, he followed his older brother Frank into the Civil War to fight under the notorious William Quantrill—but the James boys would become even

NORTH OF THE RIVER

Sights and Attractions North of the River

1. Claybrook House Historic Site
2. Gladstone Teachers Memorial
3. Jesse James Farm and Visitors Center
4. Lightburne Hall
5. Shoal Creek, Missouri
6. William Jewell College

RLDS Temple in Independence, page 107

more legendary themselves: When they returned home, they joined other former Confederates to rob banks. James' restored birthplace features the home's original furnishings, an audiovisual presentation recapping his life, and the world's largest display of James family artifacts. I-35 north to Exit 26 (Kearney), 2 miles east on Highway 92, then 2 miles north. May 1–Sept 30 daily 9–4; rest of the year Mon–Fri 9–4; Sat–Sun noon–4. Adults $3; 6–12 $1; seniors $2.70.

LIGHTBURNE HALL
301 N. Water, Liberty   **NR**
An impressive 26-room Classic Revival antebellum mansion, Lightburne Hall was constructed in 1852 near Liberty's historic square. Built by Union Army Major Alvan Lightburne, a former Liberty mayor and a founder of William Jewell College, the all-brick, 8,500-square-foot private residence has been under restoration for several years now. Although it's no longer open to the public, Lightburne Hall showcases a time when magnif-

icent plantation homes dotted these hillsides.

SHOAL CREEK, MISSOURI
7000 N.E. Barry Rd. in Hodge Park, Kansas City
816/792-2655   **NR**
This fascinating nineteenth-century living history museum comprises 17 period structures, each furnished with books, clothing, and special items that people made or took with them on their journey west. Some buildings were original and have been restored; others are replicas. Shoal Creek provides a way to step back in time through tours, special events, and native animals on site. Tue–Sat 9–3; Sun noon–4. Guided tours and special events $2, no charge under 6; all other times free.

WILLIAM JEWELL COLLEGE
Kansas St., Liberty
816/781-3806   **NR**
Three decades after Liberty was settled, town fathers founded William Jewell College in 1849. It is now one of the oldest private colleges in

Missouri. The fully accredited liberal arts school sits proudly on a hill overlooking Liberty, its 2,000 students within walking distance of the town square. The college is particularly known throughout the metro area for its outstanding music and dramatic performance series.

EAST METRO

1827 LOG COURTHOUSE
**117 W. Kansas Ave.,
Independence
816/325-7111   EM**
It's only a two-room log cabin, but this humble building on Kansas Avenue was the first courthouse in Jackson County. In the 1930s, Judge Harry S. Truman held court here while the main courthouse was being renovated. Open Apr–Oct Mon–Fri 10–2. Free.

BINGHAM-WAGGONER ESTATE
**313 W. Pacific, Independence
816/461-3491   EM**
The stately Bingham-Waggoner Estate was built in 1855 by John Lewis, an Independence pioneer. But it was artist George Caleb Bingham who made it famous. Also a community activist, Bingham painted his

popular *Martial Law* in his studio on the estate's 19 acres. In 1879 Peter Waggoner purchased the home, then remodeled it extensively. When the last Waggoner died in the 1970s, the nonprofit Bingham-Waggoner Historical Society was formed to acquire and operate the home. Much of the mansion's interior remained as it had been during Peter's residence. Tours Apr–Oct Mon–Sat 10–4; Sun 1–4. Adults $3; 6–16 $1; seniors $2.50.

CAVE SPRING INTERPRETIVE CENTER
**8701 E. Gregory at Blue Ridge Boulevard, Kansas City
816/358-2283   EM**
At the Cave Spring Interpretive Center, you've landed at one of the Santa Fe Trail's early stops. Changing exhibits describe the nature and cultural history of Kansas City, while nature trails feature a cave, spring, and wildlife habitats. The Interpretive Center offers special programs and field trips. Tue–Sat 10–5. Admission: $1.

FORT OSAGE
**BB Hwy., Sibley
816/795-8200   EM**
Fort Osage was the first U.S. outpost in the Louisiana Purchase, operating

EAST METRO

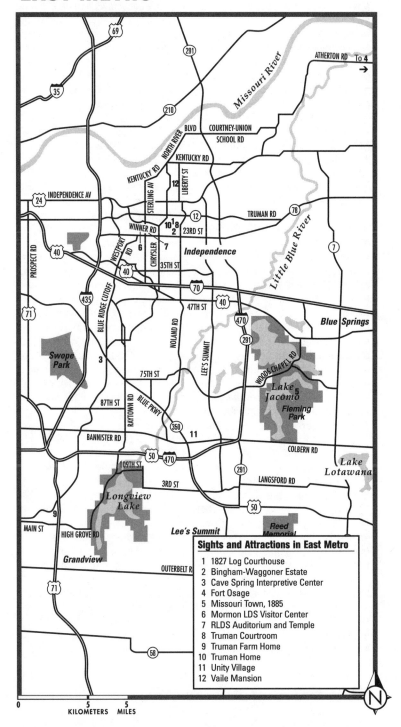

Sights and Attractions in East Metro

1 1827 Log Courthouse
2 Bingham-Waggoner Estate
3 Cave Spring Interpretive Center
4 Fort Osage
5 Missouri Town, 1885
6 Mormon LDS Visitor Center
7 RLDS Auditorium and Temple
8 Truman Courtroom
9 Truman Farm Home
10 Truman Home
11 Unity Village
12 Vaile Mansion

0   5   5
KILOMETERS   MILES

from 1808 to 1827. Overlooking the Missouri River, the site was chosen by Lewis and Clark and built under William Clark's personal direction. Now restored, the fortification showcases a variety of artifacts in the blockhouse, trading house, officers' quarters, and soldiers' barracks. Fort Osage hosts special events year-round. Take Highway 24 east to Buckner, Missouri; turn north at BB Highway (a.k.a. Sibley Street), travel 2–3 miles and watch for signs. Wed–Sun 9–4:30; Nov–Apr weekends only 9–4. Adults $3; seniors and children 5–13 $2.

HARRY S. TRUMAN COURTROOM AND OFFICE
Old Courthouse at Main and Lexington, Independence
816/795-8200, ext. 1260   EM

President Truman began his political career as a judge in this spot, overseeing a $10-million road program during the Depression and initiating the Jackson County park system. At his restored courtroom and office, visitors can view a multimedia presentation, *The Man from Independence*, and see a pictorial history of Truman's early years. Mar–Nov 9–4:30 on Fri–Sat only; closed Dec–Feb. Adults $2; 5–13 $1.

HARRY S. TRUMAN HOME
219 N. Delaware, Independence
816/254-9929   EM

Bess Wallace lived here with her mother and grandparents. When she married her childhood sweetheart, Harry Truman, in 1919, he moved in too. During President Truman's administration the residence was familiarly known as the "Summer White House," and after Truman left office in 1953 he and Bess returned to this Victorian mansion. The 33rd presi-

dent died in 1972, but his First Lady kept the house as it had been during his lifetime. Bess died a decade later, bequeathing the home to the country. Guided tours daily 9–4:45 (closed Mondays, Labor Day–Memorial Day). Tickets are $2 at the Truman Home ticket center at Main and Truman Roads. All visitors must go to the ticket office first.

MISSOURI TOWN 1855
Lake Jacomo/Fleming Park, Blue Springs
816/795-8200, ext. 1260   EM

Ever wonder about life in the 1850s? At Missouri Town 1855, more than 35 period buildings cover about 30 acres, giving you the opportunity to visit old houses, an antique church, a blacksmith shop, and reconstructed barns. Living-history interpreters show how people lived back then, as they quilt, garden, or work at the general store. Look for reenactments and other special events throughout the year. Take Highway 70 to Blue Springs exit, on the east side of Lake Jacomo. Wed–Sun 9–4:30; weekends only Nov–Apr. Adults $3; ages 5–13 and seniors $2.

MORMON (LDS) VISITORS CENTER
Corner of River Road and Walnut, Independence
816/836-3466   EM

Independence was an important destination for Mormons after founder Joseph Smith indicated that this was where Jesus Christ would return to earth. Countless numbers of his faithful flocked to the area. At the Mormon Visitors Center, you can view a historic display of Mormon life in Missouri between 1831 and 1839. The center houses plenty of artifacts; a slide show and laser disc

Why is the RLDS in Independence?

As founder of the Mormon church, Joseph Smith believed that Independence was his "city of Zion," the place where Jesus would first appear at his second coming. In fact, the leader was so convincing that converts hastened to establish a settlement in the Missouri town.

Smith, however, was killed in 1844, which sent the faithful into a tailspin. His eldest son was only 11 when Smith died; other leaders arose, but couldn't attract a sufficient following. As many as 20 splinter groups formed in the eight years following the leader's death.

By 1852, Joseph Smith III heard the call. Now 19, the prophet's son led a dissident group that refused to follow newly emerging leader Brigham Young and his doctrines, one of which was polygamy. Calling themselves the Reorganized Church of Jesus Christ of Latter Day Saints, the group claimed theirs to be the original church organized by Joseph Smith in 1830.

Now numbering some 200,000 members in more than 1,000 churches across the United States, the RLDS still believes that Independence is its spiritual home.

presentation describing church beliefs are also available. Open daily 9–9. Free.

RLDS AUDITORIUM AND TEMPLE
1001 W. Walnut, Independence
816/833-1000, ext. 1318　　**EM**
The Reorganized Church of Jesus Christ of Latter Day Saints was officially launched in 1852 when Joseph Smith III took the helm of the largest Mormon splinter group. In Independence, the massive Auditorium and the newly built Temple—with its 300-foot spiral roof that resembles a seashell—house the RLDS world

headquarters. In addition to being a place of worship, the buildings feature museum displays and guided tours. Organ recitals daily June–Sept at 3 p.m. on the 110-rank, 6,000-pipe, Aeolian-Skinner organ, one of the largest in the United States. Mon–Sat 9–5; Sun 1–5. Free.

TRUMAN FARM HOME
12301 Blue Ridge Blvd.,
Grandview
816/881-4431　　**EM**
When he was a boy, Harry Truman often stayed here on his grandparents' farm. He returned as a young

adult during his budding political career. The family farm has been restored and is now run by the National Park Service. Free tours of the house on weekends June–Aug 9–4.

UNITY VILLAGE
Highway 350 and Colbern Rd.
816/524-3550   EM
Another religious world headquarters in the area, Unity Village is the 1,400-acre home of the Unity School of Christianity. Founded in 1889 by American clergyman and educator Charles Fillmore and his wife, Myrtle, the nondenominational religion combines teachings from Christian Science, New Thought, Hinduism, Theosophy, and others. Visitors can roam Unity's well-kept grounds, which include fountains, lakes, formal gardens, a bell tower, and a cafeteria that's open to public. Tours and 20-minute slide presentation. Hours vary by season; roughly Mon–Fri 8–5; Sat–Sun 10–5. Free; goodwill offerings accepted.

VAILE MANSION
1500 N. Liberty, Independence
816/325-7111   EM
Built in 1881 by entrepreneur Harvey Vaile, this 31-room mansion is one of the United States' finest and most well-preserved examples of Victorian architecture's Second Empire style. Ceiling murals and opulent furnishings adorn the building's interior; its exterior makes for dramatic photos. Open only Apr–Oct: Mon–Sat 10–4; Sun 1–4. Adults $3; 6–16 $1.

KANSAS CITY, KANSAS/WEST

DOWNTOWN
Around 7th and Ann,

Kansas City, Kansas
913/573-5000 (City Hall)   KCK
In recent years, Kansas City, Kansas, and Wyandotte County have yearned to combine many of their government functions—and when you visit KCK's downtown civic center, it's easy to see why. Already, the two entities live happily side by side, the old Wyandotte County Courthouse across the street from the modern KCK City Hall. The venerable Sailors & Soldiers Memorial Building, "dedicated to the heroes who fought and died for their country," sits next door. Huron Park, with its municipal rose garden, offers a quiet place to stop across Ann Street.

FIRST CITY OF KANSAS
Towns of Leavenworth–Lansing   KCK
Founded in 1854, these neighboring riverfront communities comprised the first incorporated city in the Sunflower State. At Ft. Leavenworth, the oldest fort west of the Mississippi, you can see historic buildings, a museum, and a Buffalo Soldier Monument dedicated to African American soldiers.

GRANADA THEATRE
1015 Minnesota,
Kansas City, Kansas
913/621-7177   KCK
This grand old movie palace, a 1928 beauty where films were accompanied by live organ music, was des-tined for destruction when the renewed Granada Theatre Historical Society stepped in during the mid-1980s and restored the Spanish Mediterranean edifice to its former glory. The Granada is now used as a performing-arts center; its Grande Barton Theatre Pipe Organ was also restored and now accompanies

KANSAS CITY, KANSAS/WEST

Sights and Attractions in Kansas City, Kansas/West

1 Downtown
2 First City of Kansas
3 Granada Theatre
4 Grinter House
5 Huron Indian Cemetery
6 Missouri River Queen

MISSOURI
KANSAS

Missouri River

Kansas River

Riss Lake

Riverside

Wyandotte Co. Lake Park

Wyandotte County Park

LEAVENWORTH RD
PARALLEL PKWY
STATE AV
72ND ST
59TH ST
57TH ST
78TH ST
RIVERVIEW AV
KANSAS AV
MINNESOTA AV
38TH ST
31ST ST
KAW DR
INDEPENDENCE AV

MILES
KILOMETERS

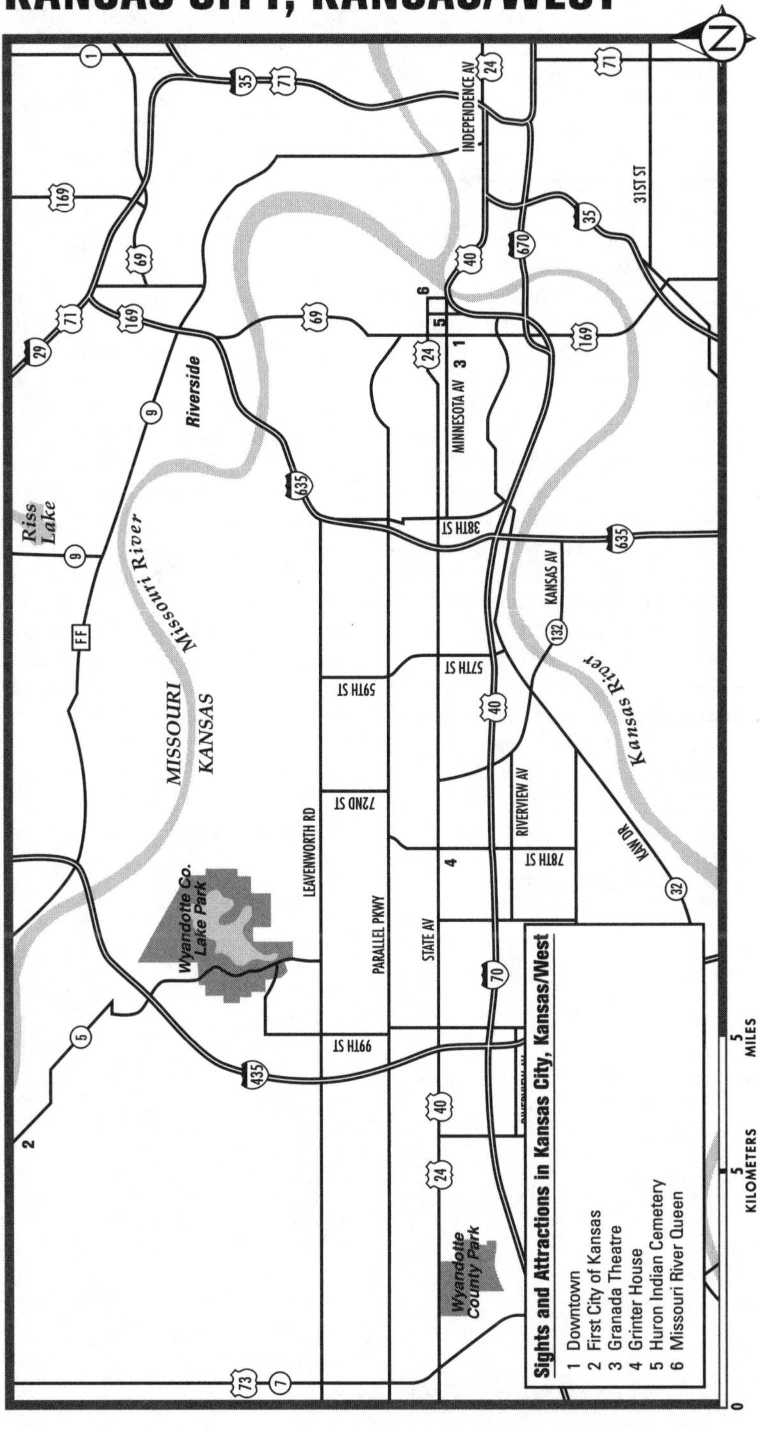

occasional showings of old movie classics.

GRINTER HOUSE
1420 S. 78th St.,
Kansas City, Kansas
913/299-0373   KCK
The first civilian post office in the Kansas Territory sat on this magnificent bluff overlooking the Kansas River. It was replaced in 1857 by a two-story Southern Colonial home that now provides a small glimpse into pre–Civil War Kansas. Guided tours Wed–Sat 10–5; Sun 1–5. Donation suggested.

HURON INDIAN CEMETERY
6th to 7th Sts., Minnesota to Ann,
Kansas City, Kansas   KCK
An eerie place nestled between downtown KCK buildings, the Huron Indian Cemetery is the final resting place for at least 400 members of the Huron tribe. Forced from Canada to Ohio to Kansas, the Hurons (who became known as the Wyandotte Indian Nation) were instrumental in establishing the first free school in Kansas and the first territorial government in their adopted homeland. The cemetery was established in 1843 and is now maintained as a city park. Eleven explanatory markers provide a fascinating glimpse into the lives of these early residents.

MISSOURI RIVER QUEEN
1 River City Dr., Kansas City,
Kansas
913/281-5300   KCK
Kansas City's only cruising excursion boat, the 600-passenger *Missouri River Queen* resembles a Victorian-style paddle wheeler. The Mighty Mo is undeniably muddy, but the voyage provides a close look at the powerful current as well as impressive views of the downtown skyline. Passengers can choose from a prime rib-dinner cruise, a Friday night family-fun cruise, a gospel entertainment cruise, a weekend brunch cruise, a moonlight cruise (during warmer weather), and a one-hour sightseeing cruise. Hours, times, and prices vary. Call for specifics.

© Hallmark Cards, Inc.

6

KIDS' STUFF

Kansas City is a kids' kind of town, from the area's many parks and play-grounds to the countless sights to see and learn from. The region offers amusement rides to try, exotic animals to touch, and educational exhibits to explore. Whether they like science or art or climbing a tree, kids can find it—and have a ball—in Kansas City.

ANIMALS AND THE GREAT OUTDOORS

DEANNA ROSE CHILDREN'S FARMSTEAD
138th St. and Switzer Rd., Overland Park
913/897-2360   JO

This 5-acre farm contains an amply stocked barnyard where kids can get close to buffalo, chickens, rabbits, pigs, lambs, ducks, and other animals. In fact, many farm residents are friendly enough to pet. The farmstead also includes picnic shelters and a nature trail. Apr–Sept 9–8 daily; Oct 9–5 daily; closed Nov–Mar. Free admission; hayrides cost $2 per person.

ERNIE MILLER PARK AND NATURE CENTER
909 N. Kansas 7, Olathe
913/764-7759   JO

Preserved in its natural state, this 113-acre park showcases ecological habitats such as grassland, upland meadow, and bottomland forest. Three short trails wind through and between the areas, giving kids an opportunity to see the wildlife that still lives there. Handy, pocket-sized reference guides make the experience even more educational. At the Nature Center, exhibits include a wildlife diorama and ecology displays. Friday nights during summer, park personnel hold family-oriented nature programs at the amphitheater. Apr–Sept

DOWNTOWN KANSAS CITY AREA

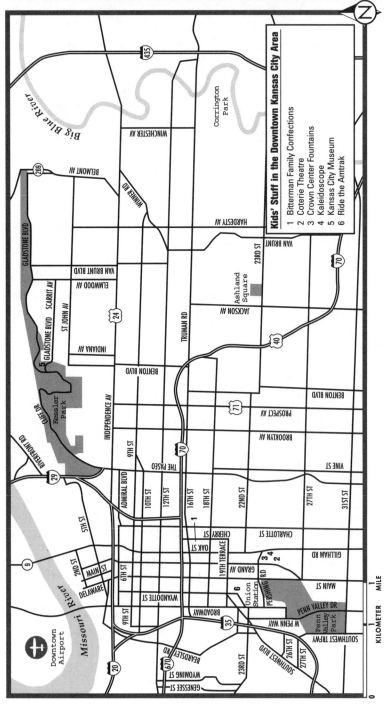

Kids' Stuff in the Downtown Kansas City Area

1 Bitterman Family Confections
2 Coterie Theatre
3 Crown Center Fountains
4 Kaleidoscope
5 Kansas City Museum
6 Ride the Amtrak

Top Ten Favorite Animals at the Kansas City Zoo
by Dr. Mark Wourms, Zoo Director

1. **Chimpanzees**. Fun, social interactions, and playful young are viewed through a 40-foot wall of glass.

2. **Meerkats**. Curious colonies have guards, babysitters, and foragers. Always a great photo.

3. **African Elephants**. The majesty and power of the largest terrestrial animal is always amazing.

4. **Red Kangaroo**. The mob can be on the path with our visitors. Joeys sticking out of pouches are wonderful discoveries.

5. **Cheetah**. Graceful. Visitors eating lunch can enjoy watching cheetah in Nanyuki Market.

6. **Giant Hornbill**. Amazing, colorful, and rare birds in Tropical Asia section.

7. **African Lions**. The "King of Beasts" can be viewed outdoors or through glass.

8. **River Otters**. These native North American "clowns" are known for their playful interactions.

9. **Our Scottish Highland Cow**, "Warf," because he is just so cute.

10. **Warthogs**. Look in the mud. These *Lion King* stars are so ugly, they're beautiful.

5 a.m.–11 p.m.; Oct–Nov 7:30 a.m.–8 p.m.; Dec–Mar 7:30–6.

KANSAS CITY ZOOLOGICAL GARDENS
I-435 and 63rd St., Kansas City
816/871-5700 CS

With its recently completed $71-million expansion, the Kansas City Zoo offers a fascinating range of natural settings for all kinds of animals, from rhinos to gorillas to meerkats. Among the zoo's newest additions are the African Safari and Australian exhibits, both replicating those continents' wild side. In 1997, the zoo will introduce a koala area—making it the only facility in a five-state region to house the cuddly critters. The zoo's new IMAX Theatre, one of the few in a zoo setting, shows films such as *The Living Sea*, narrated by Meryl Streep. Other fun stuff includes: train and pony rides, year-round sea lion presentations, and several restaurants. Daily; mid-Apr–mid-Oct 9–5; mid-Oct–mid-Apr 9–4. Ages 12 and over $5; 2–11 $2.50; under 2 free. Free admission Tue 9–noon. Parking $2.

LAKESIDE NATURE CENTER
5600 E. Gregory Blvd., Kansas City
816/444-4656 CS

CENTRAL/SOUTH KANSAS CITY

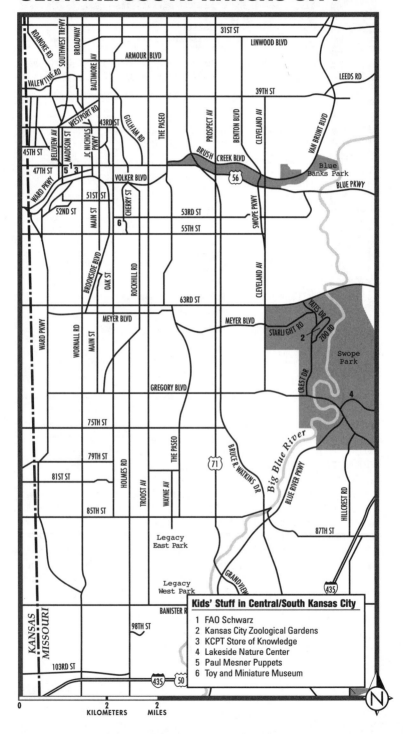

Kids' Stuff in Central/South Kansas City

1 FAO Schwarz
2 Kansas City Zoological Gardens
3 KCPT Store of Knowledge
4 Lakeside Nature Center
5 Paul Mesner Puppets
6 Toy and Miniature Museum

Like the zoo, the Lakeside Nature Center is located in Swope Park. This educational center features native Missouri animals, including birds of prey, mammals, and reptiles. Kids can learn from the center's hands-on exhibits and enlightening Saturday classes, or by hiking one of the two trails nearby. Apr–Oct Tue–Sat 9–5; Sun noon–4. Free; nominal fee for Saturday courses.

RIVERVIEW GARDEN CENTER
7851 Riverview,
Kansas City, Kansas
913/299-6184   KCK
Kids from grade school to junior high will find this commercial growing emporium a fascinating way to learn about plants. The center cultivates annuals and perennials from chrysanthemums to poinsettias, and keeps water ponds, too. An affable host, owner Mike Murray will show kids around the 10-acre garden and the 45,000-square-foot greenhouse, either by reservation or whenever families drop in. Mon–Sat 9–5; free.

FUN AND EDUCATIONAL

CROWN CENTER FOUNTAINS
Crown Center, Kansas City   DA
Running through the fountains at Crown Center isn't exactly educational, but kids certainly think it's a blast. During warmer weather, the Hallmark-owned shopping district turns on the 49 jets directly across from the center's main entrance on Grand. Some of these jets spout as high as 25 feet into the air. On hot days, fully clothed parents sometimes just can't resist either. No set hours; free.

FARMLAND INDUSTRIES RESEARCH FARM

A cheetah at the Kansas City Zoo, page 113

Ollie MacMillen/Kansas City Zoological Gardens

3705 N. 139th St., Bonner Springs
913/721-2600   KCK
The area's largest agribusiness company, Farmland Industries operates a 360-acre farm that gives a fascinating in-depth look at how the enterprise develops feed for cows, calves, pigs, and pets such as dogs and cats. Farmland stresses that this is a research facility, so tours are given only on Tuesdays and Thursdays during the third week of each spring and summer month, by reservation only. Free.

KALEIDOSCOPE
25th and Grand at Crown Center,
Kansas City
816/274-8300   DA
Run by Hallmark next door to its Visitors Center, the Kaleidoscope program exists to encourage creativity in kids between the ages of 5 and 12. Through independent, hands-on activities that involve touching, hearing, seeing, and imagining, Kaleidoscope helps children learn and experience by creating their own works of art. Reservations are required Mon–Fri

during the school year; sessions offered Sat at 11, 1:30, and 3. Free.

RIDE THE AMTRAK
2200 Main St., Kansas City
816/421-3622 DA
During the holidays, parents often take their kids to Lee's Summit, Independence, or Warrensburg to board the Amtrak train for a ride to Kansas City. From there it's a short walk to Crown Center to see Santa before the return train trip. In fact, it's possible to give the kids a real train-riding experience any time of year by making these short journeys. A round-trip ticket between Independence and Kansas City costs $8–$10 for adults; $7–$8.50 seniors. Children 2–15 ride for half price when accompanied by an adult. Limit two children per adult. Call for train schedule.

PUPPETS AND THEATER

THE COTERIE THEATRE
25th and Grand, Kansas City
816/474-6552 DA
Located on Crown Center's Level 1, the Coterie is a professional theater presenting dramatic works for the entire family. Kids, in particular, enjoy the stage company's mission to present inspiring plays that challenge stereotypes and get the audience talking. Plays set for the first half of 1997 include *Whale; African Valley Song; The Reluctant Dragon; Lyle, Lyle, The Crocodile*; and the Young Playwrights' Showcase. Individual tickets $6; call for dates and times.

THEATRE FOR YOUNG AMERICA
4881 Johnson Dr., Mission
913/831-1400 JO
In addition to its regular lineup of first-rate plays for children, TYA offers acting classes for aspiring actors aged 3½ and up throughout the year. In summer, special workshops teach dramatic skills such as storytelling and improvisation. Plays in 1997 range from *Cinderella–It's OK to be Different* to *Rumpelstiltskin* to *Anne of Green Gables*. Located on Mission Mall's second level; $5.50 all ages.

PAUL MESNER PUPPETS
Unity Temple on the Plaza
707 W. 47th St., Kansas City
816/235-2700 or 756-3500 CS
Paul Mesner puppet shows run the gamut from classic stories to educational programs, all designed to delight kids of all ages. Offbeat characters energize the shows, making them more enjoyable for adults, too. Morning and early afternoon performances during the season, ranging from the Heartland Puppetry Festival to *The Dinosaur Show*. $6.

MUSEUMS AND LIBRARIES

CHILDREN'S MUSEUM OF KANSAS CITY
4601 State Ave.,
Kansas City, Kansas
913/287-8888 KCK
Located on the lower level of the Indian Springs Shopping Center, the Children's Museum emphasizes art, history, and science with engaging exhibits such as the Magic School Bus, a mock radio station, the Slice of the City, and a model grocery. Kids both learn from and enjoy this storehouse of knowledge. Tue–Sat 9:30–5; Sun 1–5. $2.50 per person; free for children 2 and younger.

KANSAS CITY MUSEUM
3218 Gladstone Blvd., Kansas City

JOHNSON COUNTY

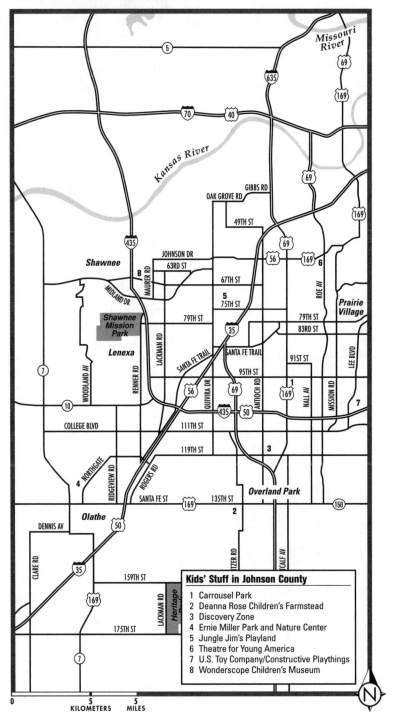

Missouri River

Kansas River

Shawnee

Shawnee Mission Park

Lenexa

Prairie Village

Overland Park

Olathe

GIBBS RD
OAK GROVE RD
49TH ST
JOHNSON DR
63RD ST
67TH ST
75TH ST
79TH ST
SANTA FE TRAIL
95TH ST
91ST ST
83RD ST
79TH ST
111TH ST
119TH ST
COLLEGE BLVD
SANTA FE ST
135TH ST
DENNIS AV
159TH ST
175TH ST

MIDLAND DR
MAURER RD
LACKMAN RD
SANTA FE TRAIL
RENNER RD
WOODLAND AV
QUIVIRA DR
ANTIOCH RD
NALL AV
MISSION RD
LEE BLVD
ROE AV
NORTHGATE
RIDGEVIEW RD
ROGERS RD
CLARE RD
LACKMAN RD
CALF AV
TZER RD

Kids' Stuff in Johnson County

1   Carrousel Park
2   Deanna Rose Children's Farmstead
3   Discovery Zone
4   Ernie Miller Park and Nature Center
5   Jungle Jim's Playland
6   Theatre for Young America
7   U.S. Toy Company/Constructive Playthings
8   Wonderscope Children's Museum

0   5   5
KILOMETERS   MILES

N

What to do with teens? Try an underground game of paintball (Chapter 10), a concert at Sandstone (Chapter 11), or a watery day at Oceans of Fun (this chapter). Teens in Kansas City also head to Country Club Plaza (Chapter 9), Crown Center's ice rink (Chapter 10), and Malibu Grand Prix, where they can test their driving skills on a half-mile track (11200 W. 87th St., Lenexa, 913/492-4949 for details).

816/483-8300   **DA**
See description in Chapter 7: Museums and Galleries.

TOY AND MINIATURE MUSEUM
5235 Oak, Kansas City
816/333-2055   **CS**
See description in Chapter 7: Museums and Galleries.

WONDERSCOPE CHILDREN'S MUSEUM
16000 W. 65th St., Shawnee
913/268-8130 (recording)
913/268-4176   **JO**
At the Wonderscope, kids will find interactive exhibits that feature every-thing from a television studio to a weather station to a "What if You Couldn't" display. Set in a former school, Wonderscope is a colorful facility that encourages parents and kids to explore together. Tue–Sat 10–5; Sun noon–5. Admission: $3.25; free for children under 3.

STORES KIDS LOVE

BITTERMAN FAMILY CONFECTIONS
1625 Oak St., Kansas City
816/221-2922   **DA**
With its wood floors and old-fashioned shelves stacked to the ceiling, Bitterman looks like a kids' paradise. The store—owned by the Bitterman family since 1936—features hard candies, chocolates, and novelty sweets, from the affordable on up. Open Mon–Fri 10–4.

FAO SCHWARZ
235 W. 47th St., Kansas City
816/931-9090   **CS**
Kids will love the giant bear that stands sentinel at the FAO Schwarz door. Inside, they can roam around the huge Plaza store and play with the electronic floor keyboard, the interactive rain forest, and the animated candy store, FAO Schweetz. Mon and Wed 10–8; Tue and Thur–Sat 10–9; Sun 10–5.

The Detonator at Worlds of Fun, page 123

Dan Feicht/Worlds of Fun

Ten Best Things to Do with Kids in the Kansas City Area

by Pam Elliott,
owner of Pam's Day Care and the 1993 Kansas Day Care Provider of the Year runner-up

1. Visit the **Deanna Rose Children's Farmstead**. Kids can pet and feed farm animals and go on hayrides in a horse-drawn wagon. Great playground and picnic area. Good for kids 1–10.

2. Ride the ***Missouri River Queen***. Take the one-hour educational cruise, plus enjoy carousel rides and an exhibit of exotic birds. Good for kids 4 and up.

3. Tour the ***Arabia* Steamboat Museum**. Children can touch some exhibits, and view artifacts taken from a Civil War–era paddle-wheel steamboat. Ages 8 and up.

4. Take a hike at the **Ernie Miller Park and Nature Center**. Offers hiking trails for all ages, with varying degrees of difficulty. The center has hands-on activities and animals on display. Kids 3–12 will enjoy these trails.

5. Visit the **Kansas City Zoo**, one of the Midwest's best. Visit the new sites: Africa and Australia. Also, take a break at the new IMAX Theatre. Ages 3 and up.

6. Ride the **Smoky Hill Railway** (502 S. Walnut, Belton). Kids can experience lifelike history as they ride a real running train down a former Frisco Railroad line, past a hobo village. The conductor will give a history lesson, and a 30-minute train movie is shown prior to the ride. Good for kids 4 and up.

7. Enjoy **Carrousel Park**. When the weather's bad, try this indoor amusement park, with rides, shows, ice cream, pizza, and other snacks. Clean and well maintained, fun for the whole family. Good for kids 3 and up.

8. Visit **Wonderscope Museum**. Hands-on activities focus on arts, sciences, and technology. Features include TV studio, space station, and hospital exhibit. The Small Wonders room is great for younger kids.

9. Tour the **NCAA Hall of Champions**. Kids who like sports can find photos, video displays, and memorabilia. Ages 8 and up.

10. Check out **Kauffman Stadium**. Visit the locker rooms, sit in the dugout and press box, see the Hall of Fame. See what only the players normally see. Call for tour schedule (816/921-2200). Ages 4 through teens.

GREATER KANSAS CITY

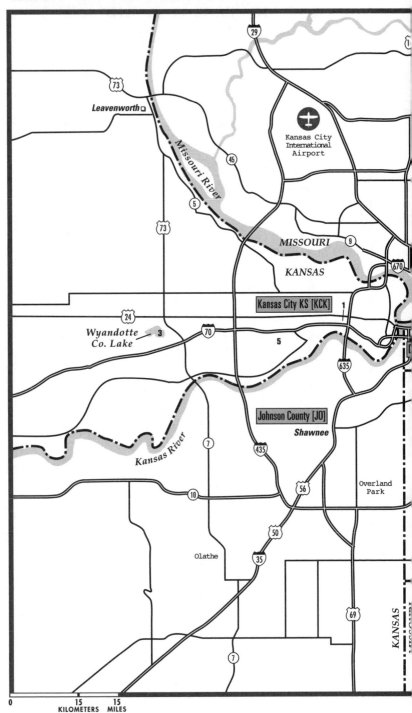

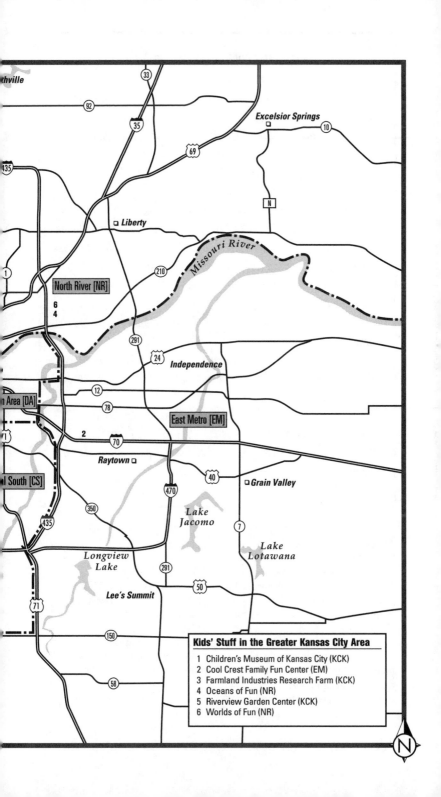

Kids' Stuff in the Greater Kansas City Area

1 Children's Museum of Kansas City (KCK)
2 Cool Crest Family Fun Center (EM)
3 Farmland Industries Research Farm (KCK)
4 Oceans of Fun (NR)
5 Riverview Garden Center (KCK)
6 Worlds of Fun (NR)

Kids Just Wanna Have Fun

Not all men with money like to have so much fun. But Lamar Hunt, owner of the NFL's Kansas City Chiefs and founder of the American Football League in 1960, also developed the dual theme parks Worlds of Fun and Oceans of Fun.

Worlds of Fun opened in 1973 with 60 rides, shows, and attractions. Based on Jules Verne's Around the World in Eighty Days, *the theme park covers five continents from Europe to Africa to America. Rides within the 170-acre park now number more than 140; the most popular these days include the Orient Express, the Zambezi Zinger, and Fury of the Nile. The Stax of Wax Rock & Roll Revue is one of the favorite shows at the park, while the Vittle Griddle is the most popular eatery.*

Oceans of Fun opened in 1982, and remains the Midwest's largest tropically themed water park. Within its 60 acres, Oceans of Fun features the Surf City Wave Pool, which holds 1 million gallons of water. In addition, a long list of water-related rides keeps the kids coming back all summer.

Although Hunt recently sold the two theme parks, his legacy remains at Worlds and Oceans of Fun. Unconfirmed reports have it that the Dallas-based entrepreneur has even been spotted whooshing down the Aruba Tuba!

KCPT STORE OF KNOWLEDGE
4705 Broadway, Kansas City
816/960-0480   CS
Sure it's for kids, but grown-ups also find plenty to play with here. The public TV-affiliated shop stocks more than 5,000 toys, games, puzzles, videos, computer software, hobby kits, and other merchandise that spans more than 60 subjects, including the arts, science, history, and foreign languages. Naturally, there's a special section dedicated to PBS programs. Mon–Sat 10–9; Sun noon–9.

U.S. TOY COMPANY/
CONSTRUCTIVE PLAYTHINGS
2008 W. 103rd Terr., Leawood
913/642-8247   JO
Get ready to spend an enjoyable afternoon—for both kids and adults—at this educational toy store. Within its two enormous warehouses set behind Gates Bar-B-Q on State Line Road, U.S. Toy stocks games and

toys for learning, plus a carnival section, one of the largest magic shops in the world, and a whole host of costumes. Open Mon–Thur 8:30–8; Fri 8:30–5:30; Sat 9–5; Sun noon–4.

THEME PARKS

OCEANS OF FUN
Exit 54 off I-435, Kansas City
816/454-4545   NR
Water, water everywhere: Oceans of Fun features watery attractions on 60 acres, including a 1-million-gallon wave pool, children's water playgrounds, giant water slides, and an adults-only pool with swim-up refreshments. 1997 hours: May 23–Sept 1 open daily at 10 a.m. Closing times vary. Adults (at least 48 inches tall or 59 years) $16.95; children 4 years to 48 inches tall $4.95; seniors 60 and up $12.50; after 4 p.m., all ages $12.50. Prices don't include tax.

WORLDS OF FUN
Exit 54 off I-435, Kansas City
816/454-4545   NR
This internationally themed park features more than 140 rides, shows, and attractions including the Sea Dragon, the Wacky Worm kiddie coaster, and the Timber Wolf roller coaster (ranked as one of top coasters in the world). One of the newest rides—the Detonator—thrusts riders straight up at 45 mph. 1997 hours: Apr 12–May 25 and Sept 6–Oct 12 weekends at 10 a.m.;

May 26–Aug 25 and Aug 30–Sept 1 daily at 10 a.m. Closing hours vary. Admission: Adults (48 inches tall to 59 years) $24.95; children 4 years to 48 inches tall $4.95; seniors 60 and up $11.95; after 4 p.m., all ages $11.95. Prices don't include tax.

PLACES TO PLAY

CARROUSEL PARK
Metcalf South Shopping Center, Overland Park
913/385-7275   JO
Set inside the Metcalf South Shopping Center at 95th and Metcalf, Carrousel Park draws families with its rides, games, prizes, food, and entertainment. The indoor theme park is available for parties during the week and open to the public Fri–Sun 10–9; kids $8 for the "Ride Pass"; adults free.

COOL CREST FAMILY FUN CENTER
10735 E. Hwy. 40, Independence
816/358-0088   EM
Within Cool Crest's 4.5 acres, families can enjoy four 18-hole miniature golf courses, an exotic bird display, a game room with video machines and pinball, and several party and patio areas set throughout the facility's gardens. The Patterson family has operated this Independence gathering spot since 1950. Winter hours: Mon–Thur noon–9:30; Fri–Sat noon–11; Sun noon–9:30. Summer:

Toy and Miniature Museum, page 118

10–10 daily. Prices vary depending on games played.

DISCOVERY ZONE
7594 W. 119th, Overland Park
913/469-1838   **JO**

An enormous room filled with elevated tunnels and slides, Discovery Zone encourages kids to expend some energy, enhancing their coordination skills. Parents, donning supplied kneepads, can join in the romp through the 4,000-square-foot play center. Another Discovery Zone's at 4420 S. Noland Rd. (373-4445) in Independence. Mon–Thur 10–8; Fri–Sat 9–9; Sun 11–7. Adults free; kids 3–12 $5.99; 1–3 $3.99; under 1 free if accompanied by another child.

JUNGLE JIM'S PLAYLAND
11010 W. 74th Terr., Shawnee
913/268-8333   **JO**

An indoor amusement park, Jungle Jim's features mini-amusement rides such as bumper cars, spinning tops, and roller coasters. Although it's recommended for kids under 12, Jungle Jim's is a great place to take the whole family. Sun–Thur 10–8; Fri–Sat 10–9 with extended summer hours. $5.99 Mon–Fri; $7.49 Sat–Sun. Adults ride free when accompanied by a child.

7

MUSEUMS AND GALLERIES

Whether it's history or art or tiny toys, Kansas City boasts a surprising number of fascinating museums. In this metropolitan area, you can view some of the finest Asian art in the country, see the entire cargo of a pre–Civil War paddle wheeler, and even discover Victorian jewelry made from human hair. Kansas City's art galleries also offer a talented array of regional, national, and international artists, whose work—from traditional to contemporary to ethnic—simply adds to the area's creative ambiance.

ART MUSEUMS

NELSON-ATKINS MUSEUM OF ART
4525 Oak, Kansas City
816/561-4000   CS
Considered one of the best art museums in the country, the Nelson contains prestigious collections of European and American art, from Caravaggio, Monet, and Rembrandt to Homer, Sargent, and Bingham. Its renowned Oriental Collection includes the Chinese Temple Room, galleries displaying furniture and porcelain, and an array of glazed T'ang Dynasty tomb figures. Outside, the Henry Moore Sculpture Garden contains 13 larger-than-life works in a landscaped setting, while four giant shuttlecocks by Claes Oldenburg and Coosje van Bruggen decorate the lawns. It's a sensory overload for arts aficionados. Tue–Thur 10–4; Fri 10–9; Sat 10–5; Sun 1–5. Adults $4; adult students with ID $2; 6–18 $1; under 6 free. Saturdays free.

KEMPER MUSEUM OF CONTEMPORARY ART & DESIGN
4420 Warwick Ave., Kansas City
816/561-3737   CS
Opened in 1994, the Kemper contains permanent and rotating exhibits by international contemporary artists. The modern glass, granite, and stainless steel building provides a harmonious setting for works by Jasper

DOWNTOWN KANSAS CITY AREA

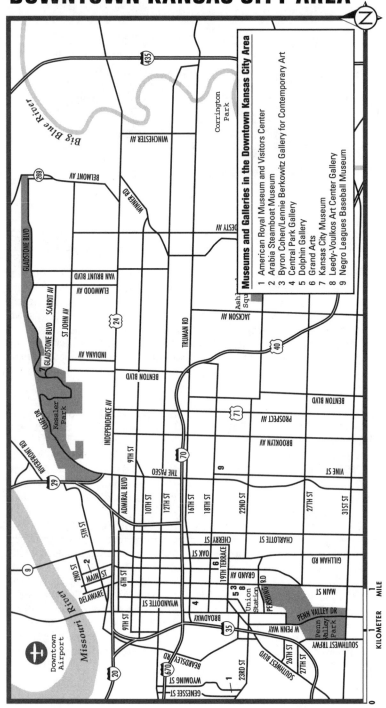

Museums and Galleries in the Downtown Kansas City Area

1 American Royal Museum and Visitors Center
2 Arabia Steamboat Museum
3 Byron Cohen/Lennie Berkowitz Gallery for Contemporary Art
4 Central Park Gallery
5 Dolphin Gallery
6 Grand Arts
7 Kansas City Museum
8 Leedy-Voulkos Art Center Gallery
9 Negro Leagues Baseball Museum

Art and Soul

William Rockhill Nelson was a zealous patron of the arts. Founder of the Kansas City Star *and financial proponent of the parks-and-boulevard system, Nelson bequeathed $11 million to the city when he died in 1915, specifically for art acquisitions. His gift, combined with another $1 million for land and a building from reclusive art patron Mary Atkins, eventually launched the now-famous Nelson-Atkins Museum of Art.*

The museum, however, wasn't started until after Nelson's wife, daughter, son-in-law, and family attorney also died. Nelson had erroneously assumed the city would provide a museum building for the collection it would amass on his behalf. When that didn't happen, Nelson's son-in-law, Irwin Kirkwood, deeded Nelson's home, Oak Hall, to the city. Oak Hall was razed; the museum broke ground in 1930.

Unlike most great museums, the Nelson-Atkins was not created from existing art collections. The trustees began buying in earnest in the early Thirties, under the direction of various art historians and consultants. Because they were starting the museum during the Depression, the trustees were able to acquire excellent pieces at relatively low prices. The Nelson, as it's known locally, finally opened its doors in 1933.

Johns, Frank Stella, and David Hockney, among others. A sculpture courtyard and the colorfully delightful Cafe Sebastienne (lunch only) make the Kemper a rewarding place to visit. Tue–Fri 10–4; Sat 10–5; Sun 11–5. Free. Cafe Sebastienne open Tue–Sun 11–3.

SCIENCE AND HISTORY MUSEUMS

AGRICULTURAL HALL OF FAME &

FARMING MUSEUM
630 N. 126th St., Bonner Springs
913/721-1075   **KCK**
As the nation's largest exhibit of artifacts relating to American farm life, the 270-acre Agricultural Hall of Fame & Farming Museum was chartered by Congress in 1960. It's now the only such institution honoring farmers. Built entirely with private funds, the museum's three major buildings chronicle the evolution of American agriculture, from the first farm truck to the steam threshing

Treasure Hunters of the Midwest

It started as a dream. It became an obsession.

Back in 1988, three families decided they would try to salvage the 180-foot sidewheeler Arabia, *which sank in 1856 after hitting a Missouri River snag. The river had shifted, leaving the boat beneath a farm field. Earlier recovery efforts had failed—in 1877, 1897, and 1974—but the Hawleys, Mackeys, and Luttrells believed they could succeed. Skeptics claimed the boat was empty; nevertheless these Independence natives remained committed.*

First, Bob Hawley designed a system to lower the water table at the riverfront field. Then the team started digging, spending four months excavating a 40-foot deep pit. Finally, they hit pay dirt: perfectly preserved—albeit wet and mud-caked—top hats, eyeglasses, tobacco, glass beads, and much, much more. After cleaning and preserving the 200 tons of booty with water and polyethylene, the families opened the Arabia Steamboat Museum in 1991. It's now one of Kansas City's unique and most popular attractions.

engine to ice harvesting tools. It's a rural extravaganza. Mid-Mar–Dec Mon–Sat 9–5; Sun 1–5. Adults $5; seniors 62 and up $4; kids 5–12 $2.50.

ARABIA STEAMBOAT MUSEUM
400 Grand, Kansas City
816/471-4030   **DA**
The mighty Missouri River swallowed hundreds of steamboats during the vessels' heyday, catching many on snags lurking just beneath the murky surface. The *Arabia* was among them, but the boat was recovered—more than a century after its sinking—by a group of determined treasure-seekers. This museum highlights the more than 200 tons of recovered goods salvaged from the

1850s steamboat, including china, jewelry, hardware, cookware, and food. A full-scale replica of the 171-foot boat deck features a 28-foot working paddle wheel. Located on the east side of the City Market complex. Mon–Sat 10–6; Sun noon–5. Adults $6.50; seniors $6; ages 4–12 $3.75.

1859 MARSHALL'S HOME & JAIL MUSEUM
217 N. Main, Independence
816/252-1892   **EM**
Built before the Civil War, this historic jail once held outlaws Frank James and William Quantrill. Within the jail, with its barred windows and double iron doors, it's possible to step into a cell and experience the sinking feel-

ing of early-frontier justice. Apr–Oct
Mon–Sat 10–5 and Sun 1–4; Mar,
Nov, Dec Tue–Sat 10–4 and Sun 1–4;
closed Jan and Feb. Adults $3; se-
niors $2.50; 6–16 $1.

HARRY S. TRUMAN
LIBRARY AND MUSEUM
U.S. 24 and Delaware,
Independence
816/833-1225   **EM**
Harry S. Truman's presidential library
provides a fascinating look at the
leader now considered by many to
be one of the finest U.S. presidents of
the twentieth century. This site contains approximately 30,000 Truman-
related objects, from gifts to personal
possessions to memorabilia. Visitors
can see Truman's Oval Office and
witness his legacy of leadership from
his stints as a captain in World War I
to judge to president. Rotating exhibits and programs illustrate the Truman presidency and the world the
Missouri native helped rebuild and
shape after he presided over the end
of World War II. Daily 9–5; closed

The Prophet *by Frank Stella at the*
Kemper, page 125

The Kemper Museum of Contemporary Art & Design

Thanksgiving, Christmas, New Year's
Day. Adults: $3; seniors and children
under 15 free.

HISTORIC LIBERTY JAIL
AND VISITOR CENTER
216 N. Main, Liberty
816/781-3188   **NR**
In this small building, Joseph
Smith—the first prophet and president of the Church of Jesus Christ
of Latter Day Saints (Mormons)—
was incarcerated from 1838 to 1839.
The museum is operated by the
Mormons, who also offer exhibits,
an audiovisual presentation, and
other information about church history at the site. Guided tours daily
9–9; free.

JESSE JAMES BANK MUSEUM
AND HISTORIC SITE
Historic Square, Liberty
816/781-4458   **NR**
Step back in time and imagine con-
ducting your bank business in this
tiny brick building. Then imagine out-
law Jesse James barreling in, ready
to relieve you of your cash. In fact,
this is the site of the first successful
U.S. daylight bank robbery during
peacetime. The original 1858 vault
and hand-scribed ledger books are
on display. Daily 9–4. Adults $2.50;
over 6 $1.

JOHNSON COUNTY
HISTORICAL MUSEUM
6305 Lackman Rd., Shawnee
913/631-6709   **JO**
Life was hard back in the pioneer
days, and this museum shows just
how difficult it truly was. Exhibits and
hands-on activities depict life on the
plains; one display is dedicated to the
trails experience in what is now
Johnson County. Tue–Sat 10–4:30;
Sun 1–4:30. Free.

From Lumber to Science

The Kansas City Museum opened its doors in 1940, in a mansion once called Corinthian Hall. Built in 1910 as the home of Robert Alexander Long, founder of the Long-Bell Lumber Company, the home was named for the six Corinthian columns that support the front portico.

Over the years, the museum increased its emphasis on exhibits that highlight science, technology, and history. Today, the facility's planetarium remains the only public planetarium in the area; its Challenger Learning Center offers simulated, hands-on space flights to stimulate interest in math, science, and technology.

The museum also has launched plans to rocket into the future. After area voters approved a bi-state cultural tax in November 1996—the first tax of any kind to cross state boundaries—the foundation for Science City in Union Station was established. Funds will go toward renovation of the 1914 train depot. Once that's completed, Science City will occupy a portion of the new space. Plans call for the Kansas City Museum to continue displaying its other exhibits from Robert Long's gracious three-story home in northeast Kansas City.

KANSAS CITY MUSEUM
3218 Gladstone Blvd., Kansas City
816/483-8300   DA
This museum features high-touch science and history exhibits that appeal to kids of all ages. The National History Hall, working soda fountain, Planetarium, and the Challenger Learning Center are only four of the major attractions. Chief exhibits in 1997 include "Good Vibrations" (Feb 1–Sept 14), demonstrating how sound travels and music is made; and "Magnetics: The Invisible Force" (Oct 11–Jan 4), which explores how magnetism works. Tue–Sat 9:30–4:30;

Sun noon–4:30. Adults $2.50; seniors and students $2; children $1.50. Planetarium tickets $3.50 each.

NATIONAL FRONTIER TRAILS CENTER
318 W. Pacific, Independence
816/325-7575   EM
The National Frontier Trails Center has become the nation's foremost museum and research facility on the West's exploration and settlement. It's a natural, since Independence was the principal jumping-off point for the Santa Fe, California, and Oregon Trails. Rotating and permanent

exhibits—including two nineteenth-century wagons—as well as an interpretive center, films, and archives all explain the "Go West" call popular in the mid-1800s. Apr–Oct Mon–Sat 9–4:30; Sun 12:30–4:30. Nov–Mar Mon–Fri 10–4; weekends 12:30–4. Adults $2.50; students 10–17 $1; children 9 and under free.

OLD SHAWNEE TOWN
57th St. and Cody, Shawnee
913/268-8772   JO
In this re-creation of an early Kansas pioneer community—operated by the Shawnee Historical Society—visitors can wander through a variety of original and reconstructed buildings, including Kansas' first jail (built in 1844), a chapel, a farmhouse, and a one-room school, among others. An adjacent park resembles the town in miniature. Grounds open Tue–Sat 10–5; Sun noon–5; closed Mon. Tours Apr–Oct only. Adults $2; children 50 cents.

STRAWBERRY HILL MUSEUM
720 N. 4th, Kansas City, Kansas
913/371-3264   KCK
Built for a prosperous family in 1887, this three-story, red brick home later became St. John's Orphanage. Now it houses exhibits that detail the lives and history of the Slavic people who immigrated to this area. The museum (named for its Strawberry Hill neighborhood) provides an intimate look at an often-overlooked ethnic group in America. Sat–Sun noon–5. Adults $3; 4–12 $1.50; under 4 free.

WYANDOTTE COUNTY HISTORICAL MUSEUM
631 N. 126th, Bonner Springs
913/721-1078   KCK
Located near the Agricultural Hall of Fame in Bonner Springs, the museum

The Nelson-Atkins Museum of Art, page 125

Convention and Visitors Bureau of Greater Kansas City

CENTRAL/SOUTH KANSAS CITY

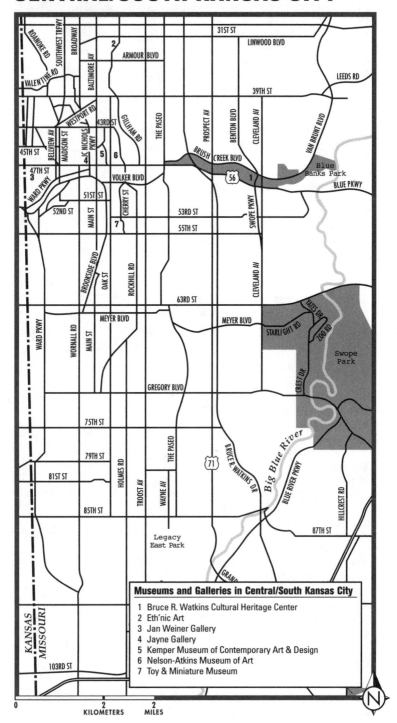

Museums and Galleries in Central/South Kansas City

1 Bruce R. Watkins Cultural Heritage Center
2 Eth'nic Art
3 Jan Weiner Gallery
4 Jayne Gallery
5 Kemper Museum of Contemporary Art & Design
6 Nelson-Atkins Museum of Art
7 Toy & Miniature Museum

presents local and regional history. Exhibits include a 1903 horse-drawn fire engine and a variety of other turn-of-the-century artifacts. Tue–Sat 10–5; Sun 1–5. Free.

SPECIALTY MUSEUMS

AMERICAN ROYAL MUSEUM & VISITORS CENTER
1701 American Royal Ct., Kansas City
816/221-9800 **DA**
The American Royal recently spent $34 million on a significant expansion that included the addition of a visitors center. Through interactive displays and a 20-minute film, visitors can learn more about the American Royal Livestock, Horse Show, and Rodeo, an annual fall event that encapsulates Kansas City's historic past as a crossroads of the cattle industry. Tue–Sat 10–4; Sun by appointment; closed Mon. Adults $3; children $2; under 2 free.

BRUCE R. WATKINS CULTURAL HERITAGE CENTER
3700 Blue Pkwy., Kansas City
816/923-6226 **CS**
Named for a much-beloved city councilman, this center was erected to honor the contributions of Kansas City's African American residents. In addition to seasonal exhibits and a research library, the center also hosts cultural events. Tue–Sat 10–6; free.

LEILA'S HAIR MUSEUM
815 W. 23rd St., Independence
816/252-4247 **EM**
Leila Cohoon, owner of the Independence College of Cosmetology, opened this museum in 1989 to feature a collection she'd begun in the Fifties. About 500 displays chronicle decorative uses for hair, most dating before 1900. Among Cohoon's most prized pieces are a scrapbook dating from 1725 to 1900 with calling cards and locks of hair; a delicately woven hair brooch; and a Victorian-era hair wreath valued at $10,000. Tue–Sat 9:30–3:30. Adults $3; seniors over 65 $1.50.

NEGRO LEAGUES BASEBALL MUSEUM
Corner of 18th St. and Vine, Kansas City
816/221-1920 **DA**
When it opened in 1994, the Negro Leagues Baseball Museum was dedicated to preserving and illuminating the history of African American baseball in America, a mission it fulfills admirably. Through interactive computer stations, uniform displays, and a photo gallery, visitors can learn about the contributions made by these gifted players. Tue–Sat 10–4:30; Sun noon–4:30. $2 over age 12; $1 ages 5–12; free under 5.

OLD OLATHE NAVAL AIR MUSEUM
1 Navy Dr., Olathe
913/768-1153 **JO**

JOHNSON COUNTY

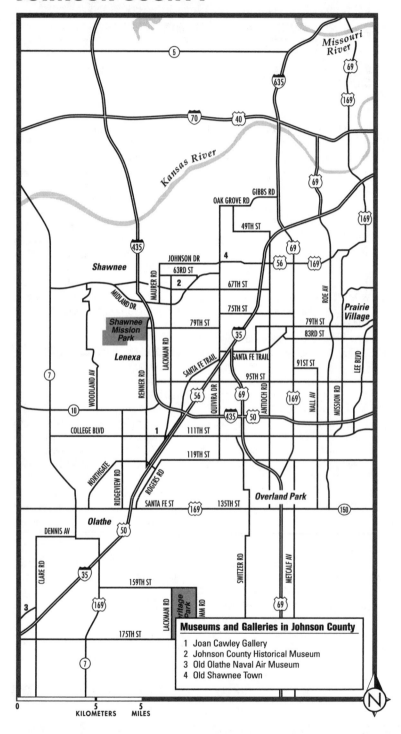

Museums and Galleries in Johnson County

1 Joan Cawley Gallery
2 Johnson County Historical Museum
3 Old Olathe Naval Air Museum
4 Old Shawnee Town

Ten Favorite Displays to See at the Toy & Miniature Museum

by William R. Robertson, renowned miniaturist and Kansas City resident

There are tens of thousands of things to see at the museum, but here goes, starting with the smallest . . .

1. An **American Indian bowl** with a pair of ⅛-inch-long frogs for handles, made by Theresa Wildflower.

2. A **carved and gold-gilded picture frame** with a 60-mesh needlepoint painting by Jim Mormon.

3. **Carved boxwood skeletons**: a 2.5-inch-high human and a 7-inch-long velociraptor, with separate teeth and claws carved from holly. Made by Lloyd McCaffery.

4. An 8-inch-high **English Georgian secretary desk** with working locks and 19 secret compartments.

5. A **sidesaddle, three-wheeled velocipede**, circa 1870s.

6. An **American Gothic–style fretwork cabinet doll house** with mid-nineteenth-century painted metal furniture. Don't miss the felt "penwipes" shaped like a bulldog with pups.

7. **Twin Manors**, a Georgian-style miniature house made from 75,000 pieces. Be sure to see its exploded-view front door.

8. A 9-foot-tall, **nineteenth-century French music box** in the shape of a château, with stained glass windows and floor, working gutters and downspouts, and gold gilt details.

9. **GeeGee's room,** a full-scale Victorian nursery filled with toys and dolls. Don't miss the Noter-Growlers, toy dogs you could rent to walk on the boardwalk in the 1890s.

10. The **maze,** a winding hallway lined with miniature room settings ranging from a turn-of-the-century Architects' Classroom to the study from the Palace of Versailles.

Honoring the naval veterans who passed through the now-mothballed Olathe Naval Air Station, this museum features awards, photographs, clothing, and other memorabilia from 1942 to 1970. It's housed at the New Century AirCenter, near Exit 210 off I-35, approximately 3 miles south of Olathe. Sat–Sun 10–5. Free.

TOY & MINIATURE MUSEUM
5235 Oak St., Kansas City
816/333-2055   **CS**
On the University of Missouri–Kansas City campus, this restored 1911 mansion contains an eye-popping collection of fine miniatures, antique doll houses, Victorian playthings, and much, much more. Far from just a

kids' attraction, the museum takes you through winding vistas of objects that amaze with their detail and artistry. Also be sure to check out the selections from Hallmark's Jerry Smith Toy Collection, a series primarily for boys. Wed–Sat 10–4; Sun 1–4; closed first two weeks after Labor Day. Adults $4; students over 12 and seniors $3.50; ages 5–12 $2.

GALLERIES

Home to the annual Plaza Art Fair, the Kansas City Art Institute and Hallmark Cards, Kansas City has become a hotbed for artistic endeavors. Galleries exist throughout the area, most holding frequent Friday-night openings. What follows is only a small sampling.

CENTRAL PARK GALLERY
1644 Wyandotte, Kansas City
816/471-7711   DA
Run by husband and wife Jim and Brenda Miles, this 9-year-old gallery features original works and prints in nearly all media. Local, regional, national and international artists are represented. Tue–Fri 9–5; Sat 10–4; Sun noon–5. Closed Mon.

BYRON COHEN/LENNIE BERKOWITZ GALLERY FOR CONTEMPORARY ART
2000 Baltimore, Kansas City
816/421-5665   DA
This contemporary gallery features rotating shows highlighting newly created paintings, sculpture, drawings, ceramics, photography, and video. Thur–Sat 11–5 and by appointment.

DOLPHIN GALLERY
2006 Baltimore, Kansas City
816/842-4415   DA

Look for budding art talent at this gallery owned by John O'Brien, including a significant representation from the Kansas City Art Institute. Artists here have created everything from modern sculpture to traditional landscapes. Tue–Fri 12:30–5; Sat noon–5; and by appointment.

ETH'NIC ART
3242 Gillham Rd., Kansas City
816/561-7600   CS
This gallery features art from around the world, but specifically taps the ethnic traditions and cultural creativity of resident artists. Tue–Sat 10–6.

GALLERY NORTH
2105 Burlington,
North Kansas City
816/421-4848   NR
Owned by Cherie Pedego, this 3,000-square-foot gallery features abstract to impressionism, original art to posters. Mon–Fri 8–6; Sat 10–4.

GRAND ARTS
1819 Grand, Kansas City
816/421-6887   DA
A nonprofit gallery, Grand Arts shows numerous works by developing artists and renowned contemporary professionals. The facility includes a working sculpture studio. Thur–Sat 10–5 and by appointment.

JAN WEINER GALLERY
4800 Liberty, Kansas City
816/931-8755   CS
New shows open every two months at this contemporary gallery in a private residence. The emphasis here is on regional and national artists with established reputations. Sat 1–4 and by appointment.

THE JAYNE GALLERY
108 W. 47th St., Kansas City

Ten Great Public Sculptures to Visit in the Kansas City Area

by Heidi Bilardo,
public art administrator for the Municipal Art Commission

1. ***Shuttlecocks*** by Claes Oldenburg and Coosje van Bruggen. At the Nelson-Atkins Museum of Art. Envision the museum's building and grounds as a badminton game being played by giants.

2. ***Sky Stations*** by R.M. Fischer. Giant aluminum sculptures placed atop the Bartle Hall Convention Center's pylons and interior sculptures installed throughout this building.

3. ***J.C. Nichols Memorial Fountain*** by French sculptor Henri L. Greber, located at 47th and Main Streets. The four equestrian figures are battling a variety of elements: an alligator, a bear, and two fish-tailed human figures; the grouping is thought to represent an allegory of rivers.

4. ***Always*** by Clement Meadmore. Large, bold sculpture located in front of the Cultural Education Center at Johnson County Community College, Quivira and College Boulevard.

5. ***Muse of the Missouri*** sculpture and fountain by Wheeler Williams, 9th and Main Streets. Bronze Greek goddess evokes mythology and history of the Missouri River.

6. ***The Scout*** by Cyrus Dallin, in Penn Valley Park, 29th and Pennsylvania. Expressive historic bronze sculpture dedicated as a memorial to the local Native American tribe in the Kansas City area.

7. ***Bull Wall*** by Robert Morris, at the American Royal Center, 1800 Genessee St. Unique sculpture combining references to Kansas City's stockyard era as well as to neolithic cave paintings in France and Goya's *Flying Bulls*. This work is at its full glory when the steam element is turned on, primarily during November's American Royal events.

8. ***Meridian and Bonfire*** by Deborah Butterfield, at the Kansas City Zoo. Made entirely from tree vines and driftwood, these cast bronze horses represent the animal humans worldwide have relied upon most heavily throughout history.

9. ***Three Figures/15 Elements*** by Joel Shapiro, at KCI Airport, along the median strip on Cookingham Drive. Three-part geometric sculptures represent the human form.

10. ***Triple Crown*** by Kenneth Snelson at Main and 27th Streets. Stainless steel, cabled tension sculpture captures an intensity of light and reflects it back onto the confluence of many roadways.

GREATER KANSAS CITY

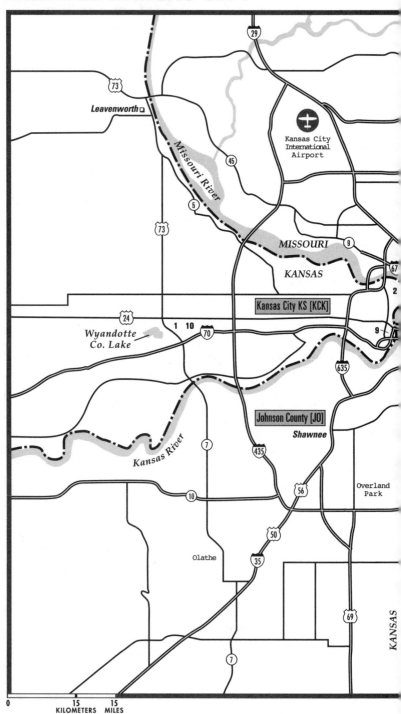

Leavenworth

Kansas City International Airport

MISSOURI

KANSAS

Kansas City KS [KCK]

Wyandotte Co. Lake

Johnson County [JO]

Shawnee

Overland Park

Olathe

Missouri River

Kansas River

KANSAS

0   15   15
    KILOMETERS MILES

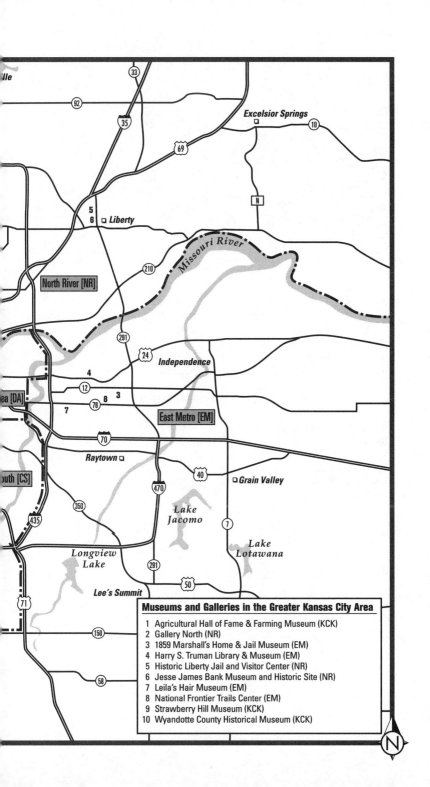

Museums and Galleries in the Greater Kansas City Area

1 Agricultural Hall of Fame & Farming Museum (KCK)
2 Gallery North (NR)
3 1859 Marshall's Home & Jail Museum (EM)
4 Harry S. Truman Library & Museum (EM)
5 Historic Liberty Jail and Visitor Center (NR)
6 Jesse James Bank Museum and Historic Site (NR)
7 Leila's Hair Museum (EM)
8 National Frontier Trails Center (EM)
9 Strawberry Hill Museum (KCK)
10 Wyandotte County Historical Museum (KCK)

The Jesse James Bank Museum, page 129

816/561-5333   **CS**

It's hard to miss this contemporary gallery if you're on the Country Club Plaza. The glass-wall front pours light onto a variety of fine artists' work, from sculpture to painting. Mon–Wed 10–7; Thur–Sat 10–9; Sun noon–5.

JOAN CAWLEY GALLERY
15500 College Blvd., Lenexa
913/599-2442   **JO**

The Joan Cawley Gallery is known for Southwestern and contemporary American fine art. It includes pottery,

engravings, and textiles in its far-south Johnson County location. Tue–Sat 10–5.

LEEDY-VOULKOS ART CENTER GALLERY
2012 Baltimore, Kansas City
816/474-1919   **DA**

Glass, ceramics, paintings—Sherry Leedy's gallery has it all. Artists from the area, as well as national and international creators, show in this downtown space. Thur–Sat 11–5 and by appointment.

8

PARKS, GARDENS, AND RECREATION AREAS

From one of the largest city parks in the country to a swath of tiny pocket preserves, Kansas City lays claim to an amazing variety of outdoor spaces. Some contain lakes within their rolling acres, others offer gardens filled with towering trees and blooming perennials. Whatever the season, the metropolitan area offers plenty of places to play and revel in nature.

PARKS

ANTIOCH PARK
6501 Antioch Rd., Merriam
913/831-3355   **JO**
This 44-acre preserve is one of the most beautiful and popular community parks in the area. Its Old Dodge Town play area appeals to kids, while parents especially enjoy the Helen S. Cuddy Rose Garden and Memorial Arboretum. Walking paths lead visitors through a nature area and near two ponds. A basketball court, tennis courts, and picnic shelters add to the park's comforts. Daily; Apr–Sept 5 a.m.–11 p.m.; Oct–Nov 7:30 a.m.–8 p.m.; Dec–Mar 7:30–6.

BRUSH CREEK PARK
47th St. and State Line to the Blue River, Kansas City
816/871-5600   **CS**
Once a concrete embarrassment, Brush Creek Park now encompasses 286 newly revitalized acres. Along the elevated path, visitors can walk, run, or skate past numerous statues and fountains, or stop off at the Bruce R. Watkins Cultural Heritage Center, the Plaza Tennis Center, the Wheeler Amphitheater in Theis Park, or any of the grassy slopes that make perfect picnic sites.

HERITAGE PARK
16050 Pflumm, Olathe
913/831-3355   **JO**

CENTRAL/SOUTH KANSAS CITY

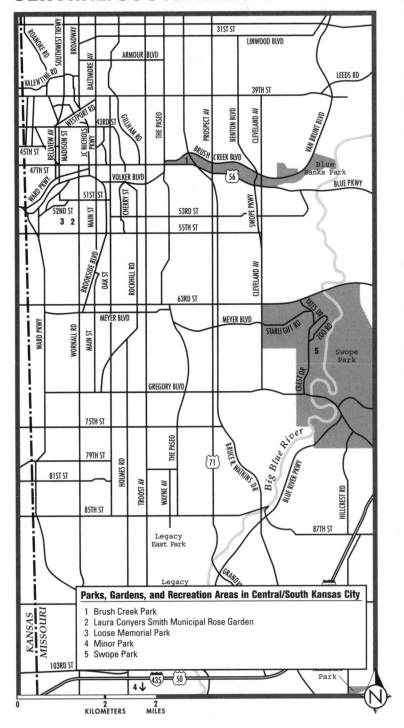

Parks, Gardens, and Recreation Areas in Central/South Kansas City

1 Brush Creek Park
2 Laura Conyers Smith Municipal Rose Garden
3 Loose Memorial Park
4 Minor Park
5 Swope Park

No More Flush Creek

Over the years, Brush Creek has been a swamp, a drainage ditch, a cesspool, and a surging flood. Today, however, waterfalls, fountains, walkways, and an amphitheater have transformed Brush Creek into a pleasant promenade.

The catalyst for the change was a 1977 flood that killed 25 people and caused $100 million in damages. A group of government engineers designed a flood control project so that such a tragedy would never happen again. At the same time, Kansas City's Parks and Recreation Department put together a beautification and recreation plan that would make the area more enjoyable, too.

When the $80-million project was nearly finished, officials discovered sewage was leaking into the waterway, which led to numerous "Flush Creek" jokes. Engineers have since corrected the problem.

Heritage Park's 1,160 acres used to be a reservation for the Black Bob Indians, a small band of Shawnee led by Chief Black Bob. Today this park features a 45-acre lake with a marina and places to fish, sailboard, and canoe. Three children's play areas, an equestrian center, softball and soccer parks, and an 18-hole golf course also provide ample outdoor activities. Picnic areas dot the landscape. Daily; Apr–Sept 5 a.m.–11 p.m.; Oct–Nov 7:30 a.m.–8 p.m.; Dec–Mar 7:30–6.

HIDDEN VALLEY PARK
North Russell Rd. and North Bennington Ave., Kansas City
816/871-5600   **NR**
Covering some 174 acres, Hidden Valley Park straddles N.E. Parvin Road just north of the Missouri River. An observation deck, playground, and hiking trails give outdoorsy types a way to escape without going far from downtown.

(ROBERT H.) HODGE PARK
7000 N.E. Barry Rd., Kansas City
816/871-5600   **NR**
Within Hodge Park's 801 acres, you can see a realistic reconstruction of an 1850s Missouri village, as well as view a native animal enclosure. The park also features an 18-hole golf course, cut by the east fork of Shoal Creek. Hodge's picnic areas are particularly scenic.

LINE CREEK PARK ARCHEOLOGICAL RESERVE
N.W. 56th St. and N.W. Waukomis Dr., Kansas City
816/587-8822   **NR**
This 137-acre park encompasses the Line Creek Archeological Museum,

Spirit of Freedom Fountain

To Kansas Citians, erecting a fountain has always been a most fitting memorial. One modernistic monument is the Spirit of Freedom Fountain *located at Cleveland and Brush Creek Boulevard. Dedicated in September 1981—one year after the death of prominent African American civic leader Bruce Watkins—the* Spirit of Freedom Fountain *honors the contributions of Kansas City's black community. The bronze, flame-like statuary, which sculptor Richard Hunt created to resemble the ebullient movement of freedom and Kansas City jazz, rises from a granite pedestal. A reflecting pool at the sculpture's base spouts water.*

which features a slide presentation and a replica of the prehistoric Hopewell Indian village. The museum also offers classes and occasional archeological digs for kids. In addition, the park has nature and hiking areas, playgrounds, picnic areas, and ball fields. Keep your eyes open for buffalo, deer, and other wildlife at the park. Sat–Sun 11–4; group reservations only on weekdays.

(JACOB) LOOSE MEMORIAL PARK
51st St. and Wornall Rd.,
Kansas City
816/871-5600   CS
This urban park was once a country club for the suburban elite; now, its 74 acres attract nearby residents, Plaza-area employees, and metro-area folks who want to bask in its rose garden, walk the path that circles the park, dip into the wading pool, swing a tennis racquet, enjoy the playground, or have a picnic. In the early mornings, you can often see the work of the mysterious Loose Park poet who scribes the sidewalk in chalk with his romantic verses.

MAPLE WOODS NATURE PRESERVE
North Prospect and 76th St.,
Gladstone
816/436-2200   NR
Kansas City sports plenty of nature preserves in and around its boundaries, but this one contains nearly 40 acres of virgin maple forest. In addition, a wildlife habitat and 6 miles of nature trails within walking distance of a residential area make Maple Woods a special place to get away without going too far.

MARTHA LAFITE THOMPSON NATURE SANCTUARY
407 N. Lafrenz, Liberty
816/781-8598   NR
The word "sanctuary" perfectly describes this 100-acre preserve that's located east of Liberty. A privately owned nonprofit facility, the park was founded by Martha Lafite Thompson, who wanted to protect wildlife and provide a place for people to appreciate nature. Three easy hiking trails wind through a restored tallgrass prairie, mature hardwood timber, and

TIP

When enough snow falls, locals often descend on area parks to practice their cross-country skiing. In particular, Loose Park is a close-in spot for cutting parallel trails through the trees.

a meadow. All are quiet, and the ideal place to experience the wilds. Organized hikes and special exhibits at the Nature Center. Take Mill Street past William Jewell College; veer right onto Richfield Road. Make a left on Lafrenz. Nature Center Tue–Sat 9–5; Sun 1–5; closed Mon. Sanctuary daily 8 a.m.–sunset. Free.

MILL CREEK STREAMWAY PARK
Along Mill Creek in Shawnee, Lenexa, and Olathe
913/831-3355   **JO**
Mill Creek Streamway Park has been in development for more than a decade, an ambitious project linking eight of the county's major streamways. Currently, the peaceful, 400-acre park provides a total of 11 miles of noncontiguous hiking and biking

Loose Park

Convention and Visitors Bureau of Greater Kansas City

trails. Access points: Lenexa (Shawnee Mission Park near shelter 8); Shawnee (west of I-435 at Shawnee Mission Parkway and Midland Drive); Shawnee (north of Shawnee Mission Parkway at 5946 Barker Rd.); Olathe (a half-mile west of Ridgeview Road on 114th Street); and Olathe (east of Woodland Avenue on Northgate Road).

MINOR PARK
Holmes and Red Bridge, Kansas City
816/871-5600   **CS**
Local families come to this park for baseball games and picnics—and for the get-away-from-it-all atmosphere close to town. Set on 235 acres just off the Big Blue River's western bank, Minor Park also includes a golf course, a Santa Fe Trail historic site, and a playground.

PENN VALLEY PARK
Pershing Rd. and Main St., Kansas City
816/871-5600   **DA**
Penn Valley Park was created at the turn of the century, as part of the comprehensive parks-and-boulevard system. Visionary architect George Kessler proposed replacing the shanties that then dotted the bluffs and ravine at Penn Valley, and the public agreed with his plan. Today, the 176-acre park contains Liberty Memorial and its World War I museum (currently closed awaiting renovation), a jogging path, tennis courts

NORTH OF THE RIVER

Parks, Gardens, and Recreation Areas North of the River

1 Hidden Valley Park
2 Hodge Park
3 Line Creek Park Archaeological Reserve
4 Maple Woods Nature Preserve
5 Martha Lafite Thompson Nature Sanctuary
6 Smithville Lake
7 Waterworks Park

Ten Favorite Birding Spots in Kansas City

by Kevin Sink,
president of the Burrough's Audubon Society

1. **Lake Jacomo and Fleming Park**. Visit the Audubon nature center and library to see a native prairie and the incredible bird-feeding station, then tour the lake roads to see waterfowl and woodland species.

2. **Lakeside Nature Center and Swope Park**. Bird and wildlife rehabilitation center and surrounding woodlands. Call the nature center (816/444-4656) for more information on specific birding sites.

3. **Ernie Miller Nature Park**. Along a wooded creek, these 113 acres are a great spot for woodpeckers, sparrows, and woodland songbirds. Impressive nature center with interpretive displays.

4. **Burr Oak Woods**. More than 1,000 acres of oak forest and prairies. Diverse habitat provides homes for a broad spectrum of birds. One of the best nature centers in the state; a great place to take the whole family.

5. **Wyandotte County Lake**. Particularly nice for birding in the fall and winter. Gulls, waterfowl, sparrows, eagles, and other raptors can be seen here.

6. **Shawnee Mission Park**. A very accessible park with woodlands, fields, and a large body of water for waterfowl. Bluebirds, hawks, Canada geese, sparrows, and other woodland species can be seen along a very good network of trails.

7. **Martha Lafite Thompson Nature Sanctuary**. This outstanding nature center has a good feeding station, interpretive displays, helpful staff, and a network of trails. Another entertaining place to take the family and see woodland species or to go on "owl prowls" with the staff.

8. **Smithville Lake**. Mid- to late November, this very large lake is a stopover for thousands of snow geese and other waterfowl. If your timing is right, you might see an eagle or two. A wide variety of habitats near the lake support woodland and grassland species.

9. **The Prairie Center**. A good example of native prairie near the metro area. Three hundred acres of grasslands are home to a host of sparrows, meadowlarks, bluebirds, and more. Of particular interest are the many species of prairie wildflowers. Something is almost always in bloom on this prairie from spring to fall.

10. **Weston Bend State Park**. About 15 minutes north of the KCI airport, this is a great place to bird. Lots of heavily timbered hills and an extensive trail system make this one of the best places around to see warblers in the spring and fall.

Kansas City's Pocket Parks

Small respites on less than an acre:
1. Murray Davis Park (40th and Main Streets), 0.09 acre
2. Andrew Drips Park (16th Street and Belleview Avenue), 0.16 acre
3. Santa Fe National Historic Trail (6201 E. 93rd St.), 0.24 acre
4. Ewing Park (107th Street and Ewing Avenue), 0.28 acre
5. Douglas Park (2632 Jarboe St.), 0.5 acre
6. Garment District Place (8th Street between Washington and Broadway), 0.76 acre
7. Lafayette Traber Garden (Woodland Avenue and Pendleton Street), 0.78 acre
8. Manheim Green (Manheim Road and 40th Street), 0.99 acre

and a ball field, and the statues *The Scout* and *Pioneer Mother.* The park is a popular venue for the Kansas City Symphony's Radio Days Concert on Labor Day and the Blues and Jazz Festival in the summer.

SHAWNEE MISSION PARK
**7900 Renner Rd.,
Lenexa–Shawnee
913/831-3355** JO
Johnson County's largest park spans

Penn Valley Park

some 1,250 acres with a lake that attracts people who want to canoe, sail, and fish. In addition, the park—dedicated in 1964—includes horseback and nature trails, an archery range, a swimming beach, a visitor center, marina, and an outdoor theater where lively summer productions are held. Shawnee Mission Park is a popular family picnic spot.

SWOPE PARK
**Swope Pkwy. and Meyer Blvd.,
Kansas City
816/871-5600** CS
Among the country's largest city parks, Swope Park comprises 1,769 acres. Within its undulating landscape are the Kansas City Zoo and its IMAX Theatre; the 7,795-seat Starlight Theatre, home to summer plays and concerts; two golf courses; the Lakeside Nature Center; athletic fields for softball, soccer, rugby, Frisbee, and more; hiking and horseback-riding trails; picnic and fishing areas; and a day camp for kids.

WATERWORKS PARK
N.E. 32nd St. and N. Oak Trafficway, Kansas City

816/871-5600 **NR**

A relatively small 57 acres, Waterworks Park is most popular for its skyline views of downtown Kansas City. In addition, its close-to-town location and steep hills make it a favorite spot for wintertime inner-tubing and sledding. In the summer, kids gather to play ball at the park's baseball diamonds.

GARDENS

LAURA CONYERS SMITH MUNICIPAL ROSE GARDEN
51st St. and Wornall Rd., Kansas City
816/871-5600 **CS**

Set in the northwest corner of Loose Park, the Laura Conyers Smith Municipal Rose Garden overflows with gorgeous, fragrant blooms from spring through fall. A full-time rosarian keeps the circular plot healthy and vivacious; in fact, the rose garden's a favorite spot for warm-weather weddings. A fountain in the garden's center adds to the aura of calm.

POWELL GARDENS
1609 N.W. Hwy. 50, Kingsville
816/697-2600 **EM**

Founded and funded chiefly by Kansas City's Powell Family Foundation, Powell Gardens occupies more than 800 acres and offers visitors

Convention and Visitors Bureau of Greater Kansas City

Henry Moore Sculpture Garden, page 153

the chance to wander through one of the largest perennial gardens in the Midwest. A Rock and Waterfall Garden intermingles with ornamental trees, shrubs, perennials, and native woods, adding winding streams and gentle cascades as accents. Throughout the summer, Powell Gardens hosts music and dance performances. The newly built Marjorie Powell Allen Chapel and the Wildflower Meadow Pavilion provide pleasant places for reflection. Daily (except Thanksgiving, Christmas, and New Year's Day) 9 a.m.–sunset. Adults $3; under 13 $1; seniors $2.50.

TRIVIA

A Brief Park Comparison

	Swope Park, KC, MO	Central Park, NYC
Size	1,769 acres	843 acres
Animals	Zoo with IMAX theater	Two zoos
Drama	Broadway-style shows	Shakespeare and puppets
Chip shots	Two 18-hole golf courses	Lawn bowling

GREATER KANSAS CITY

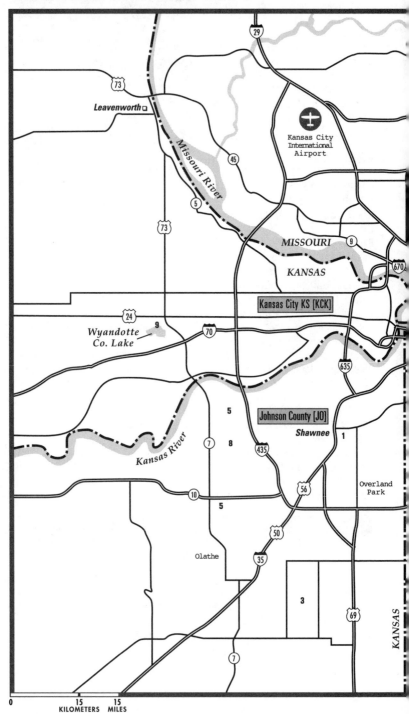

Leavenworth

Missouri River

Kansas City
International
Airport

45

5

MISSOURI

KANSAS

9

670

Kansas City KS [KCK]

24

Wyandotte
Co. Lake

9

70

635

5

Johnson County [JO]

Shawnee

1

7

8

435

Kansas River

56

Overland
Park

10

5

50

Olathe

35

3

69

7

KANSAS

73

73

29

0   15   15
KILOMETERS MILES

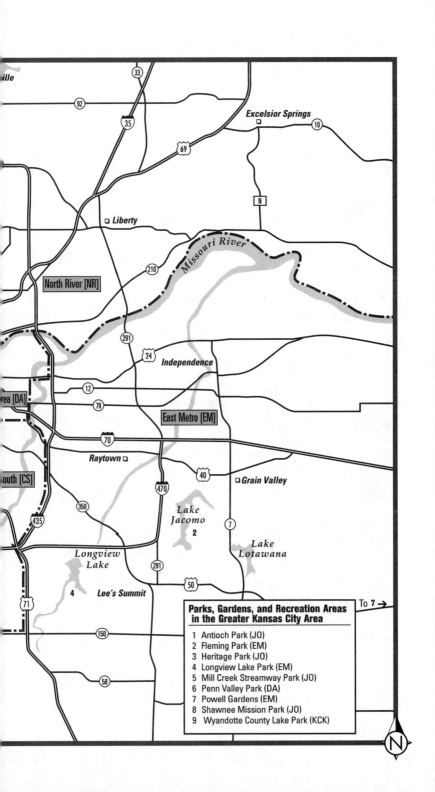

ille

Excelsior Springs

10

92

33

35

69

N

Liberty

Missouri River

210

North River [NR]

291

24 Independence

rea [DA]

12

78

East Metro [EM]

70

Raytown

outh [CS]

40

Grain Valley

470

350

Lake
Jacomo
2

7

Lake
Lotawana

435

Longview
Lake

291

50

71

4

Lee's Summit

150

58

**Parks, Gardens, and Recreation Areas
in the Greater Kansas City Area**

1 Antioch Park (JO)
2 Fleming Park (EM)
3 Heritage Park (JO)
4 Longview Lake Park (EM)
5 Mill Creek Streamway Park (JO)
6 Penn Valley Park (DA)
7 Powell Gardens (EM)
8 Shawnee Mission Park (JO)
9 Wyandotte County Lake Park (KCK)

To 7 →

N

TOP TEN

Ten Favorite Roses to Grow and View in Kansas City

by Judy Penner,
rosarian at the Laura Conyers Smith
Municipal Rose Garden, Loose Park

1. **Chrysler Imperial.** A red hybrid tea rose with a strong scent, nice form, and a long-lasting bloom.

2. **Gold Medal.** With its spicy aroma, this yellow grandiflora is great for its fragrance alone.

3. **Mr. Lincoln.** This red hybrid tea reaches heights of 5 to 6 feet and has a nice scent.

4. **Double Delight.** A red and white rose; each bloom on the bush has some color variation.

5. **Sunsprite.** Growing about 3 feet tall, this bright yellow floribunda produces lots of blooms on a single stem and maintains its color.

6. **Care Free Wonder.** I like this pink shrub rose for its hardiness.

7. **Rio Samba.** A yellow blend with pink and orange, this hybrid tea bears blooms with interesting color variations and patterns.

8. **Peace.** Its healthy strong foliage and large blooms make this yellow-blend hybrid tea a popular plant.

9. **White Lightnin'.** This rose stays very white and has a sweet fragrance.

10. **Sweet Surrender.** With pretty pink blooms, this hybrid tea dries well for potpourri.

COUNTY PARKS/ RECREATION AREAS

FLEMING PARK
South of Hwy. 40 on Woods
Chapel Road, Blue Springs
816/795-8200 (general information)
816/795-1112 (Blue Springs Lake marina)
816/795-8888 (Lake Jacomo marina) **EM**
Fifteen minutes east of Kansas City proper, Fleming Park's 7,809 acres contain three lakes, a swimming beach, marinas, and picnic shelters, as well as Missouri Town 1855, a native hoofed animal enclosure, an archery range, camping, and hiking. On summer weekends, the two largest bodies of water—Lake Jacomo and Blue Springs Lake—are magnets for boaters, fishermen, and windsurfers. Six trails wind through the area, offering bluff-top and lakefront vistas. Stop at the park headquarters for maps and more information.

A Garden of Bronze

Henry Moore was a renowned British sculptor whose enormous bronze pieces explored themes from reclining figures to mother-and-child to animal forms. Born in 1898, Moore wanted his large sculptures to be viewed in nature, set against rocks, trees, and sky.

Kansas City's Henry Moore Sculpture Garden achieves that goal. Located on the south grounds of the Nelson-Atkins Museum of Art, the sculpture sanctuary comprises the largest collection of monumental bronze pieces by Moore outside of his native country. Works include Reclining Figure; Hand; Seated Woman; *and* Three Part Object. *Another sizable group of Moore's maquettes and working models are installed in the Rozelle Court Gallery.*

In addition to the 13 outdoor sculptures, the Henry Moore Sculpture Garden contains an array of nature. More than 100 American linden, ginkgo, crab apple, Norway spruce, and river birch trees, as well as 50,000 daffodils and 10,000 Japanese yew, decorate the area.

LONGVIEW LAKE PARK
South of I-470 on Raytown Rd.,
Kansas City
816/795-8200 (general information)
816/966-8976 (marina)   EM
Longview Lake was created by the U.S. Army Corps of Engineers for flood control and recreational purposes. Open since 1986, the 4,852-acre park features a 4-mile nature trail, a 6-mile paved bicycle trail, camping, boat rentals, a marina, softball, and a golf course. Like Fleming Park, Longview also offers a fishing dock for handicapped anglers.

SMITHVILLE LAKE
Northeast of Smithville on U.S.
169 and Hwy. 92, Smithville
816/532-0803   NR
Smithville Lake covers more than

7,200 acres. Its shoreline offers two full-service marinas that provide boat rentals, equipment sales, and dining facilities. In addition, the lake has two swimming beaches and two campgrounds with more than 750 camp sites (including electrical hookups, shower, laundry, and other facilities). If you just want a day trip, choose from a waterfowl refuge, sailboat facilities, golfing, 200 picnic sites with 11 shelter houses, horseback riding, hiking trails, a visitors center, and a handicapped-accessible fishing dock. Even with all those attractions, it never seems crowded at Smithville.

WYANDOTTE COUNTY
LAKE PARK
91st St. and Leavenworth Rd.,
Kansas City, Kansas

913/299-0550   **KCK**

Wyandotte County Lake Park isn't far from town, but it certainly seems remote once you get there. The park's 1,500 acres include a 330-acre lake with marina, boat rentals, picnic shelters, tennis courts, horseback trails, and the Pierson Community Center. Kids can ride a model train on the second Saturday of each month. The National Park Service designed the lakeside boathouse. Construction began in 1935, which explains its old-time feel. From the East Lookout shelter, you can see Lansing and Leavenworth, Kansas.

Convention and Visitors Bureau of Greater Kansas City

9

SHOPPING

Although Kansas City was born near the Missouri River, commerce has spread to encompass many districts throughout the metropolis. From the Country Club Plaza's stylish boutiques to Johnson County's booming retail regions, the area now provides residents and visitors with places to buy everything from designer apparel to fishing supplies, from souvenirs to home-improvement gadgets. Note: The map in this chapter shows locations of shopping districts and malls.

SHOPPING AREAS

Downtown

Many people think downtown Kansas City lacks shopping opportunities. In fact, numerous stores there count downtown workers among their most loyal—and sometimes best—customers. Within the central business district, however, both City Center Square and the Town Pavilion gather boutiques and restaurants into convenient places for light shopping. The River Market, several blocks closer to the Missouri River, includes antiques malls, housewares boutiques, specialty shops, and the City Market.

ALL NATIONS FLAG COMPANY
114 W. 5th St., Kansas City
816/842-8798   **DA**
Founded in 1924, this locally owned flag company stocks an enormous inventory within its turn-of-the-century brick building in the River Market. All Nations carries flags from around the world, as well as holiday and special-occasion banners. Here, you can even buy the flagpole to hoist your new purchase. Prices at All Nations are reasonable, and quality is high. Mon–Fri 8:30–5; Sat 9–1.

BOB JONES SHOES
1914 Grand, Kansas City
816/474-4212   **DA**
Nothing but shoes and more shoes

TRIVIA

Whether you want a lime or a live chicken, you can find it at the City Market in the River Market area. Every Saturday and Wednesday, numerous farmers head to the historic district near downtown to peddle their produce and stock. Choices abound in the warmer seasons; between April and October, you can work your way through a cornucopia of seasonal produce.

greet you as you enter this gigantic store near downtown. Bob Jones stocks everything from designer labels to off-brand shoes, for both men and women. The back racks are where you'll find the biggest bargains. Look for the wooden Indian standing outside. Mon–Sat 9–5:30.

CHEEP ANTIQUES
500 W. 5th St., Kansas City
816/471-0092   DA
The folks at Cheep Antiques are experts at refinishing the furniture they buy, so don't expect to cull through stacks of junk. Still, there's nothing stuffy about this three-story, 30,000-square-foot antiques emporium. Cheep Antiques specializes in good-quality American antique furniture, from armoires to rockers to pie safes. Tue–Fri 9–3; Sat–Sun 9–5. Closed Mon.

OGGI
600 Central, Kansas City
816/421-1010   DA

Contemporary furnishings, lighting, and gadgets fill all four floors of Oggi's restored brick building. It's fun to wander from setting to setting, admiring the lava lamps, resting in the over-stuffed faux-leather chairs, browsing the mirrors adorned with sea glass. Oggi (say "OH-gee") charges a pretty penny for its inventory, but holds regular sales. Mon–Sat 10–6; until 8 on Thur; closed Sun.

RIVER MARKET ANTIQUE MALL
115 W. 5th St., Kansas City
816/221-0220   DA
Like many antiques malls, this one runs the gamut in goods. One dealer likes treasures from the Fifties, another collects handwoven rugs from Iran. The 25,000-square-foot mall rises several floors in a slowly re-born building near the City Market, making this a fascinating place to browse and search out hidden treasures. Mon–Fri 10:30–6; Sat 9–6; Sun 10–5.

URBAN LIVING TWO
400 Grand, Kansas City
816/221-4144   DA
In the winter, Urban Living resembles an incongruous jungle. All year long, the flower market/interiors shop bulges with colorful flowers, both exotic and ordinary, kept in buckets and sold by the stem. From protea to pussy willow, the shop gives Kansas Citians a unique way to keep spring alive. The store also features interesting garden-related items that make decorating a pure joy. Mon–Fri 9–5; Sat–Sun 7–4.

Country Club Plaza

Kansas City's shopping mecca also provides an enjoyable place just to hang around. Clothing boutiques such as Asiatica and Ann Taylor, department stores like Mark Shale and Halls Plaza, housewares boutiques from Function Junction to Pottery Barn—the list of places where you'll gladly spend your money is seemingly endless. In addition, the Plaza lures folks who want to wine and dine at its many bistros. In the summer, sidewalk cafes do a booming business.

ACCENTS
610½ W. 48th St., Kansas City
816/753-2320 CS
Women who love earrings visit Accents regularly just to see what's new. Within the store's small space they find one of the Midwest's largest selections of affordable handcrafted jewelry. Many of the pieces—necklaces and bracelets, too—were made by regional artists. Mon–Wed 10–7; Thur–Sat 10–9; Sun noon–5.

AMERICAN INDIAN STORE
500 Nichols Rd., Kansas City
816/561-0343 CS
From its location in Seville Square, the American Indian Store offers a varied selection of fine jewelry, silver, turquoise, and Native American arts and crafts, including pottery, sand paintings, and baskets. Creations come from the Cherokee, Navajo, and Zuni tribes, among others. Mon–Sat 10–9; Sun noon–5.

ASIATICA
4709 Central, Kansas City
913/931-9111 CS
Fifi White and Elizabeth Wilson launched this unique boutique by transforming antique kimonos into stylish new apparel, from jackets to scarves to handbags. Although the clothes are expensive, they're truly unusual. In addition to this small store on the Plaza, Asiatica's main location is at 4824 Rainbow Blvd. (913/831-0831). Mon–Sat 10–5:30.

THE BETTER CHEDDAR
604 W. 48th St., Kansas City
816/561-8204 CS
Look for a lot more than yellow cheese at this Plaza gourmet grocery store. Wines from famous regions, myriad kinds of extra-virgin olive oil, pasta in countless shapes

Historic Westport District, page 160

Convention and Visitors Bureau of Greater Kansas City

GREATER KANSAS CITY

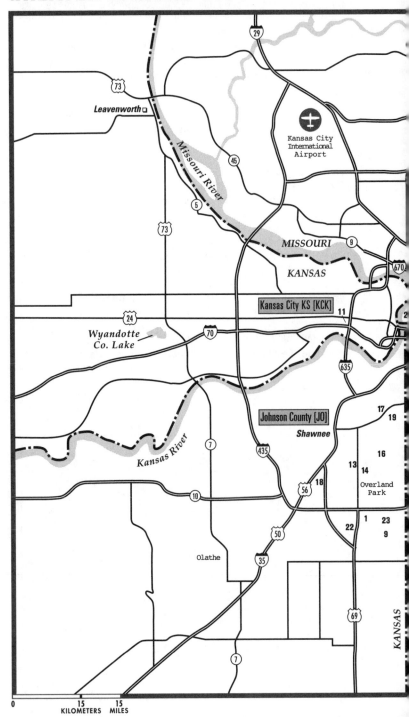

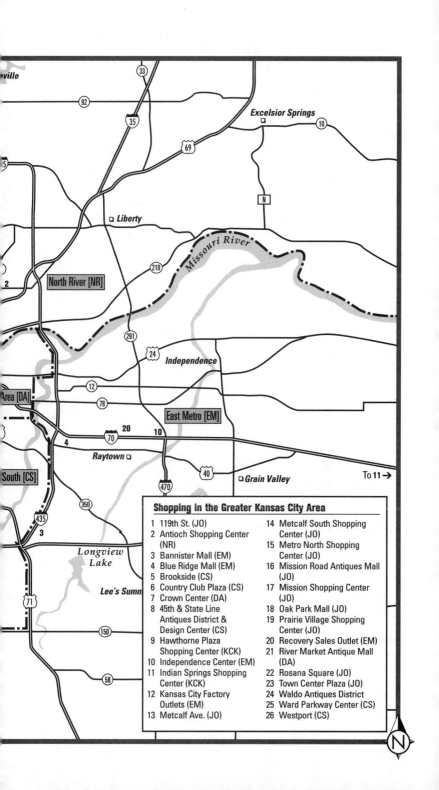

ville

Excelsior Springs

Liberty

Missouri River

North River [NR]

Independence

Area [DA]

East Metro [EM]

Raytown

South [CS]

Grain Valley

To 11 →

Longview
Lake

Lee's Summ

Shopping in the Greater Kansas City Area

1 119th St. (JO)
2 Antioch Shopping Center (NR)
3 Bannister Mall (EM)
4 Blue Ridge Mall (EM)
5 Brookside (CS)
6 Country Club Plaza (CS)
7 Crown Center (DA)
8 45th & State Line Antiques District & Design Center (CS)
9 Hawthorne Plaza Shopping Center (KCK)
10 Independence Center (EM)
11 Indian Springs Shopping Center (KCK)
12 Kansas City Factory Outlets (EM)
13 Metcalf Ave. (JO)

14 Metcalf South Shopping Center (JO)
15 Metro North Shopping Center (JO)
16 Mission Road Antiques Mall (JO)
17 Mission Shopping Center (JO)
18 Oak Park Mall (JO)
19 Prairie Village Shopping Center (JO)
20 Recovery Sales Outlet (EM)
21 River Market Antique Mall (DA)
22 Rosana Square (JO)
23 Town Center Plaza (JO)
24 Waldo Antiques District
25 Ward Parkway Center (CS)
26 Westport (CS)

and sizes. If it's food-related, Better Cheddar probably has it. Walking through the store will make you hungry, but there's plenty here to satisfy your urge to eat. Mon–Sat 9–9; Sun 10–6.

EDDIE BAUER PREMIER STORE
325 Nichols Rd., Kansas City
816/756-5390   CS
It's not Seattle, but this enormous Plaza department store stocks everything from rugged boots to dressier evening wear. You'll find all the great stuff in Eddie Bauer's catalog, as well as items that were chosen just for the company's retail operations. An Eddie Bauer Home Collection, AKA Eddie Bauer, and an outdoor gear section complete the picture. Mon–Sat 10–9; Sun 11–5.

GRANDEUR GARDENS
223 W. 47th St., Kansas City
816/561-2212   CS
Kansas Citians love their gardens. Even in winter, they're either planning for spring or decorating their homes in garden style. This shop targets these outdoor addicts with elegant pottery, distinctive paving stones, and items gardeners can hide in their gardens—from gargoyles to the Green Man. Just stepping inside Grandeur Gardens elicits that old springtime rush. Mon–Wed 10–7; Thur–Sat 10–9; Sun noon–5.

THE GREAT TRAIN STORE
4725 Broadway, Kansas City
816/561-4515   CS
The Great Train Store and its next-door neighbor, KCPT Store of Knowledge (see Chapter 6), opened within months of each other, creating a one-two punch in fun spots to shop. The train store specializes in model trains and accessories, as well as col-

lectibles, toys, books, and videos. A train runs through the store, making it easy to linger among the railroad signs, coffee mugs, T-shirts, and collector pins. Mon–Sat 10–9; Sun noon–6.

MISSOURI MEMORIES
500 Nichols Rd., Kansas City
816/931-9174   CS
What to take home from a Kansas City trip? Missouri Memories suggests Plaza Lights placemats, Kansas City jazz sweatshirts, or a six-pack of Kansas City barbecue sauce. Just about everything at this shop is affordable, from key chains to pens to stuffed animals. There's also a line of greeting cards—Hallmark, of course. Mon–Sat 10–9; Sun noon–5.

THREE DOG BAKERY
4116 Pennsylvania, Kansas City
816/753-3647   CS
Three Dog Bakery has made its owners rich and famous because the concept is so . . . bizarre! At this first-of-its-kind store, you can find the perfect gift for every woofie, from fresh-baked birthday biscuits to all-natural doggie chews. The store is so elegant, some thought at first it was a haven for humans. Bow-wow! Mon–Wed 10–7; Thur–Sat 10–9; Sun noon–5.

Westport

Although you wouldn't know it now, the area along Westport Road between Main and Southwest Trafficway was where wagon trains once loaded up before heading west. Kelly's Westport Inn and the adjacent Stanford & Sons restaurant are original buildings once owned by Daniel Boone's nephew, who operated them as supply stores. Now, Westport is home to un-

The Original Shopping Master

Back in the early part of this century, real estate developer Jesse Clyde (J.C.) Nichols built stylish homes that captivated the upwardly mobile. His plans included neighborhood amenities such as side-walks, nearby shops, and expansive landscaping. People flocked to his then-suburban communities for the chance to purchase a Nichols home.

By 1922, however, Nichols announced a scheme that was out-right revolutionary. He had purchased acreage on either side of Brush Creek, just north of his carefully manicured neighborhoods. On this property, Nichols believed he could create a retail district that would appeal to his residents and bring in the big bucks for him.

Nichols decided to limit the buildings in his retail district to three stories, except for the Spanish-style towers he would build as decoration. In fact, the entire Country Club Plaza would be created with a Spanish Renaissance and Baroque theme, using adornments such as artwork, ironwork, and fountains. The Plaza would be acces-sible by car, but would dovetail with the nearby neighborhoods, too.

When it opened in March 1923, the Country Club Plaza became the first master-planned shopping district in the country. And J.C. Nichols did, indeed, become an even wealthier businessman.

usual shopping opportunities as well as a string of restaurants and night clubs. In fact, Westport really hops on Friday and Saturday nights.

BACKWOODS
3936 Broadway, Kansas City
816/531-0200   CS
This cozy store stocks all sorts of out-door gear, from tents to hiking shoes to day packs, even though high-end rugged duds overrun much of the floor space. Look for regional outdoor books here, too. Located just north of Westport Road, Backwoods is

staffed by a knowledgeable group who can help you find the appropri-ate accoutrements for any excursion. Mon–Fri 10–7; Sat 10–6; Sun 1–5.

LOMA VISTA HARDWARE
311 Westport Rd., Kansas City
816/931-5846   CS
Todd Dean wanted to run his own business, but he wasn't sure it was the hardware store owned by his dad, Chuck. So the artistic young man set up a clothing shop in the back of Loma Vista Hardware. Now, Todd's reputation as a high-style

Three Dog Bakery, page 160

couturier has exploded nationwide. Young models, celebrities, and other hipsters come to Loma Vista for its natural fabrics, clean lines, and trendy men's and women's wear—not to mention the hardware. Mon–Fri 10–8; Sat 10–6; Sun noon–5; the hardware area opens two hours earlier each day.

NATURAL WEAR
435 Westport Rd., Kansas City
816/531-9082 CS
Mother Earth gone stylish: That's the best description of Natural Wear. Earthy colors such as beige, olive, and cayenne predominate in Natural Wear's loose and chic inventory. Accessories from earrings to handbags complete the fashion picture. Mon–Sat 10–9; Sun noon–5.

PERFECT SCENTS
4116 Pennsylvania, Kansas City
816/753-8117 CS
At this little shop you can mix and match your own shampoos, perfumes, and hand lotions from a variety of interesting scents such as rain,

patchouli, and "Chinese nights." Another store in Johnson County's Hawthorne Plaza brings the far-out to the 'burbs. Mon–Sat 10–6; Sun noon–5.

PRYDE'S OLD WESTPORT
115 Westport Rd., Kansas City
816/531-5588 CS
The ultimate kitchen store, Pryde's anchors the east end of Westport Road in its funky old building. Inside, you'll find the latest in cookware, dishes, linens, and must-have kitchen gadgets. Pryde's will gift-wrap for free and ship to anywhere in the United States. Their toll-free number lets you order more goodies no matter where you live. Mon–Sat 10–6.

WHISTLER'S BOOKS
427 Westport Rd., Kansas City
816/531-5959 CS
Whistler's went out of business for a few days in 1996, its owners frustrated by the giant bookstores opening up around town. A new owner stepped in almost immediately, and the peaceful store in the heart of Westport was saved. Set on two levels, Whistler's specializes in architecture, cooking, history, and considerably more. Mon–Thur 10–9; Fri–Sat 10–10; Sun 10–6.

THE WORLD'S WINDOW
4120 Pennsylvania, Kansas City
816/756-1514 CS
Take an around-the-world trip without ever leaving Kansas City. This interesting shop pulls together ethnic art, apparel, jewelry, and furnishings from places as diverse as Indonesia and South America. A special children's section gets kids into the global perspective, too. Mon–Sat 10–9; Sun noon–5:30.

Brookside

Throughout the older Kansas City neighborhoods, you'll come upon rows of shops built in the Twenties, Thirties, and Forties. One of the most magnetic areas sits at the crossroads of 63rd Street and Brookside Boulevard, where residents can find everything from fabrics to Halloween costumes to lawn sprinklers. Two grocery stores, a drugstore, and several lively neighborhood pubs round out the scene. Those not on diets regularly patronize Foo's Fabulous Frozen Custard for its wickedly rich desserts.

THE BEST OF KANSAS CITY
6233 Brookside Plaza, Kansas City
816/333-7900   CS
Set in a space the size of a walk-in closet, The Best of Kansas City combines locally made products into stunning gift baskets. Topsy's popcorn, Stephenson's jellies, and barbecue sauce from nearly everyone in town are only a few of the staples at this specialty shop. You can also buy items individually. Mon–Sat 10–6; closed Sun.

BLOOMSDAY BOOKS
6227 Brookside Blvd., Kansas City
816/523-6712   CS
One of the city's best used-book stores, Bloomsday is run by former lawyer Tom Shawver, who likes to know his customers and what they read. Books here are gently used, prices are reasonable, and the coffee cart serves up delicious lattes. Mon–Fri 7–7; Sat 9–6; Sun 10–5.

THE DIME STORE
314 W. 63rd St., Kansas City
816/444-7207   CS
At this store it's as though time stopped in about 1950. Undulating wooden floors hold ceiling-high shelves stocked with everything imaginable, from old-fashioned toys to cookware to scrapbooks. Chances are excellent you'll find stuff at The Dime Store that you thought wasn't even made anymore. Mon–Sat 8:30–5:30; closed Sun.

LATIN AMERICAN IMPORTS
324 W. 63rd St., Kansas City
816/361-5115   CS
¡Ay caramba! This colorful shop simply gushes with goodies from our neighbors to the south. From piñatas to candelabra to chairs and tables, Latin American Imports pulls together an impressive selection of decorative details. Mon–Sat 10–6; Sun 1–5.

Johnson County

There's a building boom in the Kansas City area, and the focus centers around Johnson County's College Boulevard and 119th Street. Town Center Plaza, for example, opened in mid-1996 with stores such as Pottery Barn, Williams-Sonoma, and Abercrombie & Fitch. The mall sits on 119th Street between Roe and Nall, surrounded by other malls featuring everything from sporting goods to maternity wear to toys. The Metcalf Avenue area, although older, is similarly lined with shopping opportunities. Out in Olathe, the Great Mall of the Great Plains will feature eight anchor stores and 175 outlet-type stores when it opens in late 1997.

119th Street

GALYAN'S
Corner of 119th & Nall, Leawood
913/661-0200   JO
Mouths drop open when people first

enter this sporting goods store. That's because Galyan's resembles a giant tree house, its soaring entrance flanked by tree trunks reaching toward second-story balcony shopping. At the back of the sports emporium, a mountain-climbing wall gives intrepid souls a place to practice their art, much to the delight of other, less-courageous patrons. Oh yes, they've got clothing, shoes, boats, backpacks, and tons of other gear for sale, too. Mon–Sat 9:30–9:30; Sun 10–6.

JACOBSON'S
Town Center Plaza, Leawood
913/696-1500   JO
One of the most deluxe department stores in town, Jacobson's features a full line of designer wear for men, women, and children. In addition, this relatively new retailer-in-town provides special services to its clientele, including personal shoppers, complimentary gift wrap, baby and bridal gift registries, free in-store alterations at no charge, and

Saks Fifth Avenue at Country Club Plaza, page 156

Country Club Plaza Merchants Association

an espresso bar. Mon–Sat 10–9; Sun noon–5.

PANACHE CHOCOLATIER
5045 W. 119th, Overland Park
913/338-5050   JO
Looking for big candy kisses, giant chocolate valentines, or a Cadillac-shaped comfit to celebrate a new car? This store started on the Country Club Plaza, but it was so popular people were traveling from miles around to purchase its delectable treats. Now with two locations, Panache is one of Kansas City's favorite confectioneries. Mon–Wed and Sat 10–6; Thur 10–8; Sun noon–5.

RESTORATION HARDWARE
Town Center Plaza, Leawood
913/327-7121   JO
Steven Gordon launched Restoration Hardware in Eureka, California, when he couldn't find parts to restore an old home. He opened his Kansas City store in late 1996—smack dab in new-home territory. Oh well, Kansas Citians with old houses flock there, too, looking for the perfect light fixture, doorknob, and paint hue. Restoration also carries soft goods, such as linens. Mon–Sat 10–9; Sun noon–5.

YANG-TRI TRADER
11934 Roe Ave., Overland Park
913/345-8977   JO
Owned by a man who's worked and traveled around the world, Yang-Tri Trader reflects that global perspective. The Hawthorne Plaza shop specializes in handwoven rugs, fine art, tribal artifacts, antiquities, and leather accessories from Africa, Asia, and Europe. It's the kind of store you just might want to move into. Mon–Sat 10–5:45; Thur until 8; closed Sun.

Metcalf Avenue

FOB KANSAS CITY
9024 Metcalf, Overland Park
913/381-8910 JO
Tables that resemble cranes, chairs that look like monkeys, vases from China and Indonesia: FOB Kansas City imports unusual furnishings from Pacific Rim countries. At FOB (which stands for "fresh off the boat"), you're as likely to find a carved teak gazebo as a set of teak salad spoons. Mon–Sat 10–7; Sun 10:30–5.

NOMADIC NOTIONS
9264 Metcalf, Overland Park
913/642-3131 JO
Beads, beads, everywhere. Nomadic Notions sells thousands of multi-colored beads, with all the supplies you need to create necklaces, earrings, and other jewelry. The shop also offers classes and re-stringing, and will custom design jewelry, too. Mon–Sat 11–8; Sun noon–5.

ORGANIZED LIVING
9050 Metcalf, Overland Park
913/642-1041 JO
Anyone trying to organize a closet, an office, a kitchen—or any other room they inhabit—will want to visit Organized Living. The store stocks furniture, as well as handy gadgets such as stacking baskets, lift-top garbage pails, and sealable canisters. Mon–Sat 9:30–9; Sun 11–6.

THE PERUVIAN CONNECTION
9256 Metcalf, Overland Park
913/648-1981 JO
Run by a friendly mother-daughter team, The Peruvian Connection features unusually stylish clothing made in Peru from soft alpaca or silky pima cotton. At this catalog-and-outlet store, you'll find scrumptious vests, sweaters, coats, and handcrafted jewelry. Mon–Wed and Sat 10–6; Thur–Fri 10–8; Sun noon–5.

Antiques Districts

45TH & STATE LINE ANTIQUES DISTRICT & DESIGN CENTER
Around 45th St. and State Line Rd., Kansas City
913/362-2002 CS
Within the little bungalows that hug State Line Road west of Westport, you'll find some 20 antiques shops and galleries. Anderson's Antiques specializes in the eighteenth and nineteenth centuries; Barkwell Antiques covers American, European, and Asian furnishings; and Cumming's Corner concentrates on turn-of-the-century lighting. Hours vary from shop to shop; Saturdays are your best bet.

WALDO ANTIQUES DISTRICT
Around 75th St. and Wornall Rd., Kansas City
816/523-9314 CS
A smaller district than the one at 45th and State Line, the Waldo area also features less-expensive goods. Still, there are several small antiques malls and individual shops whose shelves contain some mighty unusual goods. Wed–Sun 10–5; closed Mon–Tue.

OTHER NOTABLE STORES

ACT II
1507 W. 47th St., Kansas City
816/531-7572 CS
Perhaps the finest women's-apparel consignment shop in town, Act II also runs a store for men on 45th Street. Act II has strict standards, which means their clothes are almost like new. Mon–Sat 10–5:30; closed Sun.

Ten Great Places to Shop

by Tammy Edwards,
a professional shopper and owner of
Signature Image Inc., a wardrobe consulting firm

1. **Act II** (1507 W. 47th St., Kansas City). Designer consignment fashions for women at bargain prices.

2. **Button Boutique** (91st and Metcalf, Overland Park). The widest selection of exquisite clothing buttons in the area.

3. **Country Club Plaza**. One of the finest upscale outdoor shopping experiences in the world.

4. **Crown Center**. A good mix of shops set in a casual environment.

5. **Designer Shoe Warehouse** (75th and Quivira, Overland Park). Extensive selection of men's and women's shoes at discount prices.

6. **Dillard's Clearance Center** (46th and State Avenue, Kansas City, Kansas). Department-store finds at a fraction of the original prices.

7. **Genny's Women's Apparel** (College and Antioch, Overland Park). Unique clothes and accessories for all occasions.

8. **Hawthorne Plaza** (119th and Roe, Leawood). Find everything from special scents to unique fashions for the entire family.

9. **Town Center Plaza** (Between Nall and Roe on 119th Street, Leawood). A distinctive array of upscale shops in a contemporary outdoor setting.

10. **Westport** (Westport Road and Broadway, Kansas City). An eclectic mixture of specialty clothing and jewelry shops.

BARNES & NOBLE
400 W. 47th St., Kansas City
816/753-1313 CS

This bookseller has been opening stores all over the country, but Kansas City's first Barnes & Noble occupies a renovated four-story building in the heart of the Plaza. Cushy chairs and Starbucks coffee make for a great book-buying getaway. Daily 9 a.m.–11 p.m.

CHOCOLATE SOUP
7100 Wornall Rd., Kansas City
816/361-2952 CS

Moms in the know shop at Chocolate Soup for trendy kidswear. From colorful play clothes to stunning dress-up outfits, Chocolate Soup has gained a top-notch reputation. This is no bargain basement, but Chocolate Soup holds regular sales. Mon–Sat 9:30–5:30; Sun noon–5.

D&D STATUARY
3415 Merriam Dr., Merriam
913/262-2279 JO

The plethora of concrete objects at

D&D Statuary is simply mind-boggling. The company's owners have filled their huge yard with bird-baths, pots, and all manner of yard art, depicting everything from roosters to religious figures. Objects come naturally gray or stained with a green or black patina. Mon–Sat 8–5; closed Sun.

FINN'S EXOTIC BOOTS
2000 Grand Ave., Kansas City
816/221-0461   DA
You name it, and if it's a boot they'll make it at Finn's. From their location between downtown and Crown Center, Finn's offers custom boots made from alligator, ostrich, python, lizard, eel, and much, much more. Mon–Sat 10–7; Sun noon–5.

K&K FLYFISHER'S SUPPLY
8643 Grant, Overland Park
913/341-8118   JO
This former convenience store now houses one of the Midwest's largest selections of fly-fishing equipment and paraphernalia. Expert advice on casting and fly-tying; courses available, too. Mon–Fri 9:30–7; Sat 9–4; closed Sun.

LUYBEN MUSIC
4318 Main St., Kansas City
816/753-7111   CS
Kansas City's sheet-music central. In this store near the Plaza, you'll find a complete inventory of music from classical masters to contemporary hits, from vocal to piano to orchestral. If Luyben doesn't have it, they can order it. Mon–Sat 9:30–5:30; closed Sun.

MISSION ROAD ANTIQUES MALL
4101 W. 83rd St., Prairie Village
913/341-7577   JO
Perhaps the largest antiques mall in

the metro area, Mission Road presents the collections of 250 dealers in an enormous 50,000-square-foot area. The mall winds through two floors of adjoining buildings, giving antiques aficionados plenty to look at. A small cafe nestles in one corner. Mon–Sat 10–7; Sun 1–5.

MUNDY AND YAZDI
5905 Slater, Merriam
913/362-2006   JO
Forget that trip to Turkey. Mundy and Yazdi carries an amazing selection of antique, handwoven rugs from Persia, Turkey, Afghanistan—you name it. Proprietor Carol Mundy also teaches courses, complete with slides from her rug-buying trips abroad. Wed–Sat 11–5.

OLD THEATRE ARCHITECTURAL SALVAGE COMPANY
2045 Broadway, Kansas City
816/283-3740   DA
From Corinthian columns to brass doorplates to gargoyles off demolished buildings: Old Theatre's jam-packed full of treasures that make

Country Club Plaza Merchants Association

Plaza Art Fair at Country Club Plaza, page 156

brands as well. Dillard's can be pricier and a more luxurious shopping experience than Jones (see below), but the store marks down frequently so it pays to head straight for the sale racks.

HALLS   (DA, CS)
The locally owned Halls department stores provide fine shopping opportunities at two locations, Crown Center and the Country Club Plaza. Designers such as Armani, Buccelatti, and Lagerfeld reign in the clothing departments, while housewares are ruled by the likes of Wedgwood and Waterford. Expect excellent quality and high prices.

JONES STORE COMPANY (ALL ZONES)
Jones also rules the Kansas City area; you'll notice that nearly every mall has either a Jones or Dillard's as an anchor. Jones displays the same kinds of inventory as its competitor, and also holds frequent metrowide sales. Stores often command several floors, providing at least a half-day experience for the truly dedicated.

for a delightful browsing experience. There are three floors, plus a building they'll let you in next door if you ask. Tue–Sat 10–5.

WALDO PET CENTER
8011 Wornall Rd., Kansas City
816/444-4522   CS
Pet superstores have opened up in the metro area, but Waldo Pet remains a neighborhood favorite. The large store features an enormous selection of fish, both fresh and saltwater. Mon–Fri 10–9; Sat 10–6; Sun noon–5.

MAJOR DEPARTMENT STORES

DILLARD'S   (ALL ZONES)
This ubiquitous Kansas City department store features a wide range of men's and women's apparel, as well as kids' clothing, housewares, and furniture. Famous brands range from Liz Claiborne to Ralph Lauren, but Dillard's offers less-expensive house

SHOPPING MALLS

Kansas City has as many malls as other U.S. metro areas; they're just not always obvious. Prairie Village Shopping Center, for example, sits in the middle of a tree-lined residential district, but features a respectably sized Jones Store as anchor.

The area's four largest malls span the area geographically: Oak Park Mall in Johnson County, Bannister Mall in southern Kansas City, Metro North in Kansas City North, and Independence Mall in the East Metro area.

ANTIOCH SHOPPING CENTER
Antioch and Vivion Rds.,
Kansas City
816/454-1200   **NR**
Stores include Burlington Coat Factory, Antioch Music Center, and Sears (700,000 square feet).

BANNISTER MALL
I-435 and Bannister Rd.,
Kansas City
816/763-6900   **EM**
Stores include Sears, Dillard's, and J.C. Penney (1.2 million square feet).

BLUE RIDGE MALL
I-70 and Blue Ridge Blvd.,
Independence
816/353-5555   **EM**
Stores include Jones Store, Montgomery Ward, and Anderson's Book Shop (974,000 square feet).

CROWN CENTER
2450 Grand, Kansas City
816/274-8444   **DA**
Stores include the upscale Halls department store, Victoria's Secret, and Hallmark LIVE! (400,000 square feet).

HAWTHORNE PLAZA SHOPPING CENTER
119th and Roe, Overland Park
913/469-5100   **JO**
Stores include Jos A Bank, Talbot's, Tivol, and The Gallery (113,540 square feet).

INDEPENDENCE CENTER
I-70 and Hwy. 291, Independence
816/252-0608   **EM**
Stores include Jones Store, Dillard's, and Sears (1.1 million square feet).

METCALF SOUTH SHOPPING CENTER
95th St. and Metcalf,
Overland Park
913/649-2277   **JO**
Stores include The Gap, Jones Store, and Kids at Heart (950,000 square feet).

METRO NORTH SHOPPING CENTER
Hwy. 169 and Barry Rd.,
Kansas City
816/436-7800   **NR**
Stores include Musicland, Brandsmart, and Dillard's (1.2 million square feet).

MISSION SHOPPING CENTER
Johnson Dr. and Roe,
Roeland Park
913/262-3000   **JO**
Stores include Dillard's, Brentano's Bookstore, and Limited Express (344,350 square feet).

OAK PARK MALL
95th St. and Quivira,
Overland Park
913/888-4400   **JO**
Stores include M.C. Sports, J.C. Penney, and Dillard's (1.2 million square feet).

PRAIRIE VILLAGE SHOPPING CENTER
69th and Mission, Prairie Village
913/561-3456   **JO**
Stores include Jones Store, Toon Shop, and B. Dalton Bookseller (350,000 square feet).

ROSANA SQUARE
119th and Metcalf, Overland Park
913/842-7023   **JO**
Stores include Discovery Zone, Jenkins Music Company, and Nill Brothers Sporting Goods (444,000 square feet).

TOWN CENTER PLAZA
119th between Roe and Nall,
Leawood

913/498-1111   **JO**
Stores include Abercrombie & Fitch, Barnes & Noble, and Jacobson's (650,000 square feet so far).

WARD PARKWAY CENTER
86th St. and Ward Pkwy., Kansas City
816/363-3545   **CS**
Stores include Montgomery Ward, Dillard's, and J.M. Porter's (860,000 square feet).

DISCOUNTERS/FACTORY OUTLETS

INDIAN SPRINGS SHOPPING CENTER
46th St. and State Ave., Kansas City, Kansas
913/287-9393   **KCK**
The backbone of this entire shopping center is Dillard's Clearance Outlet. Department stores from around the region send this retail store the discontinued goods and items they can't sell. Clothes, though, occupy miles of racks. Prices are amazing—Carole Little blouses for $10; Calvin Klein jeans for $8—and they continue to drop as the season progresses. The

rest of the mall continues to experiment with other discounters, but it's hard to predict who'll still be there as you read this. Mon–Sat 10–9; Sun noon–5.

KANSAS CITY FACTORY OUTLETS
1306 W. Old Hwy. 40, Odessa
816/230-5662   **EM**
You've got to drive 20 miles east to reach this factory outlet mall, but plenty of folks do it regularly. Once there, you'll find 45 stores, including Spiegel, Mikasa, and Nine West shoes. There's a food court midway in the mall, so you can rest before tackling the second half. Mon–Sat 10–9; Sun 11–6.

RECOVERY SALES OUTLET
139000 E. 35th St., Independence
816/252-9212   **EM**
The inventory at RSO changes daily, depending on the salvaged goods that come through its doors. At this freight reclaimer you'll find everything from designer wedding gowns at half price to $2 compact discs. Regulars come often, just so they don't miss anything. Recovery Sales Outlet is open Mon–Fri 9–8, Sat 9–6, and Sun noon–6.

10

SPORTS AND RECREATION

Kansas Citians love the outdoors. Besides the natural greenways that course through the city's heart, the area boasts lakes perfect for sailing, streams ideal for fishing, and trails tailor-made for hiking. Even in winter, Kansas City's natural side beckons locals and visitors alike to stretch their legs, breathe some fresh air, and come out and play. Note: The map in this chapter shows locations of professional sports venues.

BIKING

INDIAN CREEK AND TOMAHAWK GREENWAY BIKING & HIKING TRAILS
I-435 and Lee Blvd., Leawood
913/451-9165   JO
These urban-suburban paths run more than 10 miles along the northern edge of I-435 and the surrounding area. But once you're riding, it seems like the world is far away. Get on the trail at Leawood Park (actually south of the freeway, but accessible from Lee Boulevard) or at many points including Corporate Woods North and South and Indian Creek Recreation Center. The Tomahawk Trail eventually ends at College Boulevard and Highway 69. Riders and hikers will find nature

information and exercise stations along many parts of the path.

LONGVIEW LAKE
South of I-470 on Raytown Rd., Kansas City
816/795-8200   EM
Longview Lake is a popular destination for all kinds of outdoor enthusiasts, including those who want to experience nature on a street bike. A paved, 6-mile bicycle trail traverses much of the western side of the lake, between O'Donnell Park and picnic shelter 14 near the marina. Cyclists pass through wooded areas and across a wooden bridge.

LITTLE BLUE TRACE
Hwy. 78, Independence
816/795-8200   EM

EAST METRO

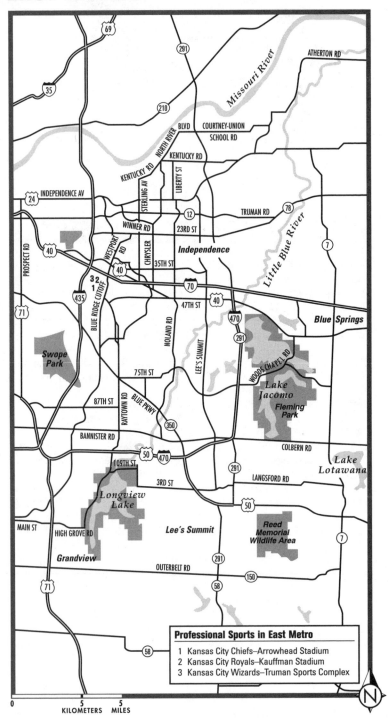

ATHERTON RD

Missouri River

69

35

291

210

NORTH RIVER BLVD

COURTNEY-UNION SCHOOL RD

KENTUCKY RD

KENTUCKY RD

24 INDEPENDENCE AV

STERLING AV

LIBERTY ST

12

TRUMAN RD

78

WINNER RD

23RD ST

7

PROSPECT RD

40

WESTPORT RD

CHRYSLER

35TH ST

Independence

Little Blue River

3 2
1

435

BLUE RIDGE CUTOFF

40

70

40

71

47TH ST

NOLAND RD

LEE'S SUMMIT

470

291

Blue Springs

Swope Park

75TH ST

WOODS CHAPEL RD

Lake Jacomo

87TH ST

RAYTOWN RD

BLUE PKWY

350

Fleming Park

BANNISTER RD

COLBERN RD

Lake Lotawana

50
470

109TH ST

3RD ST

LANGSFORD RD

291

Longview Lake

50

MAIN ST

HIGH GROVE RD

Lee's Summit

Reed Memorial Wildlife Area

7

Grandview

OUTERBELT RD

291

150

71

58

58

Professional Sports in East Metro

1 Kansas City Chiefs–Arrowhead Stadium
2 Kansas City Royals–Kauffman Stadium
3 Kansas City Wizards–Truman Sports Complex

N

0   5   5
KILOMETERS   MILES

Among the many areas for trail bicycling, the Little Blue Trace provides a relatively easy opportunity to get out into the wilds. An 8-mile round trip, the trail starts at the Blue Mills Road shelter off Highway 78. The crushed-rock surface takes some of the hazard out of the off-road trip.

Cycling Clubs

Kansas City is packed with two-wheel enthusiasts. For more information, see the Biking in Kansas City section in Chapter 2.

BOATING

BLUE SPRINGS LAKE
South of Hwy. 40 on Woods Chapel Rd., Blue Springs
816/795-1112 (marina)   EM
Blue Springs Lake is one of three lakes within Fleming Park, and the only one available for unlimited powerboating. People flock to the lake's 725 liquid acres for powerboating, water-skiing, tubing, and jet-skiing. The lake also features a full-service marina with rental boats, concessions, tackle, bait, and slip rentals. Rental prices for fishing and pontoon boats range from $10–$25/hour, $25–$80/four hours, and $45–$150/day.

LAKE JACOMO
East of I-435 on Woods Chapel Rd., Lee's Summit
816/795-8888   EM
At 970 acres, Lake Jacomo in Fleming Park is one of Jackson County's prime boating lakes. Jacomo includes a full-service marina, concessions, lakeside gasoline pumps, and fishing bait and tackle. Those eager to navigate upon the waters

can rent crappie boats, bass boats, canoes, and two- and four-seat pedal boats. Prices range from $6–$15/hour, $15–$45/four hours, and $20–$70/day.

LONGVIEW LAKE
South of I-470 on Raytown Rd., Kansas City
816/966-8976   EM
Set between Kansas City and Grandview, Longview Lake covers 930 acres, with ample opportunities for powerboaters, water-skiers, jet-skiers, and pontoon boaters. At the lake's marina, you can rent a variety of vessels, plus stock up on marine supplies, gasoline, tackle, and bait. The carp that school around the marina love to be fed. Rental prices for fishing and pontoon boats range from $10–$25/hour, $25–$80/four hours, and $45–$150/day.

SHAWNEE MISSION PARK LAKE
7900 Renner Rd., Lenexa–Shawnee
913/888-4713   JO
Shawnee Mission is Johnson County's largest park and includes a 150-acre stocked fishing lake. It's a serene setting, with wooded slopes coming right down to the shoreline. A boathouse on the north shore rents canoes, fishing boats with trolling motors only, and pedal boats. Canoes cost $4/each half-hour; fishing boats rent for $10/hour; and pedal boats cost $4/each half-hour.

SMITHVILLE LAKE
Northeast of Smithville on U.S. 169 and Hwy. 92, Smithville
816/532-0803   NR
Compared to the others in the area, Smithville Lake is gigantic, covering 7,200 acres and with two full-service marinas that offer boat rentals,

equipment sales, and dining facilities. Families come here to enjoy the relatively uncrowded lake and the easy access (five multilane boat-launch ramps). The southern half of the lake is available for water-skiing and inner-tubing throughout the year. Boat rental ranges from $15–$65/hour, $75–$210/day.

WYANDOTTE COUNTY LAKE
91st St. and Leavenworth Rd., Kansas City, Kansas
913/299-8488   KCK
A 60-year-old boathouse sits along Wyandotte County Lake's shore, offering concessions and boat rentals (canoes, paddle boats, and fishing boats). The 330-acre lake is small but provides a relaxing way to spend time on the water. Boats rent for $6.25–$12.50/hour. Boathouse open 8 a.m.–dark. Closed Tue.

BOWLING

AMF COLLEGE LANES
10201 College Blvd., Overland Park
913/451-6400   JO
Bowling buffs will find 32 lanes, seven billiard tables, and a lounge among the many amenities of this popular South Kansas City center, just across the street from the Dou-bletree Hotel. League play is popular, but open lanes can nearly always be had. Rates are $2–$3/game; $2 shoe rental. Mon–Fri 9 a.m.–midnight; until 3 a.m. Sat–Sun.

NKC PRO BOWL
505 E. 18th Ave., North Kansas City
816/221-8844   NR
With 48 lanes, this is by far the largest bowling facility in the Kansas City area, a fact that's made it popular for more than four decades. Lanes are $2/game weekdays; $2.50/nights and weekends. Shoes rent for $1.50. But bowling's just the beginning: NKC also offers nine pool tables, go-carts ($4/5-minute ride), 18 holes of miniature golf ($5), and four batting cages ($1/20 pitches). Mon–Thur 9 a.m.–midnight; until 3 a.m. Fri–Sat; and until 11 p.m. Sun.

PREMIER BOWLING & RECREATION
11400 E. Hwy. 350, Raytown
816/356-5955   EM
This ranks as one of the area's newest bowling centers, open just six years. That means the 32-lane facility offers some of the latest equipment and amenities. Besides the lanes, you'll find pool tables, a large dart area, and a 75-game arcade room. When the games on the floor become too much, you can

Ten Places to Reflect on Nature

by Marty Kraft,
Kansas City Earth Day organizer, environmental educator, and director of the Heartland All Species Project

Finding a place to commune with nature requires traveling to two places. One is a geographic location, and the other is a receptive place in your mind. After you've arrived at your destination, notice everything above, below, near, and far. See yourself as part of the scene. Simply be a human in the flow of being. Some of the many places to practice around Kansas City:

1. Walk by the spring at **Cave Springs Interpretive Center**.

2. Feel the contrast between the surrounding mowed lawn and the grove just south of the tennis courts in **Loose Park**.

3. Drive along **Cliff Drive** and see the cliffs formed by the Missouri River; look out across the river valley.

4. See the river valley from bluff to bluff at the Missouri River, one block south of downtown **Parkville**.

5. Visit the **Maple Woods Nature Preserve**, the largest grove of sugar maples west of the Mississippi.

6. Hike along the hill south of the **Lake of the Woods in Swope Park**.

7. Stop by the beautiful wooded hillsides at **Roanoke Park**, (38th Street and Roanoke).

8. See the native prairie grasses at the **Prairie Center** in Olathe.

9. Experience the beautiful rolling, wooded hills at **Wyandotte County Lake Park**.

10. Walk along the **Big Blue River at Minor Park** at Red Bridge, just west of Holmes.

relax in Premier's 150-seat sports bar and watch the big-screen TV. Note: League play occupies all lanes nearly every night from 6–8:30. Premier Bowling & Recreation is open Sun–Thur 10 a.m.–midnight; until 2 a.m. Fri–Sat. Lanes cost $2.35 per game during day hours; $2.60 at night. Shoes $1.50.

CAMPING/BACKPACKING

In addition to campgrounds listed in Chapter 3, the Kansas City area offers several wilderness reserves with hiking and primitive camping.

RIVER BLUFF RESERVE
Courtney Rd., Sugar Creek

816/795-8200   **EM**

On the bluffs overlooking Sugar Creek's LaBenite Park and the southern banks of the Missouri River, the River Bluff Reserve contains a section of the historic Lewis & Clark Trail. There are no campgrounds as such, but you can pitch a tent under the stars. To find the 263-acre reserve, go north on Highway 291; exit on Courtney Road.

MONKEY MOUNTAIN RESERVE
South of I-70, Grain Valley
816/795-8200   **EM**

On this 855-acre reserve you'll find hiking trails; fishing ponds; and places to picnic, cross-country ski, and ride horses. Even the most dedicated primitive campers will be glad for the reserve's restrooms. Head east from I–70 until you're just past Grain Valley; Monkey Mountain's to the south on old U.S. 40.

LANDAHL PARK RESERVE
East Truman Rd.,
Independence
816/795-8200   **EM**

The scenic Landahl Park Reserve includes trails that range from .6 to 3.6 miles and cover wooded hills and hidden vales. In warm weather, the Conservation Department holds target-shooting and outdoor educa-

tion courses in several open areas, although campers can easily avoid the groups on this 1,397-acre reserve. Landahl is 2 miles west of Highway 7 on Truman Road. The park also includes playing fields, picnic shelters, and restrooms.

CANOEING

BLUE RIVER PARKWAY
Blue River, Kansas City
816/795-8200   **CS**

A greenbelt lines the Big Blue River, beginning at Swope Park and winding southward approximately 12 miles to the Kansas–Missouri state line. The parkway is a special spot for hikers, and local canoeists treasure the waters of the Blue, too. A put-in ramp can be found near 131st Street and Holmes Road. **Beware:** The normally quiet waters can rise quickly and become treacherous during year-round flooding situations.

Canoe Rentals

Canoe rental in Kansas City is rare outside of local lake marinas, but A-1 Rental, 14891 E. Highway 40, Kansas City, 816/373-0234, offers a boat-

paddles-and-lifejackets package for $20/day or $30/weekend.

FISHING

Kansas City is riddled with lakes, streams, and rivers—which makes fishing a popular pastime. In these parts, fisherfolk reel in largemouth bass, walleye, crappie, channel cat, striped bass, bluegill, and carp, among other species.

Since the region covers two states and 11 counties, fishing permits vary. In general, however, in Missouri you'll need a $3 daily non-resident   fishing permit and in Kansas a $15, five-day nonresident fishing license. Aside from major waters such as Smithville, Jacomo, Blue Springs, Longview, and Wyandotte County Lakes (see Boating section), fervent fishers might want to try these spots:

JAMES A. REED MEMORIAL CONSERVATION AREA
13101 Ranson Rd., Kansas City
816/524-1656   EM
This wildlife refuge contains 11 lakes connected by easily accessible roads. Regular catches here include crappie, bluegill, and catfish; a catch-and-release trout season takes place in the fall. Take Highway 50 east to Ranson Road, then go south. Just east of Lee's Summit.

SHAWNEE MISSION PARK
7900 Renner Rd.,
Lenexa–Shawnee
913/831-3355   JO
This 150-acre Johnson County lake regularly attracts anglers seeking everything from bluegill to bass to carp. Rainbow trout, however, draw the most significant crowd, soon

after the fish are stocked each spring and fall. Boat rental is available.

LAKE OLATHE
625 Lakeshore Dr., Olathe
913/764-6163   JO
Fish stalkers have 170 watery acres for hunting grounds at this south Kansas City lake. With any luck they'll find catfish, crappie, bass, and even trout. The area near the fishing pier is sown annually with Christmas trees, providing new cover and nesting areas for the fish.

FITNESS CLUBS

GOLD'S GYM FAMILY FITNESS CENTERS
816/931-9888   DA, CS, JO, NR, EM
Gold's sports six locations in the Kansas City metro area, offering workout equipment such as stationary bicycles, stair-steppers, Nautilus machines, and free weights. Some also have swimming pools. $10/day or $25 for seven days. Open Mon–Fri 6 a.m.–11 p.m.; Sat 8–8; Sun 9–7.

MOFFETT'S GYM
12244 W. 63rd St., Shawnee
913/268-6808   JO
This local gymnasium features circuit training, aerobics classes, free weights, and massage. In addition, the fitness club provides child care. No towels or locks. $5/day or $20/week. Open 5 a.m.–10 p.m. Mon–Fri, 6 a.m.–7 p.m. Saturday, and 10–5 Sunday.

YMCAS
816/561-9622   DA, CS, JO, NR, EM
913/371-4400   KCK
The YMCA of Greater Kansas City includes ten branches, some with pools. You'll also find weight rooms,

indoor and/or outdoor tracks, and locker-room facilities at many of the clubs. The YMCA of Kansas City, Kansas, has two facilities, similarly equipped. Hours and fees vary.

GAMBLING

Riverboat gambling was approved in Kansas City in 1993. Soon after, as many as a dozen companies filed applications to operate casinos in the area (although gaming officials have licensed only five). Citing safety concerns for vessels that originally planned to cruise the swift Missouri River, regulators soon allowed the boats to moor. Although some look like riverbank buildings, all are still required to actually float.

Competition, of course, is keen among these waterborne wagering wonders, which means they all offer a similar assortment of games, ranging from blackjack to craps, slot machines to Caribbean stud poker.

ARGOSY CASINO
I-635 and Hwy. 9, Riverside
816/746-7711 NR
The Argosy was Kansas City's first riverboat casino, brought to the area from Illinois in late 1993. This was one of the only vessels that actually cruised the river with gambling underway, in the days before moored boats were allowed. Now set in Riverside, five minutes from downtown Kansas City, Missouri, on Hwy. 9, the boat offers aisles and aisles of gaming tables, along with several restaurants. Argosy Casino is open daily from 8 a.m.–2 a.m.

HARRAH'S CASINO NORTH KANSAS CITY
Hwy. 210 and Chouteau Trafficway, North Kansas City
816/472-7777 NR
Harrah's opened its North Kansas City facility in late 1994 with an enormous building beside its floating casino. Inside, Harrah's offers three restaurants, in addition to the one aboard the North Star riverboat, a replica nineteenth-century paddle wheeler. Sun–Thur 8 a.m.–2 a.m., until 3 a.m. Fri–Sat.

FLAMINGO HILTON CASINO KANSAS CITY
920 Main, Kansas City
816/474-8300 DA
The first Kansas City casino on the south bank of the Missouri River, the colorful Flamingo Hilton puts its gambling all on one floor. The facility offers several restaurants and lounges, as well as live entertainment. Open daily 8 a.m.–2 a.m.

SAM'S TOWN
I-435 and Hwy. 210, Kansas City
816/414-7777 NR
Inside, Sam's Town looks like a Victorian village, its restaurants and sports bar providing a promenade to the boat entrance. On the boat, gambling takes place on three decks. Open daily 10 a.m.–5 a.m.

STATION CASINO
I-435 and Birmingham Rd., Kansas City
816/414-7000 NR
When it opened in early 1997, Station Casino became Kansas City's largest riverboat-gambling operation. The twin-boat complex features movie theaters, a children's play zone, a 1,400-seat arena, and a microbrewery—in addition to a substantial gam-

Truman Sports Complex, page 189

ing area. By mid-1997, the Las Vegas company expects to open a hotel, nine restaurants, and a nongambling arcade. Daily 8 a.m.–5 a.m.

GOLF

Daily greens fees at the following public courses range from $15–$25 depending upon day of the week.

CRACKERNECK GOLF COURSE
18800 E. Hwy. 40, Independence
816/795-7771 EM
Whether you believe this course's distinctive name derives from a "hanging tree" once used by Jesse James or from some Southern "crackers" who moved into the area in the late 1800s, this 18-hole course offers both challenges and easy access. It's found where Hwys. 291 and 40 intersect, just south of I-70.

DEER CREEK GOLF CLUB
7000 W. 133rd St., Overland Park
913/681-3100 JO
Deer Creek has a noble heritage: The 18-hole course was designed by Robert Trent Jones Jr. In addition, it's received several *Golf Digest* rankings, including Top 3 Best New Public Courses in 1989 and 3½ stars for Places to Play in 1993.

HERITAGE PARK GOLF COURSE
16445 Lackman, Olathe
913/829-4653 JO
One of the newest public golf courses in the metro area, Heritage Park Golf Course renders a variety of water features among its 18 holes. In fact, the course crosses and parallels three lakes and Coffee Creek.

HODGE PARK GOLF CENTER
7000 N.E. Barry Rd., Kansas City
816/781-4152 NR
This 18-hole, Kansas City–run course is especially scenic, winding through wooded, rolling hills. The east fork of Shoal Creek also cuts a small swath, lending a natural air to the game.

LONGVIEW LAKE GOLF COURSE
South of I-470 on Raytown Rd.,
Kansas City

Ten Favorite Hikes in the Kansas City Area

by Bill Eddy,
co-author of *Hiking Kansas City*

1. **Watkins Mill State Park Trail**. A paved circuit through varied terrain around Williams Creek Lake north of Kansas City. The quiet walker stands an excellent chance of seeing deer (6 miles east of Kearney off Highway 92).

2. The **Landahl Nature Preserve**. Northeast of Blue Springs, the area contains several trails through woods and uplands, including the nature trail with the Indian name Washingsabba.

3. The **Bethany Falls Trail at Burr Oak Woods**. Walk past the remains of settlers' cabins and below limestone bluffs, where one may find spring-blooming columbine.

4. **Larry Mattonen Memorial Trail**. One of Fleming Park's seven trails, this new one travels through deep woods and along the lake shore.

5. **Blue River Parkways Trail**. The north segment of the trail, in the Red Bridge area, follows an abandoned railroad right of way along bluffs with views of the Blue River.

6. The **Mill Creek Streamway Trail**. This Johnson County system is a paved route that will soon extend from Olathe to the Kansas ("Kaw") River. The north segment, from Shawnee Mission Park to and around Nelson Island in the river, is a favorite.

7. **West Ridge and Harpst Valley Trails**. These connecting trails at Weston Bend State Park pass up, down, and through wooded hills, and along high bluffs that offer spectacular views of the Missouri River.

8. **Wallace State Park**. The well-developed loop trail system, just south of Cameron, Missouri, provides a deep-woods experience close to that in national forests, with valleys, thick forests, and open hilltops.

9. **Clinton Lake**. This 12,000-acre preserve near Lawrence, Kansas, has nearly 100 miles of trails. The George Latham Trail, in the Woodbridge Primitive Area, provides an excellent hike around a peninsula, with woods, meadows, rock outcroppings, and sightings of birds and other wildlife.

10. **Prairie Center**. West of Olathe, this native prairie grasslands preserve has a trail through the prairie and adjacent forest. The trip includes streams, lakes, old stone fences, and a buffalo wallow.

Detailed information on these and other trails can be found in Hiking Kansas City *by William B. Eddy and Richard O. Ballentine.*

816/761-9445 **EM**

Jackson County's first golf facility sits on the east side of Longview Lake with vistas of the water. The complex includes a total of 27 holes—an 18-hole championship course and a nine-hole executive course—plus a driving range and clubhouse.

PAINTED HILLS GOLF COURSE
7101 Parallel Pkwy.,
Kansas City, Kansas
913/334-1111 **KCK**

On the hills overlooking Kansas City (Kansas) Community College, Painted Hills offers greens fees on its 18-hole championship course at lower rates than others around town. The clubhouse has become a KCK place to meet.

PARADISE POINTE
CHAMPIONSHIP GOLF COURSE
18212 Golf Course Rd., Smithville
816/532-4100 **NR**

Sculpted out of the hilly land that surrounds Smithville Lake, Paradise Pointe combines relaxing play with geologic challenges. Paradise Pointe is the only public golf complex in the Kansas City area with two 18-hole championship courses, a driving range, and a four-hole golf academy.

SWOPE PARK GOLF COURSES
6900 Swope Memorial Dr.,
Kansas City
816/523-9081 **CS**

Set in urban Swope Park, this course's 18 holes ramble through wooded hills overlooking east Kansas City. Also in Swope Park, the Blue River Golf Course abuts the private Hillcrest Golf Club and the Big Blue River.

TOMAHAWK HILLS PUBLIC
GOLF COURSE
17501 Midland Dr., Shawnee

913/631-8000 **JO**

Tomahawk Hills was built in 1910 and remains the oldest golf course still played in the metro area. Set among rolling hills adjacent to Shawnee Mission Park, Tomahawk Hills ranks as one of Kansas City's most challenging public courses. Its 18-hole, championship layout runs 6,000 yards.

HIKING

BLUE AND GRAY PARK RESERVE
Hwy. 50, near Lone Jack
816/795-8200 **EM**

This Jackson County park offers two wooded trails, but the most interesting is the Lone Jack Civil War Trail. Approximately 15 miles long, the trail follows county roads from the Blue and Gray Park Reserve to Missouri Town 1855. Hikers pass through oak and hickory hardwood forests and encounter a variety of wildlife. (Missouri Town 1855 lies on the eastern shore of Lake Jacomo.)

BLUE RIVER PARKWAY
Blue River, Kansas City
816/795-8200 **CS**

Among the parkway's trails is the very scenic, and moderately easy, 4.5-mile (one way) Blue River Parkway Nature Trail between Kenneth Rd. and Red Bridge. Much of the trail follows the river, allowing hikers to see wildlife that includes birds, rabbits, squirrels, and the occasional deer and beaver.

FLEMING PARK
South of Hwy. 40 on Woods
Chapel Rd., Blue Springs
816/795-8200 **EM**

Fleming Park features seven trails, from the .75-mile Missouri Town–Clermont Nature Trail to the 1.5-mile

Rock Ledges Nature Trail, a loop that begins at shelter 14. Directions to these paths can be found at the park headquarters on Woods Chapel Road.

PRAIRIE CENTER
26325 W. 135th St., Olathe
913/856-8832 JO

Much of this preserve's 300 acres are open prairie with nature trails through wildflowers such as larkspur, sunflowers, and goldenrod. Animals also frequent this verdant prairie; you just might see owls, deer, or coyote. The buffalo wallow dates back an estimated 150 years.

RIVER BLUFF TRAIL
Hwy. 291, Kansas City
816/795-8200 EM

The River Bluff Trail, in River Bluff Park near Courtney, is a twisting, hilly, 2.4-mile trek. You'll encounter a 100-foot drop-off at one point. A walkable, historic 13.5-mile section of the Lewis & Clark Trail starts at River Bluff Park as well. The trail heads east, often following county roads, to the mouth of the Little Blue River then follows the levee to Fort Osage.

HORSEBACK RIDING

BENJAMIN RANCH WEST
6401 E. 87th St., Kansas City
816/765-1100 EM

Russian immigrant Hyman Benjamin started with 40 acres in 1885. Today Hyman's descendants, Howard Benjamin and his son, Ben, run the 250-acre Benjamin Ranch and maintain about 200 acres of their property as a preserved natural wilderness, with riding trails winding through the rugged terrain. Reservations requested. 8a.m.–dusk in nonwinter months. $18.50/hour; $32.50/two hours.

HOT-AIR BALLOONING

Kansas City's nearby wide-open spaces make hot-air ballooning popular. A variety of companies rise to meet the demand, primarily flying May–Nov.

AERONAUTICAL ADVENTURES
103rd and Metcalf, Overland Park
913/649-0004 JO

The St. Louis–based Petrehn family has flown balloons since 1972, and several members hold world flying records. In Kansas City, between six and ten passengers can fly together in one of the company's 15 balloons. The one-hour flights include refreshments, followed by a champagne reception back on the ground. Year-round flights, contingent on weather conditions. $155/person; packages available.

BALLOON SAFARIS
11560 W. 95th St., Overland Park
913/649-2050 JO

Balloon Safaris' pilots have taken passengers aloft since 1981. The 2.5- to 3-hour experience includes a briefing session, up to 1.5 hours in flight, and a champagne party on landing. As many as seven passengers may ride together. Flights cost $145/person, but ask about ongoing specials.

HUNTING

Hunters relish the opportunities available in Kansas and Missouri. Both states offer a variety of game seasons including deer, turkey, pheasant, quail, dove, rabbit, squirrel, duck, and goose. Additionally, many areas offer firearm, muzzleloader, and archery seasons. Hunting licenses are required for all but those hunting on land they own.

MISSOURI DEPARTMENT OF CONSERVATION
Kansas City Metro Office
8616 E. 63rd St., Kansas City
816/356-2280 EM
A Missouri's resident license costs $9 small-game; $15 combined small-game and fishing; $11 deer or turkey; and $15 archery deer and turkey. Nonresidents pay $5 daily small-game; $60 annual small-game; $75 turkey; $75 archery deer; and $110 firearm deer.

KANSAS DEPARTMENT OF WILDLIFE & PARKS
Kansas City District Office
14639 W. 95th St., Lenexa
913/894-9113 JO
An annual Kansas general hunting license costs $15.50 for residents and $65.50 for nonresidents, however a 48-hour nonresident waterfowl license is available for $20.50. Additional deer tag and state and federal waterfowl stamp fees may apply.

Public Areas

Hunting on public land is strictly controlled. Several special deer hunts, for example, have been held in recent years in Jackson County's Fleming Park, due to an overly large deer population. Call the state telephone numbers above for more information.

Private Areas

HUNTING SPORTS PLUS
710 W. Main, Blue Springs
816/228-8700 EM
This group provides hunting access to 200,000 acres of private land in Kansas, Missouri, and contiguous states. Game options include quail, pheasant, prairie chicken, deer,

turkey, duck, and geese. Guides available.

MID-AMERICA GAME BIRD ASSOCIATION
11920 Grandview Rd., Grandview
816/761-3636 EM
Specializing in game birds including duck, pheasant, quail, and geese, the Mid-America Game Bird Association opens some 125,000 acres in both Kansas and Missouri to hunters. Arrangements may also be made to hunt deer and fish. Guides available.

ICE SKATING

AMF ICE CHATEAU
8788 Metcalf, Overland Park
913/648-0129 JO
Located indoors with its sister AMF West bowling center, this 85-by-185-foot rink is large enough to host regulation United States Figure Skating tests and competitions. The chateau is open Mon, Tue, Thur–Fri 10–5;

Hospital Hill Half-Marathon, page 184

Convention and Visitors Bureau of Greater Kansas City

Wed 10 a.m.–12:30 a.m., Sat–Sun 2–4 and 8–10:30. $5.50–$6; $2 skate rental.

CROWN CENTER ICE TERRACE
2450 Grand, Kansas City
816/274-8411 DA
Between November and March, the Crown Center Ice Terrace is one of the most popular places in town. The free-form tent over the outdoor rink sets the stage for an enjoyable afternoon or evening of skating. In the summer, the rink becomes a stage. Mon–Wed and Sat 10–6; Thur–Fri 10–9; Sun noon–5. Adults $4.50; children 12 and younger $3.50; seniors 60 and over free.

PAINTBALL

JAEGERS SUBSURFACE PAINTBALL
9300 N.E. Underground,
Kansas City
816/452-6600 NR
Quite possibly the world's only underground paintball field, Jaegers features 180,000 square feet of subterranean space at a year-round 56 degrees. Within the facility, players can choose from six to ten different games. Located east of I-435 and just north of the Missouri River. Tue–Fri 6–10:30; weekends 9 a.m.–10:30 p.m. A two-hour session, including gun and paintballs, averages $24.

KANSAS CITY PAINTBALL FIELD
15 S.W. 3rd St., Lee's Summit
816/524-7600 EM
Warriors at the Kansas City Paintball Field find themselves battling it out on 40 wooded acres with a stream that runs through the property. There are two games available at the site; the $20 fee includes a high-tech pump gun, 100 paintballs,

enough fuel for 350 rounds, a mask, goggles, ear protection, and lunch. Weekends 10–4.

ROLLER SKATING

SKATE WORLD
I-35 and Shawnee Mission Pkwy.,
Merriam
913/262-0711 JO
This popular rink offers a variety of options for skaters of every skill level. Among the sessions: Friday Teen Skate from 7:30 to 10:30 p.m., with a sock-hop party for the final 30 minutes, $5.50. Saturday morning, the rink hosts a $2.50 learn-to-skate session from 9:30 to10:30; and Wednesday is Retro Music Night, featuring music from the Seventies, Eighties, and Nineties from 8 to 10:30, $5.

NORTHLAND ROLLADIUM SKATE CENTER
1020 S. Kent, Liberty
816/792-0590 NR
North of the River skate buffs enjoy this rink, with its selection of inexpensive packages. Wednesday night's Cheap Skate, for example, allows skating from 7 to 9 for $1 and a $1 skate rental fee. On Friday from 7 to 11, Super Session participants pay $4.50, with free skate rental. And those new on wheels can try the beginners class Saturday afternoon from 1 to 2 for only $3.50.

RUNNING & ROAD RACES

Running routes and regular runners abound in Kansas City. You'll even see fanatical folks jogging through the snow. Competitive road races range from the nationally ranked Hospital Hill Half-Marathon to the

Ten Favorite Kansas City Running Routes

by Garry Gribble,
owner of Garry Gribble's Running Sports and a marathon finisher in all 50 states

1. **Indian Creek Trail** in Overland Park, east between Switzer and Mission Road.

2. **Shawnee Mission Park** trails offer a variety of scenery.

3. **Martha Lafite Thompson Nature Trail**. This Liberty trail is beautiful.

4. **Loose Park**. This run features a view of the Plaza; go through scenic neighborhoods by heading south on Summit to Valley Road.

5. **Mill Creek Park** is a circular trail at J.C. Nichols Parkway.

6. **Overland Park Arboretum**. This one offers much in southern Johnson County, near 179th Street and Antioch.

7. **Longview Lake**. The trails here provide a scenic view of eastern Jackson County.

8. **Burr Oak Trails**. In Blue Springs off Highway 7, these are a must run.

9. **The Levee Run**. This Lawrence route is rural, but good running.

10. **Parkville River Trail**. This one, in Parkville, Missouri, hugs the Missouri River.

10,000-runner Michael Forbes Trolley Run to the Groundhog Run, a 10K threading through an underground system of limestone caves.

For information about competitive races and fun runs, call Kansas City Track Club 816/333-7223.

SAILING/SAILBOARDING

HERITAGE PARK
16050 Pflumm Rd., Olathe
913/831-3355 JO
This 1,160-acre park in south Johnson County sports a 45-acre lake,

the only waters within the Johnson County Parks & Recreation Department that offer sailboarding rentals. The lake's on the north end of the park, accessible from either 159th Street or Pflumm Road. Boardsailors can cruise by Black Bob Island—more of an islet, actually—that can be rented for private parties. Rentals $12/hour, $30/four hours, $60/day.

LAKE JACOMO
East of I-435 on Woods Chapel Rd., Lee's Summit
816/795-8888 EM
Fleming Park's largest lake offers 970

acres for boat sailors. The limited-horsepower regulations on pontoon and fishing boats keep the waters calm. The lake has a full-service marina, boat rentals, concessions, tackle, bait, dock fishing, and boat ramps. Dolphin Sr. sailboats rent for $10/hour, $25/four hours, and $45/day. Although sailboard rentals are no longer available on the lake, Jacomo—especially near the dam—is a favorite with local boardsailors. One-day permit: $15.

LONGVIEW LAKE
**South of I-470 on Raytown Rd.,
Kansas City
816/795-8200   EM**
Winds can get gusty at this 930-acre lake, making it a prime spot for windsurfing. Board rentals are not available, but those with their own equipment will have plenty of open area for tacking, jibing, and long runs. The boat ramp at Longview Marina, near the dam, makes a good launch site. The marina also sells the required one-day permit ($15). Personal flotation devices are required, and boardsailing is limited to Mon–Thur.

SHAWNEE MISSION PARK
**7900 Renner Rd.,
Lenexa–Shawnee
913/888-4713   JO**
Johnson County's largest park features a 150-acre lake that's a good spot for beginning boat sailors. Besides sailing

classes, organized through Johnson County's Parks & Recreation Department, the park's boathouse rents Sunfish sailboats from late spring through early fall. Rentals $30/four hours or half-day; $60/full day.

SKIING

FLEMING PARK
816/229-8980   EM
During January and February, the Jackson County Parks & Recreation Department holds cross-country ski classes at Fleming Park (weather permitting). Rentals are available. Call for more details.

LANDAHL PARK RESERVE
**East Truman Rd., Independence
816/795-8200   EM**
Landahl Reserve is popular with cross-country skiers because of the many trails that wind through the hilly, 1,397-acre reserve. Look for the trailheads at the Truman Rd. and Argo Rd. shelters. The reserve is 2 miles west of Hwy. 7 on Truman Road.

SNOW CREEK
**1 Snow Creek Dr., Weston
816/386-2200   NR**
Yes, the Kansas City area has a nearby downhill-ski area. Hoping to capitalize on local ski fanatics—I-70 is filled with Kansas Citians who drive the 600 miles to ski the Colorado Rockies—Snow

Creek opened in 1985. The slopes are in a hilly region 5 miles north of Weston, Missouri, and include nine intermediate trails, two triple chairlifts, and two beginner areas served by three rope tows. Snow Creek can make its own snow and has lighted slopes for night skiing. A day-lodge with a cafeteria and lounge make for great après-ski relaxation. Lessons available. Mid-Dec–mid-Mar; Sun 9–8, Mon–Thur 1–10, Fri 1–11, Sat 9 a.m.–11 p.m., and Fri and Sat midnight–6 a.m. Adults $17–$28, depending on session, $32–$45 with ski rental; $17 seniors all sessions, $29 with rental; $14 children 12 and under all sessions, $26 with rental.

SWIMMING

Thanks to Kansas City's hot and humid summers, outdoor swimming pools abound. Year-round swimming options, open to nonmembers and other visitors, are most easily found at health clubs and other facilities open to the general public. YMCA, for example, offers more pools across a greater portion of the metropolitan area than any other organization.

YMCA OF GREATER KANSAS CITY
3100 Broadway, Kansas City
816/561-9622   All Zones
Of the ten YMCAs in Greater Kansas City, seven have swimming pools, and five offer indoor or indoor and outdoor pools. Hours and rates vary. A one-day pass for nonmembers generally ranges $5–$10.

TENNIS

EISENHOWER RECREATION CENTER

2901 N. 72nd St.,
Kansas City, Kansas
913/299-1118   KCK
Four lighted courts

HAPPY ROCK PARK
76th St. and Antioch, Gladstone
816/468-1200   NR
Four lighted courts

INDIAN CREEK RECREATION
7401 W. 103rd St., Overland Park
913/341-4350   JO
Eight courts

PLAZA TENNIS CENTER
4747 J.C. Nichols Pkwy.,
Kansas City
816/561-5120   CS
Fourteen lighted courts on the Country Club Plaza. Regular courts, $4–$8 depending on time and day; two practice courts, no charge.

SANTA FE PARK
2800 Santa Fe Rd., Independence
816/325-7360   EM
12 courts (six lighted)

Sailing at Lake Jacomo, page 185

Convention and Visitors Bureau of Greater Kansas City

America's Stadium Capital

Today's sports fans file into multilevel arenas filled with super suites, concierge service, gourmet dining, and high-tech sound and video systems. They have three Kansas City sports architecture companies to thank for the experience.

It was in the late Sixties that the Kansas City Chiefs Football Club ordered the first-ever U.S. stadium dedicated solely to a professional football team. For design, the owners tapped Kivett & Myers of Kansas City, Missouri.

After local officials asked, "What about baseball?" the architects suggested two separate stadiums, one for each sport, which would operate as a single entity. Despite going some $20 million over budget, the projects were deemed a success. Arrowhead debuted in the fall of 1972; Royals Stadium (later renamed Kauffman Stadium) opened the next spring and was the last baseball-dedicated facility built until Chicago's Comiskey Park opened in 1991. The dual facilities were dubbed the Harry S. Truman Sports Complex.

Since then, Kivett & Myers' protégés have created the nation's big three sports architecture firms, all still based in Kansas City: HOK Sports, Ellerbe Becket, and HNTB Corp. All compete for commissions from major- and minor-league teams, colleges, and Olympic committees around the world. From England to Malaysia, Manitoba to Hong Kong, these firms set the cutting edge.

HOK created, among others, Chicago's New Comiskey Park, Miami's Joe Robbie Stadium, and the New Hong Kong Stadium. HNTB designed Vancouver B.C.'s Place Stadium and Indianapolis' Hoosier Dome, and Ellerbe Becket is responsible for Jack Kent Cooke Stadium for the Washington Redskins and the 1996 Olympic Stadium/Atlanta Braves Ballpark.

SPECTATOR SPORTS

Auto Racing

KANSAS CITY INTERNATIONAL RACEWAY
9201 Noland Rd., Kansas City
816/358-6700 EM
This is the Kansas City area's drag-racing capital. Fans, including many of the race drivers' and crews' families, meet at the raceway from the end of May through the end of October for bracket drag racing. Gates open Saturdays at 2:30, and races generally run until 10. Grudge, or practice, racing takes place each Wednesday beginning at 6. Sat $10, Wed $8; children under 12 free.

LAKESIDE SPEEDWAY
5615 Wolcott Dr.,
Kansas City, Kansas
913/541-8692 KCK
Lakeside features a half-mile, semi-banked asphalt track with stand seating for 5,000. Racing fans come at 8 on Friday nights between April and September to watch four car classes: NASCAR/Winston Racing series modifieds, 4-cylinder pony stocks, street stocks, and charger stocks. Adults $10; children under 6 free.

Horse and Greyhound Racing

THE WOODLANDS
9700 Leavenworth Rd.,
Kansas City, Kansas
913/299-9797 KCK
This dual-track racing complex features both horses and dogs. Two modern buildings are fully enclosed, making both the grandstands and clubhouses all-season. The Woodlands stages greyhound racing year-round, while the thoroughbred and quarter horses race mid-Aug–early Nov. Wed and Sat 1 and 7 p.m.; Thur–Fri 7 p.m.; Sun 1 p.m. Closed Mon–Tue. General admission $1.50; clubhouse $3.50.

PROFESSIONAL SPORTS

KANSAS CITY ATTACK
1800 Genessee, Kansas City
816/474-2255 DA
You know about outdoor soccer; how about indoor soccer? The Kansas City Attack belong to the National Professional Soccer League with a regular season that runs late Oct–Mar.

KANSAS CITY BLADES
1800 Genessee, Kansas City
816/842-1063 DA
The Kansas City Blades were purchased in March '96 by the founders of the International Hockey League's newest team, the Grand Rapids Griffins. Soon after, the Blades secured a National Hockey League affiliation with the San Jose Sharks. The Blades' season runs Oct–Apr; tickets $10–$18.

KANSAS CITY CHIEFS
One Arrowhead Dr., Kansas City
816/924-9400 EM
Members of the National Football League, the Kansas City Chiefs play their home games at Arrowhead Stadium in the Harry S. Truman Sports Complex. A majority of the stadium's 79,100 seats are occupied by season-ticket holders, but true gridiron fans will want to try landing a ticket anyway. Ticket prices average about $35; parking's extra. For pre-game festivities, Arrowhead is the site of one of the world's largest tailgate parties, as countless fans arrive early to picnic before the contest begins.

TRIVIA

Kansas City football fans are rabid; tens of thousands show up for games clad in red-and-gold Chiefs gear to passionately cheer on their team . . . despite the fact that the Chiefs—even with revered quarterback Joe Montana in the 1993–94 seasons—haven't made it to the Super Bowl since 1970. Still, fans haven't given up hope. Arrowhead Stadium remains sold out for years to come, and the search for another Len Dawson–like quarterback continues.

KANSAS CITY EXPLORERS
Hale Arena, Kansas City
913/362-9944   **DA**

This World Team Tennis group has played in Kansas City since 1993. The Explorers' 1996 guest-player roster included the likes of tennis bad-boy John McEnroe. The Explorers play at Hale Arena next to Kemper. Tickets $20–$45.

KANSAS CITY ROYALS
One Royal Way, Kansas City
816/921-8000   **EM**

Arrowhead Stadium, home of the Chiefs

Convention and Visitors Bureau of Greater Kansas City

The Kansas City Royals have witnessed a youthful resurgence of late, releasing veteran stars in favor of up-and-comers. The team continues to work at rebuilding, always reaching for a repeat of that glorious 1985 season when the Royals won the World Series. Tickets $5–$14.

KANSAS CITY WIZARDS
706 Broadway, Kansas City
816/472-4625

This flashy new team started out in 1995 as the "Wiz"—until the jokes became unbearable. No matter what you call it, this Major League Soccer team, launched by Kansas City Chiefs owner Lamar Hunt and his family, provides exciting action. The Wizards play at the Truman Sports Complex in a season that runs Apr–Sept. Tickets $10–$13.

Convention and Visitors Bureau of Greater Kansas City

11

PERFORMING ARTS

What shall we see tonight? The options are nearly endless when it comes to Kansas City's performing arts. Whether it's a rousing rendition of Beethoven's Fifth, a spirited "Dance of the Sugar Plum Fairy," or a stirring choral ensemble singing Handel's Messiah, *you can find it in this town. Kansas City has a major symphony, many smaller musical orchestras, several dance companies, traveling arts series, and enough live theater to make it one of the best drama-oriented towns in the country. What do you want to see? How will you ever decide? Note: The map in this chapter shows locations of major performing arts venues.*

THEATER

AMERICAN HEARTLAND THEATRE
2450 Grand, Suite 314, Kansas City
816/842-9999   DA
The American Heartland Theatre presents Broadway-style comedies, musicals, mysteries, and dramas throughout the year, using local theatrical talent and visiting headliners. Set on Crown Center's Level 3, the theater is a well-appointed facility with a stage that extends into the audience. Seats rise sharply from the stage, giving all an unobstructed view. There's a full-service bar in the lobby at intermission, although the American Heartland allows you to

take your drink into the performance, too. Recent performances include *Greater Tuna, A Wonderful Life,* and *Dial "M" for Murder.*

HEART OF AMERICA
SHAKESPEARE FESTIVAL
4800 Main, Suite 402, Kansas City
816/531-7728   CS
The annual Heart of America Shakespeare Festival was a fortuitous addition to Kansas City's theater scene, bringing thousands to Southmoreland Park each summer to enjoy the Bard for free. In the hilly esplanade opposite the Nelson-Atkins Museum of Art, the equity company presents high-quality performances that have

DOWNTOWN KANSAS CITY AREA

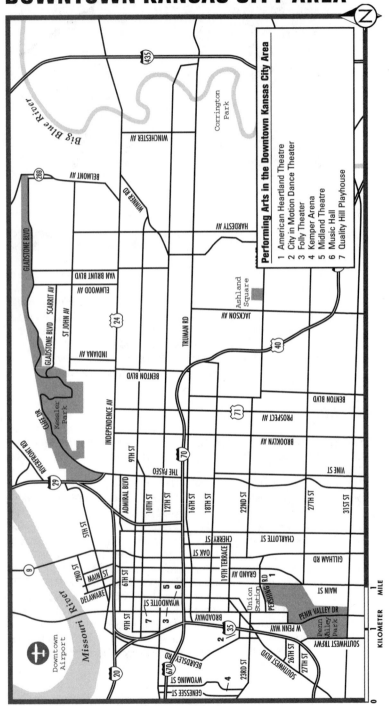

Performing Arts in the Downtown Kansas City Area

1 American Heartland Theatre
2 City in Motion Dance Theater
3 Folly Theater
4 Kemper Arena
5 Midland Theatre
6 Music Hall
7 Quality Hill Playhouse

included *Romeo and Juliet, A Midsummer Night's Dream,* and *The Tempest. Richard III* is scheduled for 1997. Plays run nightly for about two weeks in midsummer. Fans bring blankets and picnics early to be sure they get close to the stage. Southmoreland Park is at 47th Street and Oak, east of the Country Club Plaza.

MARTIN CITY MELODRAMA & VAUDEVILLE COMPANY
13340 Holmes Rd., Kansas City
816/942-7576   CS

Not content to present mere melodrama, the Martin City Melodrama & Vaudeville Company adapts old standards to its highly wacky purposes. Productions in the past have included *The Three Little Pigs, or Hamletta; Jezebel, or Gone With the Men;* and *The Invisible Man, or No Guts, No Glory!* The evening's entertainment—held way out south in an old wood-frame theater building—also includes a rousing vaudeville revue.

MISSOURI REPERTORY THEATRE
4949 Cherry, Kansas City
816/235-2700   CS

The Missouri Repertory Theatre has entertained Kansas Citians ever since one muggy night in June 1964, when the theater troupe staged Emlyn Williams' *The Corn is Green* in an old playhouse on the UMKC cam-

pus. Now the professional company presents five plays each season, between September and May, and *A Christmas Carol* every December in its intimate facility, still on the university grounds. Recent plays have included Moliere's *The Misanthrope,* translated to the art deco period in a lavish, three-tier set; Sophocles' famed Greek story of *Antigone;* and *The Belle of Amherst,* the one-woman play that highlights the life of Emily Dickinson.

QUALITY HILL PLAYHOUSE
303 W. 10th St., Kansas City
816/474-7529   DA

This small theater specializes in off-Broadway dramas, comedies, and musicals in a season that lasts all year. The playhouse is an intimate setting that makes the theater company's productions especially memorable. Recent plays have included *Me and Jezebel,* the story of Bette Davis' month-long stay with author Elizabeth Fuller; *Hi Hat Hattie,* the tale of Oscar-winning African American actress Hattie McDaniel; and *Noel and Gertie,* the lively play about Noel Coward and Gertrude Lawrence.

STARLIGHT THEATRE
Swope Park, Kansas City
816/363-7827   CS

When it opened more than 40 years

...vorite Haunt

TRIVIA

Although it's a tradition that seems to have started years earlier, the Missouri Repertory Theatre's annual production of *A Christmas Carol* was launched in 1981. The professional acting company had moved to its new Helen F. Spencer Theatre on the UMKC campus only two years before, and the facility was perfect for a holiday extravaganza. The Dickens play took full advantage of the new theater's state-of-the-art facilities, using lighting, sound, trap doors, and special effects to create the show's rich imagery.

Ironically, some believe the apparitions who visit Scrooge each year aren't the only ghosts to haunt the Mo. Rep. In 1957, a former Broadway actress died of a heart attack in the lobby of the now-demolished University Playhouse, the company's previous location. Unexplained events and unusual noises on the Spencer stage lead many to believe the actress' ghost still performs for the Kansas City troupe.

---

ago, Starlight Theatre symbolized the revival of legitimate theater in Kansas City. Today, it's one of only two professional, self-producing outdoor theaters in America. The theater, set in the midst of 1,700-acre Swope Park, has concentrated largely on Broadway shows and national concert attractions during its summertime season. Recent productions have included *Evita, Little Shop of Horrors,* and *Guys and Dolls.*

THEATRE IN THE PARK
7799 Renner Rd., Lenexa
913/831-3355   JO
Every summer, Shawnee Mission Park hosts a variety of outdoor musicals in its amphitheater. All locally cast and directed, the plays often include full-scale Broadway-style productions. Recent performances have included *Damn Yankees, Alice in Wonderland,* and *The King and I.* Performances begin after dark, at 8:30 p.m.

THEATER LEAGUE
301 W. 13th St., Kansas City
816/421-7500   DA
Set in downtown's sumptuous Music Hall, the Theater League sponsors professional touring companies that focus on big-production musicals, both new plays and revivals. Recent stage shows have included *Kiss of the Spider Woman, Smokey Joe's Café,* and *West Side Story.*

UNICORN THEATRE
3820 Main St., Kansas City
816/531-7529   CS
The Unicorn has made a name for itself throughout the region for producing more daring plays. Set in an intimate midtown theater, the small Equity company specializes in adventurous off-Broadway plays and original work. Recent productions have included *At the Feet of Doves* by local playwright Ron Simonian; the first two works in the *Angels in Amer-*

ica series; and *Keely and Du,* a drama emotionally portraying both sides of the abortion issue.

CLASSICAL MUSIC AND OPERA

FRIENDS OF CHAMBER MUSIC
4643 Wyandotte, Suite 201, Kansas City
816/561-9999   DA

During its 18-concert season, the Friends of Chamber music imports a variety of established and new chamber music artists from around the globe to play at the Folly Theater in downtown Kansas City. Running from fall to spring, the Friends' series have included such recent guests as the Melos String Quartet, the Amsterdam Baroque Orchestra and Choir, and the Ying String Quartet.

KANSAS CITY CAMERATA
4949 Cherry, Kansas City
816/235-2700   CS

Founded in 1991, the Kansas City Camerata now plays seven concerts during its annual September- to-May

The Folly Theater, page 199

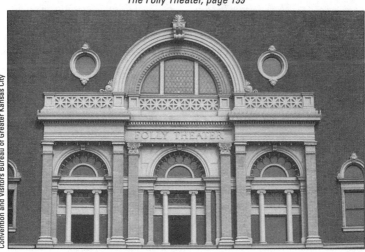

Convention and Visitors Bureau of Greater Kansas City

season. The well-respected group performs a classic repertoire, from eighteenth- and nineteenth-century masterpieces to unusual and contemporary music. Most performances are held at Unity Temple on the Plaza (708 W. 47th St., Kansas City); recent soloists have included cellist Allison Eldredge, pianist/conductor Shuang Guo, and violinist Ben Sayevich.

KANSAS CITY CHAMBER ORCHESTRA
11 E. 40th St., Kansas City
816/960-1324   JO
During its five-concert season, the Kansas City Chamber Orchestra provides first-rate small-ensemble music at the acoustically appealing Yardley Hall at Johnson County Community College and the Old Mission United Methodist Church at Shawnee Mission Parkway and Mission Road. Recent series include "Mozart Mania" and "Baroque by Candlelight" featuring pieces by Handel, Scarlatti, and Telemann.

KANSAS CITY CHORALE
201 Westport Rd., Kansas City
816/931-7669   CS
The Kansas City Chorale is a 22-voice professional chorus that not long ago became the first United States singing ensemble to appear on Great Britain's Nimbus record label. Holding several concerts each season at churches around the metro area, the Chorale has recently performed

pieces by Brahms, Mozart, and a world premiere of a work by local composer Jean Belmont.

KANSAS CITY SYMPHONY
1020 Central, Suite 300, Kansas City
816/471-0400   DA
After a decade, Kansas City Symphony Maestro Bill McGlaughlin recently announced that his departure will follow the 1997–98 season, which may mean the symphony could undergo some changes. Under McGlaughlin's direction, the symphony—which was launched in 1982—plays 12 concerts in its annual Classical Series between September and May. In addition, a seven-concert NightLights Pops Series teamed the orchestra with major jazz, country, and pop artists. McGlaughlin also developed the Family Series and Casual Concerts, three each, for people learning to appreciate classical music. Highlights of the 1996–97 season: Marvin Hamlisch guesting in a NightLights concert and Itzhak Perlman performing Beethoven's Violin Concerto at the Truman Anniversary Concert on May 5, 1997.

LYRIC OPERA OF KANSAS CITY
1029 Central, Kansas City
816/471-7344   DA
The oldest performing-arts organization in Kansas City, the Lyric Opera stages four operas each season in its 1,642-seat Lyric Theatre. Dedicated to promoting American artists and works, the Lyric also believes in

Top Ten Classical Favorites Played by the Kansas City Symphony

by Tiberius Klausner,
concertmaster of the Kansas City Symphony

1. Beethoven's Symphony No. 5
2. Brahms' Symphony No. 1
3. Elgar's The Enigma Variations
4. Mahler's Symphony No. 1
5. Mendelssohn's Symphony No. 4 ("Italian")
6. Mozart's Symphony No. 41 ("Jupiter")
7. Mussorgsky's Pictures at an Exhibition
8. Schumann's Symphony No. 4
9. Shostakovich's Symphony No. 5
10. Verdi's Requiem

opera as theater, to be sung in English. Recent productions have included *The Marriage of Figaro, La Boheme,* and *H.M.S. Pinafore.*

RLDS TEMPLE & AUDITORIUM
River & Walnut, Independence
816/833-1000 **EM**
The world headquarters of the Reorganized Church of Jesus Christ of Latter Day Saints features two outstanding organs that are frequently shared with the community. During summer, staff organists give free concerts at 3 p.m. on Sundays. The rest of the year, the RLDS invites musicians to stage concerts on the Auditorium's 110-rank, 6,000-pipe organ and on the Temple's 102-rank pipe organ. Recent concerts have included Brahms' *Requiem,* the Durufle and Faure Requiems, and the annual performance of Handel's *Messiah.*

UMKC CONSERVATORY OF MUSIC
4949 Cherry, Kansas City
816/235-2700 **CS**

The acclaimed Conservatory of Music at the University of Missouri–Kansas City holds more than 350 concerts annually, both by students and professionals. The Conservatory offers graduate programs in orchestral and solo instruments as well as voice, and many students perform regularly for the public at White Recital Hall in the Center for Performing Arts. Recent concerts have included Mike Parkinson and the Conservatory Jazz Orchestra; faculty cellist Nina Gordon; and the Musica Nova/Dance.

WILLIAM JEWELL COLLEGE FINE ARTS PROGRAM
William Jewell College, Liberty
816/781-8250 **DA**
Not solely an educational institution, William Jewell College also sponsors a nationally recognized arts series that features nearly two dozen productions a year. Major performers, from vocal groups to orchestras to dance companies and theater troupes, travel to

T|I|P

Every summer, the State Ballet of Missouri stages its free Balletomania throughout the metro region. Performances are held outdoors at places such as Powell Gardens, Loose Park, and Crown Center Square. Check the *Kansas City Star* for times and places in late August and early September or call 816/931-2232.

Kansas City as part of the program, playing primarily at downtown's Music Hall or Folly Theater. Recent performances have included pianist André Watts, the Bolshoi Ballet Ensemble, and The Acting Company in *Arms and the Man.*

DANCE

CITY IN MOTION DANCE THEATER
700 W. Pennway, Kansas City
816/472-7828 **DA**
The founders of this experimental dance company renovated an old brick church near downtown, then put together a company that performs an annual series. Local choreographers and dancers are in the spotlight here; concerts are energetic and fun.

KANSAS CITY FRIENDS OF ALVIN AILEY
201 Wyandotte, Kansas City
816/471-6003 **DA**
Kansas City is the second home of the Alvin Ailey American Dance Theatre. Each fall, the Kansas City Friends of Alvin Ailey host the New York–based company in a two-week residency. The lively dance troupe holds public performances at the Midland Theatre and conducts in-school programs throughout the area.

STATE BALLET OF MISSOURI
706 W. 42nd St., Kansas City
816/931-2232 **CS**
The only fully professional ballet company in Missouri, the State Ballet of Missouri performs both classical and contemporary works during its three-program season each year. The Ballet recently acquired a new director, after 15 years under Todd Bolender. Already, William Whitener—who's worked with the Joffrey Ballet and Twyla Tharp—has brought his own perspective to performances at the Midland. Recent concerts include "Night Shadow (*La Sonnambula*)," "Souvenirs," and "Western Symphony."

WESTPORT BALLET THEATRE
3936 Main St., Kansas City
816/531-4330 **CS**
The Westport Ballet Theatre has become famous for its outdoor performances in Midtown during the summer. A mix of professional dancers and students, the Westport Ballet schedules dancing al fresco at the Westport Marketplace, 41st and Pennsylvania. Last summer's program included George Balanchine's "Tarantella," a romantic dance suite inspired by Gershwin, and a newly commissioned jazz selection. The group also showcases its talents in concerts at the Folly Theater.

Kansas City Symphony, page 196

CONCERT VENUES

FOLLY THEATER
**12th and Central Sts.,
Kansas City**
816/474-4444   **DA**

The Folly was not the first theater built in Kansas City but it happens to be the oldest one still standing downtown. Now this painstakingly restored neo-Palladian burlesque house features a variety of theater and concerts on stage. Placed on the National Register of Historic Places, the Folly is home to the Folly Jazz series, the Friends of Chamber Music series, the William Jewell Fine Arts Program, and many other events.

JOHNSON COUNTY COMMUNITY COLLEGE
12345 College Blvd., Overland Park
913/469-4445   **JO**

The college's 1,400-seat Yardley Hall provides a welcoming venue for arts groups such as the symphony and chamber music ensembles, but JCCC holds its own performing-arts series, too. Performances have included notables such as pianist Michael Wolf,

humorist Mark Russell, and the musical *Zorba.*

KEMPER ARENA
1800 Genessee St., Kansas City
816/421-6460   **DA**

Although primarily a sporting venue—hosting everything from the NCAA basketball finals to the American

TRIVIA

The Folly Theater was erected at the turn of the century as one of the more than ten legitimate theaters in town. Like the others, it regressed from vaudeville to burlesque over the years. It remained standing even after theater's "golden era" ended in the 1920s. In the early Eighties, the Folly underwent a $4-million renovation when interest in theater and historic preservation resurged.

Don't even think of trying to sneak food or alcohol into Sandstone Amphitheatre. Coolers are not allowed, and meticulous guards check backpacks, bags, and purses.

Royal Barbecue & Rodeo— the 16,300-seat Kemper also offers concerts and other events. Set southwest of downtown in the West Bottoms, Kemper has recently been visited by Eric Clapton, bluesman extraordinaire and onetime member of the legendary Yardbirds and Cream; AC/DC, the scorch-the-earth rock group with hits including "Highway to Hell" and "Money Talks"; and the Ice Capades.

MIDLAND THEATRE
1228 Main, Kansas City
816/471-8600 DA
This elegantly ornate facility was built for $4 million in 1927 by Loew's as a movie theater, marking a new day for moving pictures. Now, several performing-arts groups hold their events in the 2,800-seat venue, including the Friends of Alvin Ailey and the State Ballet of Missouri. This stunning building is now listed on the National Register.

MUSIC HALL
1310 Wyandotte St., Kansas City
816/274-2900 DA
Located within Municipal Auditorium, this art deco masterpiece hosts a variety of fine arts programs. Originally opened in 1936—in the midst of the Depression—the Music Hall was recently restored. Anyone who appreciates architecture should notice the rotunda above the grand staircase; the building's light fixtures were the inspiration for the new *Sky Stations* atop Bartle Hall's pylons next door.

SANDSTONE AMPHITHEATRE
633 N. 130th St., Bonner Springs
913/721-3400 KCK
Located west of town in Bonner Springs, Sandstone is a natural amphitheater with 6,700 permanent seats. Terraced lawns add space for another 11,000 fans. From April through October, top recording acts perform under the stars. Past performances have included Bonnie Raitt, Phil Collins, and Chicago.

BUYING TICKETS

Nearly every performing-arts group in Kansas City sells tickets through their own box office (see listings for phone numbers). In addition, Ticketmaster sells tickets to most major events in the area (phone 816/931-3330).

American Heartland Theatre, page 191

Convention and Visitors Bureau of Greater Kansas City

Convention and Visitors Bureau of Greater Kansas City

12

It's understandable that Kansas City has an active nightlife scene. This is, after all, the place where jazz and blues greats such as Charlie "Yardbird" Parker, Count Basie, and Joe Turner jammed their ways through numberless late-night sessions. These days, Kansas City has no less to offer. From hole-in-the-wall saloons where you can swill $1 bottles of beer to sophisticated cabarets serving vodka martinis and highbrow music, from two-step taverns to rock 'n' roll-eramas—the Kansas City metro area gives night owls multiple ways to unwind in style. Note: The map in this chapter shows the location of all Central/South Kansas City night spots.

DANCE CLUBS

BLAYNEY'S
415 Westport Rd., Kansas City
816/561-3747 CS
Blayney's loves its live music, and its clientele appreciate the club's eclectic approach. Each night, the Westport tavern features a different musical style, from reggae to rock to rhythm and blues. Blayney's even spotlights jazz and blues in its intimate location. Bands have included The Nace Brothers, Jhamm, and Tequila Mockingbird, as well as the Roland Allen Blues Jam and K.C. Brass and Electric. Mon–Sat till 3 a.m. Covers vary.

EPICUREAN LOUNGE
7502 Troost, Kansas City
816/333-8383 CS
The Epicurean draws a rousing group of regulars to dance to both live and recorded music. In addition, the lounge has become a magnet for local musicians who want to test their talents in regular jam sessions. Hosting a largely African American crowd, the Epicurean has been a long-time success on Troost Avenue. Mon–Sat 5 p.m.–2 a.m.; closed Sun. $5 cover at 7 p.m.

KIKI'S BON TON MAISON
1515 Westport Rd., Kansas City

CENTRAL/SOUTH KANSAS CITY

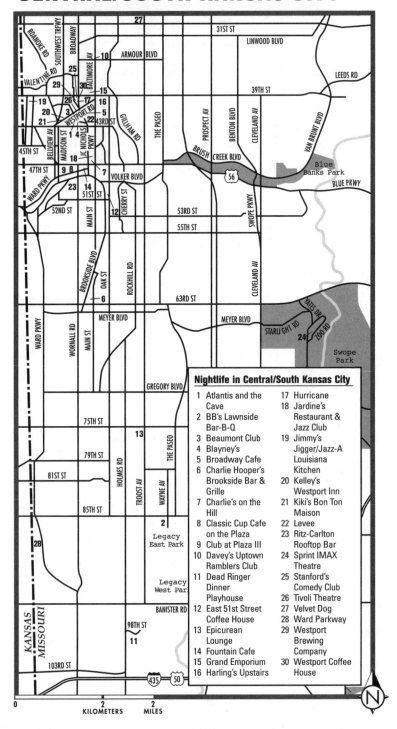

Nightlife in Central/South Kansas City

1. Atlantis and the Cave
2. BB's Lawnside Bar-B-Q
3. Beaumont Club
4. Blayney's
5. Broadway Cafe
6. Charlie Hooper's Brookside Bar & Grille
7. Charlie's on the Hill
8. Classic Cup Cafe on the Plaza
9. Club at Plaza III
10. Davey's Uptown Ramblers Club
11. Dead Ringer Dinner Playhouse
12. East 51st Street Coffee House
13. Epicurean Lounge
14. Fountain Cafe
15. Grand Emporium
16. Harling's Upstairs
17. Hurricane
18. Jardine's Restaurant & Jazz Club
19. Jimmy's Jigger/Jazz-A Louisiana Kitchen
20. Kelley's Westport Inn
21. Kiki's Bon Ton Maison
22. Levee
23. Ritz-Carlton Rooftop Bar
24. Sprint IMAX Theatre
25. Stanford's Comedy Club
26. Tivoli Theatre
27. Velvet Dog
28. Ward Parkway
29. Westport Brewing Company
30. Westport Coffee House

816/931-9417 CS

Get ready for a Cajun party at Kiki's, where the house band is the Bon Ton Soul Accordion Band. This Louisiana-style restaurant was opened by Richard and Kiki Lucente back in 1987 so that Kiki could cook and Richard could play his wild Cajun music. It's been a rollicking good time ever since. Restaurant opens daily for lunch and dinner; music Wed 9:30–midnight and Sat nights 10:30–1.

LAND OF OZ
5648 State Ave.,
Kansas City, Kansas
913/287-8686 KCK

This brightly colored building on the western edge of Kansas City, Kansas, serves up everything from country to salsa to ballroom dancing. As for food, you'll find a barbecue drive-through, all-you-can-eat taco nights, a 6 p.m. buffet, and karaoke nights. Did we say brightly colored? Look for a teal exterior with purple doors and pink, yellow, and green flags. Oh, and there's a painted mural on the side, too. Call for current schedule.

THE LEVEE
16 W. 43rd St., Kansas City
816/561-2821 CS

The Levee's a fun neighborhood bar whose regular band, Hothouse, plays highly danceable tunes, from Sixties and Seventies favorites to more recent rock 'n' roll. Set in a wood-frame building northeast of the Country Club Plaza, the Levee also books guest artists like Boko Maru, The Bidets, and Camp Harlow. The outdoor deck is popular in warm weather. Open nightly until 1 a.m. Closed Sundays.

OLDE MILL BALLROOM
168 S. Main, Parkville

816/505-2300 NR

Ballroom dancing seems to be experiencing a mini-comeback—at least in Parkville at the Olde Mill Ballroom. Don Hoagland and his band provide the tunes for ballroom dances such as the fox trot, tango, and rumba on Friday nights and Sunday afternoons. $6.

MUSIC CLUBS

Jazz

For information on who's playing around town, call the Kansas City Jazz Ambassadors Hotline, 816/753-5277.

CLUB 427
427 Main St., Kansas City
816/421-2582 DA

Open since July 1995, Club 427 has quickly become one of the city's best jazz venues. The upscale club—which also serves a delicious menu of fish, pastas, and salads—has provided a winning showcase for local jazz talent such as Steve Miller, Karrin Allyson, and the Pat Morrissey Trio. The restaurant's open Mon–Sat; live music Tue–Sat 6:30–11.

CLUB MARDI GRAS
1600 E. 19th St., Kansas City
816/842-8463 DA

One of the notorious music haunts in the historic 18th & Vine District, Club Mardi Gras still contributes an irresistible locale for upcoming jazz and blues talent to play together. Some of the musicians at Club Mardi Gras include King Alex & the Untouchables, Everette DeVan, and the Tim Perryman Quintet. Mon–Thur 4–midnight; Fri–Sat till 1; closed Sun.

THE CLUB AT PLAZA III
4749 Pennsylvania, Kansas City

Kansas City skyline at night

816/753-0000 **CS**
Beneath the venerable Plaza III steakhouse lurks a jammin' spot for jazz geniuses. Previously called the City Light Jazz Club, this spot attracts both national acts and local artists. Performers have included everyone from saxophonist Bobby Watson and pianist Henry Butler to vocalist Queen Bey and ensemble David Basse & the City Light Orchestra. Wed–Sat 6–midnight; music Wed–Thur 7–11 and Fri–Sat 8:30–12:30.

THE ELBOW ROOM CAFE
7820 Quivira, Lenexa
913/268-6466 **JO**
Set in a suburban shopping center, The Elbow Room surprises with its casually elegant style. Those eating lunch or dinner will find a variety of selections including stuffed beef tenderloin, rosemary-scented pork loin, and rack of lamb. On Mondays and Tuesdays, The Elbow Room offers live jazz duos featuring the likes of Charlie Gatschet, Bryan Hicks, Bob Bowman, Rod Fleeman, Steve Swanson, and Mike Metheny. The

Elbow Room is open Mon–Thur 11–10; Fri 11–11:30; Sat 4:30–11:30.

IVY'S RESTAURANT & JAZZ CLUB
240 N.E. Barry, Kansas City
816/436-3320 **NR**
Ivy's is the place for live jazz in the Northland. Owners Sam and Carol Cross have recently redesigned both the restaurant and the club, and have increased the number of nights patrons can enjoy Kansas City jazz. Ivy's now offers live jazz on Thursdays, Fridays, and Saturdays featuring talent that includes Angela Hagenbach, Dave Stephens, and Russ Long. Reservations are recommended. Music Thur 6–10; Fri–Sat 8–midnight.

JARDINE'S RESTAURANT &
JAZZ CLUB
4536 Main St., Kansas City
816/561-6480 **CS**
Jardine's has emerged as a hot jazz spot in Kansas City, where noted local musicians such as Karrin Allyson, Mike Metheny, and Lisa Henry perform regularly. At Jardine's you can hear live jazz as many as

Ten Best Jazz Venues in the Kansas City Area

by Vanessa Barnard,
president of the Jazz Ambassadors, a local nonprofit organization dedicated to the support of local jazz

1. **Club 427**. Newest addition to Kansas City's jazz scene. Top entertainment with wonderful acoustics, great food, and a New York–style atmosphere in the historic River Market area.

2. **The Phoenix Piano Bar & Grill**. Hot spot for the after-work downtown crowd with music continuing into the night. Good bar-type food. The place to see and be seen.

3. **Club Mardi Gras**. On the corner of 19th and Vine in the original jazz district, this club has been the home of all the jazz greats such as Charlie Parker and Count Basie. The history (and the ghosts) live on.

4. **Jardine's**. Best late-night jam session on Friday and Saturday nights (until 3). Fabulous food, and the music is smokin' with musicians.

5. **Mutual Musicians Foundation**. Best late-late-night jam session in the historic jazz district. Open to the public on Saturday nights, the jam session begins around midnight and lasts until . . . Come ready to party until sunrise and hear the best Kansas City has to offer.

6. **Jazz-A Louisiana Kitchen**. Spicy Cajun food, mixed with some of the hottest bands in town delivers a winning combination. Live music Wednesday through Sunday. Prepare to eat, drink, and dance in a fantastic and fun New Orleans setting.

7. The **Kansas City Blues & Jazz Festival**, Penn Valley Park. Held the third weekend in July, this is simply the best. Featuring three days of live local and the biggest names in national blues and jazz acts. One of the finest festivals you'll find across the country.

8. **18th & Vine Jazz Heritage Festival**. Held the third weekend of August, this weekend-long festival offers some of the best local and national talent free of charge to the public.

9. **The Club at Plaza III**. Restaurant upstairs and intimate jazz club downstairs. Food also served in the club. Wonderful steaks, romantic atmosphere, and some of the greatest talent in jazz around.

10. **Annual Jazz Lovers Pub Crawl**. Held each year in June, Kansas City crawls to approximately 20 clubs around town. Transportation is provided by bus, and a one-time admission fee allows access to all the clubs. One of the year's best events designed to kick off the summer jazz season, sponsored by the Kansas City Jazz Ambassadors.

seven nights a week, plus sit in on several weekly jams. Drummer Tommy Ruskin hosts a jam every Saturday afternoon from 3 to 6. No cover, an eclectic menu, and a cozy jazz-club ambience.

JOHN'S FOOD & DRINK
928 Wyandotte, Kansas City
816/474-5668 DA
As long as the weather's nice—from March through October—this downtown establishment offers live music on John's Big Deck, otherwise known as the roof. It makes for an amiable live-music venue, and features some get-down blues musicians, such as Blue 88, Terry Hancock, and Fast Johnny. Wed–Thur 6–11; Fri–Sat 9–2.

MUTUAL MUSICIAN'S FOUNDATION
1823 Highland, Kansas City
816/471-5212 DA

TOP TEN TOP TEN

Top Ten Song Requests in Kansas City
by Tim Whitmer,
popular Kansas City jazz pianist and bandleader who plays regularly at The Phoenix.

1. Kansas City
2. What a Wonderful World
3. Route 66
4. Let the Good Times Roll
5. Georgia
6. When the Saints Go Marching In
7. In the Mood
8. All of Me
9. Unforgettable
10. St. Louis Blues

Set in the historic 18th & Vine District, the Mutual Musicians Foundation is a living shrine to jazz history. Designated a National Historic Landmark in 1981, the foundation was where Charlie Parker, Jay McShann, and other jazz legends got started. These days, the foundation packs in fans for weekend after-hours jazz jams. Music starts around midnight on Fridays and Saturdays and can go until dawn, depending upon who shows up to play. The foundation can also arrange pub crawls for people who want to hear authentic jazz in locales throughout the Kansas City area.

PHOENIX PIANO BAR & GRILL
302 W. 8th St., Kansas City
816/472-0001 DA
The cozy Phoenix is a relaxing neighborhood pub with big-name musical talent. The affable Tim Whitmer and his K.C. Express often hold the stage, but the Phoenix hosts other talented musicians, too. The Max Groove Band, Dave Stephens' Martini Bash, and the Toni Oliver Quartet play here, and other entertaining jam sessions take place as well. Local entertainers often head to the Phoenix for their own record-release parties. Music Mon–Sat until 1 a.m. Closed Sundays.

Blues

BB'S LAWNSIDE BAR-B-Q
1205 E. 85th St., Kansas City
816/822-7427 CS
One of Kansas City's unique barbecue joints sits in a ramshackle roadhouse on the south side of town. There, blues lover Lindsay Shannon and his wife, Jo, opened BB's Lawnside Bar-B-Q, a restaurant that combines their passionate interests in blues and barbecue. A founder of the Kansas City Blues Society, Lindsay

owns more than 5,000 recordings and presents a weekly blues radio show. Wednesday through Saturday nights at BB's, blues artists such as Bill Laursen, Little Hatch, and the Lonnie Ray Blues Band keep the music alive.

GRAND EMPORIUM
3832 Main St., Kansas City
816/531-1504 CS
The Grand Emporium has gained a national reputation among blues cognoscenti—and rightfully so. The loud, smoky club has hosted the likes of John Lee Hooker, Koko Taylor, and B.B. King. But the Grand Emporium's excursions into jazz, alternative rock, and world music have been successful, too. Featuring nightly performances, the Grand Emporium has hosted everyone from Marcus Roberts to El Vez & his Memphis Mariachi Band. Cover charges vary depending on the artist.

HARLING'S UPSTAIRS
3941 Main St., Kansas City
816/531-0303 CS
Originally a blues venue, Harling's

Upstairs also strays into alternative and world music, especially of the Irish variety. Every Saturday afternoon, a blues jam session heats up the joint. Harling's hosts artists such as Eddie Delahunt, Mama Ray & Rich Van Sant Band, and Ceili's Muse. Music most Wed–Sat.

QUINCY'S
I-70 at Sports Complex, Kansas City
816/737-4719 EM
Located in the Adam's Mark Hotel, near the Truman Sports Complex, Quincy's attracts an impressive roster of talented artists. A small club frequented both by residents and visitors, Quincy's roster includes popular blues crooner Ida McBeth, the get-down-and-have-fun Scamps, and the rocking group Retro. Mon–Fri 4:30–3; Sat–Sun 7:30–3.

THE ROXY
7230 W. 75th St., Overland Park
913/236-6211 JO
On Sundays, The Roxy features an open blues jam with the BWB band that many consider to be one of the best groups of its kind. Guest

The J.C. Nichols Fountain on the Plaza at night

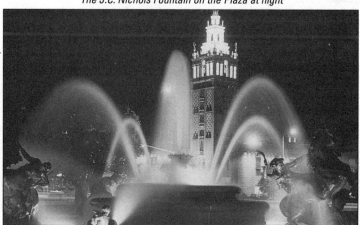

Convention and Visitors Bureau of Greater Kansas City

performers at The Roxy have included Albert Flasher, Charlie & the Stingrays, and No Parking. A dance floor and three pool tables add extra activities to the roster. Nightly 10:30–1:30.

Rock

ATLANTIS AND THE CAVE
3954 Central, Kansas City
816/753-0112 CS
Young party animals head to this two-bars-in-one complex. Atlantis offers Top 40 dance music and, with 160-plus video screens, the largest light and video show in the region. The Cave features live bands in an underground, cave-like atmosphere. Wed–Sat 9–3. Thur $1 drinks.

DAVEY'S UPTOWN RAMBLERS CLUB
3402 Main, Kansas City
816/753-1909 CS
They say this unobtrusive joint was once the hangout of corrupt politicians who gathered in the back room to hammer out deals. These days, though, the club hosts a wide mix of groups including Tuesday in Stone, Bubble Boys, Puddle of Mudd, Reverb Brothers, and In a Sick Way. Live music every night but Sunday.

THE HURRICANE
4048 Broadway, Kansas City
816/753-0884 CS
One of the most popular places in town, The Hurricane features everything from alternative rock bands to solo acoustic guitarists. Popular artists have included the likes of Tina & the B Side, Big Rude Jake, Molotov Grasshopper, Jason & the Scorchers, and Pamper the Madman. Music five to six nights a week; open nightly until 3.

NIENER'S BAR & GRILL
815 N. Noland Rd., Independence
816/461-6955 EM
A popular spot for local rock bands, as well as traveling rock 'n' roll acts, Niener's attracts groups like Synergy, Joker, and Unit. The Independence club also hosts frequent open jam sessions, where musicians gather to collaborate on classic and new rock songs.

Country and Western

THE BEAUMONT CLUB
4050 Pennsylvania, Kansas City
816/561-2668 CS
Music at this Westport club tends to be recorded but that doesn't stop the two-steppers who fill the largest wooden dance floor in the city. A mechanical bull ride and lots of special events, from boxing matches to dance contests, keep Beaumonters busy.

GUITARS & CADILLACS
11950 S. Strang Line Rd., Olathe
913/829-8200 JO
Country's the usual gig at Guitars & Cadillacs, but the Olathe club sometimes hosts touring groups from other genres. The dance floor is ample enough to allow for line dancing as well as partners. The bar's actually a private club, but memberships are available.

PUBS AND BARS

BONNIE LYNN'S
6825 N. Oak, Gladstone
816/436-0070 NR
At Bonnie Lynn's you'll find a no-nonsense kind of place that features nightly themes, from old country to karaoke to rock 'n' roll on weekends.

The Phoenix Piano Bar & Grill, page 206

Food runs the gamut, too, from all-you-can-eat catfish to Mexican and spaghetti. Two pool tables, jukeboxes, and darts give the active plenty to do.

CHARLIE HOOPER'S BROOKSIDE BAR & GRILLE
12 W. 63rd St., Kansas City
816/361-8841 CS
If you want an obscure European imported beer, you'll likely find it at Hooper's. A convivial neighborhood bar in Brookside, Hooper's features 35 different kinds of beer on tap and another 140 bottled varieties, as well as other drinks and a grill menu.

JIMMY'S JIGGER/JAZZ-A LOUISIANA KITCHEN
1823 W. 39th St., Kansas City
816/561-7977 CS
On the southeast corner of State Line Road and 39th Street, Jimmy's Jigger has long attracted everyone from blue-collar workers to medical students who walk across the street from the University of Kansas Medical Center. Jazz-A Louisiana Kitchen

bought into the Jigger and brought some of the area's most notable live music to the mix.

KELLY'S WESTPORT INN
Westport Rd. at Pennsylvania Ave., Kansas City
816/753-9193 CS
This long, narrow tavern occupies the oldest building in Kansas City. Here, a new drawing, sign, or handbill tacked over the old is considered a major change in decor. Once the site of an outfitter serving the Santa Fe Trail, Kelly's is famous for its flowing booze, no-frills atmosphere, and its extremely devoted crowds.

LIQUID LOUNGE
333 Southwest Blvd., Kansas City
816/421-6888 DA
Neon greets you, both outside and in at the Liquid Lounge. A true happy-hour club in an old brick storefront near downtown, the lounge serves no meals, but does provide live music several nights a week. On Saturdays, alternating bands play jazz, blues, and rock.

Count Basie, page 201

How many different martinis are there? At the swanky, Forties-style Velvet Dog, you'll find a total of 16. The club attracts an after-work, Midtown yuppie crowd eager to try a new cocktail concoction and the Dog's eclectic Italian fare.

WESTPORT BREWING COMPANY
4057 Pennsylvania, Kansas City
816/931-2739   CS
A decidedly younger crowd fills the Westport Brewing Company to the rafters. The club features nightly events such as discount drinks on Tuesdays, disco tunes on Wednesdays, and discounted drinks and munchies for women on Thursdays. Dancing after 10 p.m.

Drinks with a View

CHARLIE'S ON THE HILL
4558 Main St., Kansas City
816/931-3400   CS
The restaurant has changed hands recently, and the food here has improved. In addition, Charlie's sports a back deck with a killer view of the Country Club Plaza.

CLASSIC CUP CAFE ON THE PLAZA
301 W. 47th St., Kansas City
816/753-1840   CS
The Classic Cup surrounded its deck with a high wooden fence, then filled the space with umbrella-topped tables. The expanse attracts a see-and-be-seen sort of crowd.

FOUNTAIN CAFE
102 W. 47th St., Kansas City
816/561-0066   CS
During warm weather, the Fountain Cafe's rooftop deck provides an arbored, European ambiance. The view of the J.C. Nichols fountain, the

NORTH KANSAS CITY BAR & GRILL
1613 Swift, North Kansas City
816/421-4332   NR
The North Kansas City Bar & Grill is the epitome of the neighborhood pub, supplying juicy burgers, a pool table, juke box, and video games to its diverse and loyal crowd. The motto: "If you're not here to have fun, you'd better go somewhere else."

THE QUAFF
1010 Broadway, Kansas City
816/471-1918   DA
Downtown workers gather here after a hard day to belly up to the long bar and order a burger. The Quaff is also near Quality Hill, a renewed residential area for urban pioneers, and a number of loft developments that attract those who long for life near the heart of the big city.

THE VELVET DOG
400 E. 31st St., Kansas City
816/753-9990   CS

Convention and Visitors Bureau of Greater Kansas City

Giralda tower, and general Plaza passersby is stunning. Live music on weekends.

RITZ-CARLTON ROOFTOP BAR
401 Ward Pkwy., Kansas City
816/756-1500   CS
Even the elevator up to the Rooftop Bar affords a magnificent view of the Country Club Plaza just to the north. The atmosphere here ranges from chic to Brooks Brothers. Live music nightly in the Rooftop Restaurant next door.

COFFEEHOUSES

BROADWAY CAFE
4106 Broadway, Kansas City
816/531-2432   CS
Owned and operated by a twentysomething entrepreneur, the Broadway Cafe was one of the first coffeehouses in the area. Its sidewalk is a favorite hangout during warm weather months.

EAST 51ST STREET COFFEE HOUSE
318 E. 51st St., Kansas City
816/756-3121   CS
This coffeehouse is near the UMKC campus, offering delicious pastries

with its java. In addition, the spot hosts a weekly songwriters' circle and one-person local acts. The bar offers beer on tap and wine as well.

JAVA CUP COFFEE HOUSE
9637 W. 87th St., Overland Park
913/385-5282   JO
Retired microbiologist Lisa Lim opened this coffeehouse in the summer of 1995, offering bagels, sandwiches, and quiche with her coffee. On Saturday afternoons, members of the Kansas City Symphony provide live classical music.

WESTPORT COFFEE HOUSE
4010 Pennsylvania, Kansas City
816/756-3222   CS
In addition to a tasty bean and brew, the Westport features open jazz and blues jams, classical guitar lunches, and performances from groups like the Midtown Jazz Quartet.

COMEDY CLUBS

THE COMEDY CLUB AT OVERLAND PARK
6920 W. 105th St., Overland Park
913/385-5653   JO
This club, located in the Metcalf 103 Shopping Center, brings in national

Who appears regularly in Kansas City area dinner theaters? Frequent performers include Don Knotts of *The Andy Griffith Show*, Jamie Farr from *M*A*S*H*, Marion Ross of *Happy Days*, and Elinor Donahue from *Father Knows Best*.

comedians while providing a place for rising local comics. Acts that have hit the Overland Park venue include James Inman from Seattle; Mark Gross, who's been on *Comedy Central;* and Hank McGill, winner of the Jay Leno Comedy Search. Sun–Thur 8 p.m. $7; Fri–Sat 7:30 and 9:45 $9.

KANSAS CITY COMEDYSPORTZ
512 Delaware St., Kansas City
816/842-2744   DA

Like the popular British TV show *Whose Line is it Anyway?* Kansas City ComedySportz relies on audience participation for its improvisational theater. Quick-thinking, athletically minded comedy teams must deliver their on-the-spot humor within a set time, then the audience acts as judges. ComedyCourtz sets the show in a courtroom. Wed–Sat; various times. Adults $10; seniors and students $8 on select performances.

LIGHTEN UP IMPROVISATION COMPANY
323 W. 8th St., Kansas City
816/474-4386   DA

Another downtown improv company, Lighten Up stages a variety of performances. The company's "Play It by Ear" sessions start with audience-suggested topics; "Theatresports" pits two teams against each other; and "Outside the Lines" features improvisational comedy with no rules and no scripts. Fri–Sat; times and prices vary. Call for details.

STANFORD'S COMEDY CLUB
504 Westport Rd., Kansas City
816-753-1450   CS

Kansas City's first comedy club has recently returned to its original location, above the restaurant with the same name. The club brings in a variety of touring acts, from Frankie Bastille to Tommy Chong, and also holds an open-mike night every Monday. Nightly. $6 during the week; $9 weekends.

DINNER THEATERS

DEAD RINGER DINNER PLAYHOUSE
99th and Holmes, Kansas City
816/789-7529   CS

One of the newest dinner theaters in Kansas City, Dead Ringer combines its dramatic performances with the all-American fare at Sherlock's Steakhouse. Recent plays have included *Ouija Board to Death* and *Frosty the Hitman*. Possible 1997 productions include *Ice Scream of Genie* and *Star Trek: The Next Incineration*. $35 inclusive.

MYSTERY CAPERS DINNER PLAYHOUSE
7148 W. 80th St., Overland Park
913/454-3340   JO

The entertaining Mystery Capers Dinner Playhouse holds forth during its season at the Italian eatery Tony Ferrara's Restaurant, whose pasta specialties have become legendary. Recent productions have included *Buried to the Mob* and *Murder Under the Mistletoe*. $37.50 inclusive.

NEW THEATRE RESTAURANT
9229 Foster St., Overland Park
913/649-7469   **JO**

The only year-round, equity theater in Kansas, New Theatre Restaurant has been noted by the *Wall Street Journal* as "the best in their business." The building, erected especially for the theater, includes a revolving stage, a state-of-the-art sound system, and a buffet created by an on-site chef and staff of 15. Some of the most memorable performances at this enjoyable venue have included *You Can't Take it With You* starring Don Knotts and *Never Too Late* with Elinor Donahue, among others. Tue–Sun evenings and some matinees; $17.95–$33.95.

MOVIE HOUSES OF NOTE

With 1,821 screens in 232 theaters in the United States and Japan, Kansas City–based AMC Theatres has become the world's second-largest movie chain. CEO Stan Durwood has tried several new movie-watching ideas on his friends and neighbors in the Midwest, giving the area first crack at a variety of theatrical innovations. Other notable theaters in the area are:

ENGLEWOOD THEATER
10917 E. Winner Rd.,
Independence
816/252-2463   **EM**

The historic Englewood shows movie classics, from *Patton* to *How the West Was Won*.

FINE ARTS THEATRE
5909 Johnson Dr., Mission
913/262-4466   **JO**

An intimate neighborhood theater, the Fine Arts showcases art and independent films. You can rent videos in the front corner of the lobby.

SPRINT IMAX THEATRE
Kansas City Zoo, Kansas City
816/871-4629   **CS**

The screen at this IMAX theater is 50 by 80 feet, about ten times the size of a standard movie screen. The first IMAX located at a zoo, the Sprint IMAX has shown *Special Effects* and *Stormchasers,* among other specially filmed works.

TIVOLI THEATRE
425 Westport Rd., Kansas City
816/756-1030   **CS**

A tiny art house in Westport, the Tivoli has often been the only theater in town showing daring or foreign films. Lines form for favorably reviewed flicks.

TRIVIA

As a young man, Kansas City native Walt Disney rented a tiny studio above a cafe on 31st Street, where he experimented with animation. His Laugh-O-Gram Films made very little money; in fact, his stenographer typed menus for the diner below in exchange for free lunches for the staff. Disney left Kansas City in 1923; his first Mickey Mouse film debuted six years later.

Ten Favorite Places to See a Movie in Kansas City

by Patti Broyles Watkins,
director of the Film Commission of Kansas City, Missouri

1. **IMAX at the Kansas City Zoo**. A great venue right in the zoo in an architecturally splendid setting.

2. **Nelson-Atkins Museum of Art Auditorium**. A place to see experimental film series in a beautiful atmosphere that's free with museum admission.

3. **Plaza Theatre**. A beautiful old theater. I like to sit in the balcony for first-run movies.

4. **Independence 20**. Always a great selection and wonderful high-backed seats with adjustable armrests.

5. **Tivoli**. A small independent-film venue in an intimate setting; like watching with a group of friends.

6. **Fine Arts Theatre**. Always showing smaller art films that may not make it to Kansas City otherwise.

7. **Tivoli Manor Square**. Showcases a wide variety of independent films. Both Tivoli theaters are in Westport, which offers great places to eat and drink for a total movie experience.

8. **Westglen**. Terrific screens, seats, and sound system. Great for pictures with special effects as in *Apollo 13* or *Waterworld.*

9. **Englewood**. Usually shows old movie classics on the big screen. Wooden benches.

10. **Film festivals**. Film Fest Kansas City; Kan Film Festival; Tivoli has several featured series.

WARD PARKWAY
8600 Ward Pkwy., Kansas City
816/333-2046   **CS**
In the 1960s, hometown cinema company AMC Theatres decided to install two screens in the neighborhood Ward Parkway Shopping Center. It was a way for the company to maximize its movie-renting dollar—but it was also the first multiplex in the nation. Now, Ward Parkway features 20 different screens on two levels of the center, while larger and larger multiplexes spring up across the country.

Lawrence Convention and Visitors Bureau

13

DAY TRIPS

Day Trip: Lawrence

Distance from Kansas City: about 45 minutes; 35 miles

Kansas Citians have a soft spot in their hearts for Lawrence because so many of them graduated from the highly regarded **University of Kansas** there. But there's more to it than that: The college town has a decidedly hip atmosphere that's downright magnetic.

Since it's a college town, start at the university, which perches atop **Mount Oread**. Founded in 1866, KU now boasts an enrollment of more than 25,000 students; the institution has been recognized by such publications as *U.S. News & World Report* and *Barron's* for providing a high-quality education at relatively low cost. Moreover, the picturesque campus was noted as one of the nation's most beautiful by architect Thomas Gaines in his book *The Campus as a Work of Art.*

The **Spencer Museum of Art** at KU features 11 well-stocked galleries and is best known for its Asian art, seventeenth- and eighteenth-century European paintings, and nineteenth- and twentieth-century American paintings. In fact, the Spencer is considered one of most comprehensive university art collections in the United States. (Mississippi Street; Tue–Sat 10–5; Thur until 9; Sun noon–5; closed Mon; free.) **Lied Center**, also on the KU campus, is a recently opened $14.3-million multipurpose facility that provides a state-of-the-art setting for concerts, plays, and other performances. You can view the building Mon–Fri 9–5; check local newspapers for events ranging from the National Song and Dance Ensemble of Tibet to *The Sleeping Beauty on Ice* to The Who's *Tommy.*

Such artistic endeavors are only partly why Lawrence was named No. 15 in author John Villani's *The 100 Best Small Art Towns in America* (Santa Fe, N.M.: John Muir Publications, 1996). The town also features venues such as

KANSAS CITY REGION

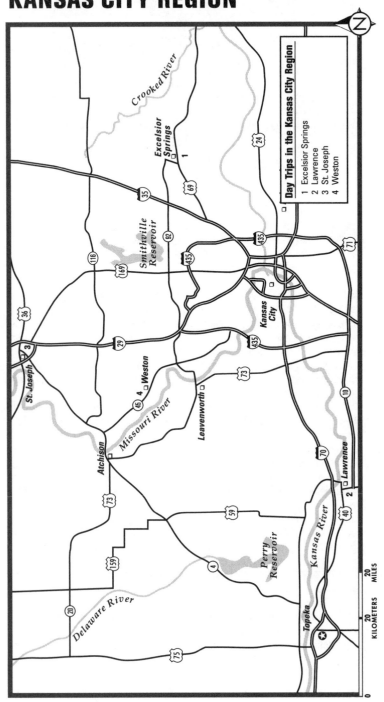

Day Trips in the Kansas City Region

1 Excelsior Springs
2 Lawrence
3 St. Joseph
4 Weston

Crooked River

Excelsior Springs
1

35

69

24

435

435

Smithville Reservoir

92

116

169

71

36

Kansas City

29

435

Weston
4

St. Joseph
3

45

73

10

Leavenworth

Missouri River

Atchison

70

73

Lawrence
2

59

40

159

Perry Reservoir

4

Kansas River

20

Delaware River

Topeka

75

20
MILES

20
KILOMETERS

0

the **Lawrence Arts Center,** housed in the 1904 Carnegie Library building at the corner of 9th and Vermont (Mon–Fri 9–5; Sat 9–3; closed Sun). The Lawrence Art Guild, the annual Indian Art Show, and Roy's Gallery—among other places—also provide ample opportunities to experience art.

Actually, Lawrence's **downtown** is a work of art. A classic main-street setting, Massachusetts between the Kansas River and South Park affords prime strolling opportunities. Antiques shops, funky clothing boutiques, and bookstores sit tooth by jowl with popular hangouts like the **Eldridge Hotel**, which still welcomes guests in its turn-of-the-century rooms; **Teller's,** an Italian restaurant in a restored bank building; and the **Free State Brewery**, one of the first brew pubs in the Midwest, and certainly among the most beloved.

Outdoorsy types will want to try the hiking, biking, and volkswalk trails along the **Kansas River** in Lawrence. Trails snake along a 10-mile stretch on one side of the riverfront and, opposite, along the levee. Other trails wind through town, but remember that Lawrence's hills may leave you puffing. You can get a map showing walkways and bike paths at the Visitors Information Center in the historic Union Pacific Depot (across the river from downtown) or at the Parks and Recreation office at 6 E. 6th St.

Three miles southwest of Lawrence, **Clinton Lake** lures those who want to boat, swim, fish, hike, or camp within its 7,000 acres. The marina at **Clinton State Park** offers complete facilities for boating and fishing, including rentals and licenses (go west on 23rd Street, then follow the signs).

Shoppers will want to know that two factory outlet malls occupy Lawrence.

Robidoux Row Museum, page 221

The older one, **Lawrence Riverfront Factory Outlets**, just north of downtown on the banks of the Kansas River, features some 50 stores, including Bass, Mikasa, and J. Crew. The new mall, **Tanger Factory Outlet Center**, is just south of I-70. Its stores include Adolfo II, Liz Claiborne, and Reebok.

Getting there: You can drive to Lawrence on I-70, or take I-435 in Kansas City then continue west on Highway 10. I-70 becomes a toll road at Bonner Springs, so expect to pay a few dollars if you take that route.

Day Trip: Excelsior Springs

Distance from Kansas City: about 30 minutes; 25 miles
Some folks might say that Excelsior Springs is a Kansas City suburb; certainly, enough people commute the 25 miles to work downtown. But the charming burg looks more like it was plucked out of the 1940s and dropped intact into the heartland. Soaring elm and oak trees cover the steep hills that surround the town; quaint storefronts line the narrow streets.

In the actual 1940s, people such as Franklin D. Roosevelt and Harry Truman used to venture to Excelsior Springs for the **healing waters.** Siloam Springs, which bubbles up from under the mountain of the same name, is the only natural source of iron-manganese water in the United States. In fact, five specific mineral waters are found here, more than in any other location in North America or Europe.

Although the mineral waters had long been revered by American Indians for their medicinal qualities, Excelsior Springs' town fathers discovered them shortly after they incorporated their city in 1880. In 1888, the **Elms Hotel** opened its doors and quickly became the place for healthful soaking. In fact, Truman was lapping up the Elms' healing powers himself the night he was elected president in 1948.

Golfers will want to try the Excelsior Springs Golf Club, an old English-style club built in 1915, which makes it one of the oldest courses in the region. Set on Excelsior Springs' eastern boundary—next to the Municipal Airport in Ray County—the 18-hole course offers a full-service pro shop and a clubhouse that was built around an original 1825 log cabin. For more information, call 816/637-3731.

During the past decade or so, the hotel has changed hands several times, becoming dowdier and dowdier in the process. Yet another new owner took over in mid-1996, and has promised renovation; in the meantime, the hotel's pools, spas, and themed water rooms remain an unusual and relaxing attraction (Regent and Elms Boulevard; 816/630-2141).

As an adjunct to the Elms, the historic **Hall of Waters** was built in 1937 to be the finest and most complete health resort in America. Inside, you'll find a swimming pool, water-bottling facility, and the world's longest water bar. You can still get a massage, salt rub, or hot mineral water bath and steam in the cavernous art deco building now on the National Historic Register (201 E. Broadway; Mon–Fri 8–5; free admission to the building, fees for spa services).

Four miles north of Excelsior Springs on Highway 69, you'll come to **Watkins Mill State Park,** one of the largest state parks in Missouri. Within this 1,000-acre area are walking and biking trails, fishing, swimming, camping, picnic shelters, and the 100-acre Williams Creek Lake. The park also includes **Watkins Woolen Mill State Historic Site,** the country's only nineteenth-century textile factory with its original machinery still intact. Built by Waltus Watkins in 1861, the three-story mill and factory spun wool into yarn, then turned it into cloth and blankets. Watkins opened at the right time; he did a booming business during the Civil War. Next door, you can visit **Watkins' elegant home,** built in 1850, as well as the **Mt. Vernon Church** (1871), and **Franklin School** (1856). Tours Mon–Sat 10–4; winter, Sun 11–4; summer, Sun noon–6.

Getting there: *Go north on I-35; take Highway 69 and exit at Excelsior Springs.*

Day Trip: Weston

Distance from Kansas City: approximately 45 minutes; 40 miles

Back in 1837, Weston's first settlers discovered that the rich black soil bordering the Missouri River was perfect for growing the hemp and tobacco from their native Virginia, Kentucky, and Tennessee. By 1853, Weston was the second largest port in Missouri; steamboats plied the waters, carrying the town's two big moneymakers to market. Today, you can still see evidence of Weston's booming days. More than 100 **antebellum buildings and homes** have been preserved within a 22-block area in and around downtown Weston, now designated a National Historic District.

But Weston wasn't frozen in time. In fact, the **downtown area** has become a haven for artists, antiques dealers, retailers, and restaurateurs, who've filled the four-block stretch with plentiful places to prowl. The **Missouri Bluffs Boutique and Gallery,** for example, features an eclectic mix of apparel and accessories. Nearby, The **Avalon Cafe** is set in an antebellum home once called White Lace. **O'Malley's Pub** serves its Irish libations in the limestone cellars of the old **Weston Brewing Company,** which is once again producing suds; **Pirtle's Winery** has a tasting room and shop in a cavernous 1867 German church; and **The McCormick Country Store,** an outlet for **McCormick Distilling Co.,** pays tribute to Weston resident Benjamin J. Holladay, who learned that the natural limestone spring water flowing through the area was the secret to creating fine whiskey. Up on a slight hill, chef Cheryl Mock creates a cozy, fine-dining experience in an 1845 home called **The Vineyards.**

For those who want to learn more about Weston's past, the **Weston Historical Museum** displays artifacts and photos from Weston's glory days in the mid-nineteenth century (601 Main St., Tue–Sat 1–4; Sun 1–5:30; free). The **Herbert Bonnell Museum** depicts life in the late 1800s, including a farmhouse, outbuildings, and tools (May–Oct weekends 1–5; free).

One of the best antebellum homes open to the public once belonged to Col. James A. Price and his wife, Russella Warner Price. Russella was the great-granddaughter of Daniel Boone, while husband James was Robert E. Lee's cousin. Built in 1857, the home was occupied until the couple's last descendant passed away in 1991; the **Price-Loyles House** still contains nearly everything the family owned through five generations (718 Spring St., Wed–Sat 10–5; tours available other times).

Midwest Living magazine named Weston one of the best towns in the Midwest in which to hunt for quality antiques. Start your search on Main Street at Tobacco Road Antiques, Bo Jingles, or The Painted Lady. The Old Brewery Antiques Mall (500 Welt St.) is one block east of Main, behind City Hall.

One mile south of Weston on Highway 45, **Weston Bend State Park** comprises 1,133 acres of wooded hillsides, walking and biking trails, camping, and picnic areas. Adjacent to the Missouri River, these native lands are where the Sac, Fox, and Kansa Indians once hunted game. The old Leavenworth Road at the rear of the park provides panoramic views of the Missouri River.

Getting there: Take I-29 north, then go west on Highway 45.

Day Trip: St. Joseph

Distance from Kansas City: approximately 1 hour; 60 miles

St. Joseph dates from 1826 when Joseph Robidoux established an Indian trading post on these bluffs overlooking the Missouri River. The town grew into a major trade center; in 1843, the Frenchman incorporated the town and named it after his patron saint, St. Joseph. You can see where the town's founder lived by visiting the restored homes at the **Robidoux Row Museum** (3rd and Poulin; May–Sept Tue–Fri 10–4; weekends 1–4).

St. Joseph's ties are surely with the West: the town outfitted thousands of Forty-niners when gold was discovered in California. But St. Joseph's most famous link westward came just prior to the Civil War, when the Pony Express was born. Indeed, history buffs will want to check out St. Joseph's **Pony Express National Memorial,** the birthplace of the famous delivery service and one of 13 museums within the city. The memorial honors the company's founders and the hardy riders (led by Johnny Fry and his pony, Sylph), who saddled up and lit out for Sacramento—nearly 2,000 miles west—on April 3, 1860 (914 Penn St., Mon–Sat 9–5; Sun 1–5; open an hour later June–Sept).

Coincidentally, that same date 22 years later marks the central event of another St. Joseph landmark. It was April 3, 1882, when Bob Ford gunned down his fellow gang member, the infamous Jesse James, in what's now known as the **Jesse James Home Museum** (12th and Penn Streets, Mon–Sat 10–4; Sun 1–4; one hour later June–Aug). Other museums also capture pieces of St. Joseph's past. An internationally famous Native American collection appears at the **St. Joseph Museum** (1100 Charles; Mon–Sat 9–5; Sun 1–5); the **Knea-Von Black Archive** features two floors of local and national black history exhibits, from a simulated underground railroad to a 1920s kitchen (1901 Messanie, Mon–Fri 10–5).

St. Joseph also offers wonders of the art world, thanks to 12 women with a passion for art who founded the St. Joseph Art League in 1913. Today, the

TRIVIA

The Kemper name in St. Joseph's Albrecht-Kemper Museum and in Kansas City's Kemper Museum of Contemporary of Art indeed refer to the same family. Along with his family's foundations, R. Crosby Kemper, head of Kansas City's United Missouri Bank, is a huge arts patron who has directed millions to the arts in both communities.

Like Kansas Citians, St. Joseph residents approved riverboat gambling several years ago. And in the same fashion as its neighbors down river, the St. Jo Frontier Casino doesn't actually ply the Missouri. Instead, gamblers stand nearly solid-ground steady before the blackjack, craps, video poker, and slot machines on board. Open daily; "cruise" times vary.

Albrecht-Kemper Museum of Art, boasting a new 21,000-square-foot wing, houses one of the Midwest's most diverse collections of eighteenth-, nineteenth-, and twentieth-century American art. Visitors can see colonial portraiture, Albert Bierstadt's rugged landscapes, and the paintings of George Caleb Bingham (2818 Frederick; Tue–Sat 10–4; Sun 1–4).

Shoppers head to St. Joe for the plethora of antiques stores, including the **Robidoux Landing Antique Mall** (720 Felix) and the **Penn Street Square** (122 Penn). **Howard's Church Artisan's Studios & Gallery** was an 1880 church where Jesse James once attended services; the renovated house of worship now provides a venue for the area's fine artists to create, display, and sell their work (12th and Penn). And the **Stetson Hat Factory Outlet** (3601 S. Leonard Rd.) lets shoppers buy its famous headgear at direct-from-the-manufacturer prices.

Getting there: Take I-29 north, then follow signs to downtown.

IMPORTANT PHONE NUMBERS

EMERGENCY
Police, 911
Fire Department, 911
Ambulance, 911

MAJOR HOSPITALS
Baptist Medical Center, 816/276-7000
Children's Mercy Hospital, 816/234-3430
Independence Regional Health Center, 816/836-8100
Liberty Hospital, 816/781-7200
Menorah Medical Park, 913/345-3600
Overland Park Regional Medical Center, 913/541-5000
Shawnee Mission Medical Center, 913/676-2000
St. Luke's Hospitals, 816/932-6200
University of Kansas Medical Center, 913/588-5000

EMERGENCY MEDICAL CARE
Ask a Nurse, 913/676-7777
Kansas City Free Health Clinic, 816/753-5144
Truman Medical Center East (Lee's Summit), 816/373-4415
Urgent Care Center Midtown, 816/753-5454
Walk-in Health Care of Olathe, 913/780-0030

VISITOR INFORMATION

Convention & Visitors Bureau of Greater Kansas City, 816/221-5242
Brochures, maps, and other information available from the Downtown Information Center in the City Center Square (1100 Main, Suite 2550) Mon–Fri 8:30–5 and from the Plaza Visitor Information Center at the Clock Tower (222 W. 47th St., across from FAO Schwarz). Recorded information on events and activities: 816/691-3800.

Kansas City, Kansas, Convention & Visitors Bureau, 913/321-5800

Overland Park, Kansas, Convention & Visitors Bureau, 913/491-0123

Kansas City Internet Addresses
http://www.kansascity.com
http://www.experiencekc.com

CITY TOURS

SHOW-ME KC GRAYLINE TOURS
913/268-5252
Seasonal tours during warmer weather; $10 Kansas City only; $15 including Independence. Call for times and availability.

KANSAS CITY TROLLEY
816/221-3399
Major stops between downtown and the Plaza every 30 minutes, Mon–Sat 10–6; Sun noon–6. Adults $4; seniors 65 and up and children 6–12 $3.

CAR RENTAL

AVIS
Three locations in the metro area, including Kansas City International Airport, 800/331-1212

BUDGET RENT-A-CAR
Six locations in the metro area, including Kansas City International Airport, 800/527-0700

ENTERPRISE RENT-A-CAR
Twenty-six locations throughout the metro area, including Kansas City International Airport, 800/325-8007

HERTZ
One location in the metro area, at Kansas City International Airport, 800/654-3131

THRIFTY
Three locations in the metro area, including Kansas City International Airport, 800/367-2277

CITY MEDIA

DAILY NEWSPAPER
Kansas City Star

BUSINESS NEWSPAPERS
College Boulevard News
Johnson County Business Times
Kansas City Business Journal
Kansas City Small Business Monthly

WEEKLY/COMMUNITY
Kansas City Kansan
Sun Newspapers

ENTERTAINMENT/ALTERNATIVE NEWSPAPERS
New Times
Pitch Weekly

ETHNIC NEWSPAPERS
Dos Mundos (Latino)
Kansas City Call (African American)
Kansas City Jewish Chronicle

MAGAZINES
Ingram's
Kansas City Magazine

COMMERCIAL TELEVISION STATIONS
KCPT Channel 19 (PBS)

KCTV-5 (CBS)
KMBC TV-9 (ABC)
KSHB TV/Channel 41 (NBC)
KSMO TV-62 (Ind.)
WDAF Channel 4 (Fox)

RADIO STATIONS
KPRS 103.3 FM/soft rock/r&b
KPRT 1590 AM/soft rock
KBEQ 104 FM/country
KCCV 760 AM/Christian
KCMO 95 FM/oldies
KCMO 810 AM/talk
KISS 107.3 FM/rock
KLTH 99.7 FM/light
KMBZ 980 AM/news
KUDL 98 FM/soft rock
KXTR 96.5 FM/classical
KYYS 102 FM/rock

BABYSITTING

Most major hotels can arrange for reputable babysitting services in your hotel room. In addition, the following companies provide child care at your location:

A-1 TINY TOTS PRE-SCHOOL & SITTER SERVICE
2534 Queen Ridge
Independence, MO 64055
816/461-8636

TLC CHILD CARE SERVICES
8080 Ward Pkwy.
Kansas City, MO 64114
816/444-6400

BOOKSELLERS

ANDERSON'S BOOKSHOPS
5429 Center Mall, Kansas City
816/454-7677

B. DALTON BOOKSELLERS

Oak Park Mall: 11391 West 95th St., Overland Park, KS, 913/888-1416
Bannister Mall: 5600 East Bannister Rd., Kansas City, 816/966-0014
Metro North Mall: 400 Northwest Barry Rd., Kansas City, 816/ 436-5250
Independence Center: 2020 Independence Center, Independence, 816/795-8210
Ward Parkway Mall: 8600 Ward Pkwy., Kansas City, 816/333-2047
Prairie Village: 3925 W. 69th Terrace, Prairie Village, KS, 913/362-6772

BARNES & NOBLE BOOKSELLERS

420 W. 47th St., Kansas City 816/753-1313
4751 W. 117th St., Leawood, KS 913/491-4535
19120 E 39th St., Independence 816/795-9878

BOOKSHOP AT BROOKSIDE

116 W. 63rd St., Kansas City 816/444-8187

BORDERS BOOKS & MUSIC

9108 Metcalf Ave., Overland Park, KS 913/642-3642
12055 Metcalf Ave., Overland Park, KS 913/663-2356

BRENTANOS

4715 Johnson Dr., Mission, KS 913/384-5236

THE COMPLETE TRAVELER

7321 W. 80th St., Overland Park, KS, 913/648-1560

KANSAS UNION BOOKSTORE

University of Kansas
Kansas Union, Level 2,
Lawrence, KS
913/864-4640

RAINY DAY BOOKS

2812 W. 53rd St., Kansas City, KS 913/384-3126

RAVEN BOOKSTORE

8 E. 7th St., Lawrence, KS 913/749-3300

THE READING REPTILE BOOKS AND TOYS FOR YOUNG MAMMALS

4120 Pennsylvania Ave., Kansas City 816/753-0441

WALDENBOOKS

Bannister Mall: 5600 East Bannister Rd., Kansas City, 816/761-6755
Metcalf South: 9641 Metcalf Ave., Overland Park, KS, 913-642-2755
Crown Center: 2450 Grand Ave., Kansas City, 816/474-8774
Independence Center: 1042 Independence Center, Independence, 816/795-8077
Oak Park Mall: 11689 W. 95th St., Overland Park, KS, 913-888-3367
Metro North: 400 Northwest Barry Rd., Kansas City, 816/436-5566
Ward Parkway SC: 8600 Ward Pkwy., Kansas City, 816/523-4580
Blue Ridge Mall: 4200 Blue Ridge Blvd., Kansas City, 816/737-2584

WALDENBOOKS & MORE

7311 Quiviera, Shawnee, KS 913/962-1428

WHISTLER'S OF WESTPORT

427 Westport Rd., Kansas City 816/531-5959

DISABLED ACCESS INFORMATION

ACCESSIBLE ARTS

1100 State Ave.
Kansas City, KS 66102
913/281-1133

MULTICULTURAL RESOURCES

BLACK CHAMBER OF COMMERCE OF GREATER KANSAS CITY
1601 E. 18th St.
Kansas City, MO 64108
816/474-9901

GAY/LESBIAN INFORMATION
6300 Main St.
Kansas City, MO 64113
816/737-0700

HISPANIC CHAMBER OF COMMERCE OF GREATER KANSAS CITY
6601 Stadium Dr.
Kansas City, MO 64129
816/221-5772

KANSAS CITY MINORITY SUPPLIERS DEVELOPMENT COUNCIL
3017 Main St.
Kansas City, MO 64108
816/931-9672

MID-AMERICA ARTS ALLIANCE
912 Baltimore
Kansas City, MO 64106
816/421-1388

POST OFFICES

Post offices are located throughout the metro area. The main post offices in the major areas include:

KANSAS CITY, MISSOURI, POST OFFICE
315 W. Pershing
Kansas City, MO 64108
816/374-9180

KANSAS CITY, KANSAS, POST OFFICE
5215 Richland Ave.
Kansas City, KS 66106
913/321-0482

SHAWNEE MISSION POST OFFICE
6029 Broadmoor
Mission, KS 66202
913/831-5350

INDEPENDENCE POST OFFICE
301 W. Lexington
Independence, MO 64050
816/836-1440

PUBLIC HOLIDAYS

New Year's Day, President's Day, Memorial Day, Independence Day, Labor Day, Thanksgiving, Christmas

TIME AND TEMPERATURE

816/844-1212

INDEX

Titles from John Muir Publications

Rick Steves' Books

Asia Through the Back Door, $17.95
Europe 101: History and Art for the
Traveler, $17.95
Mona Winks: Self-Guided Tours of
Europe's Top Museums, $18.95
Rick Steves' Baltics & Russia, $9.95
Rick Steves' Europe, $18.95
Rick Steves' France, Belgium & the
Netherlands, $15.95
Rick Steves' Germany, Austria &
Switzerland, $14.95
Rick Steves' Great Britain & Ireland,
$15.95
Rick Steves' Italy, $13.95
Rick Steves' Scandinavia, $13.95
Rick Steves' Spain & Portugal, $13.95
Rick Steves' Europe Through the Back
Door, $19.95
Rick Steves' French Phrase Book,
$5.95
Rick Steves' German Phrase Book,
$5.95
Rick Steves' Italian Phrase Book, $5.95
Rick Steves' Spanish & Portuguese
Phrase Book, $7.95
Rick Steves' French/ German/Italian
Phrase Book, $7.95

City·Smart™ Guidebooks

All are $14.95 paperback.
City·Smart Guidebook: Cleveland
City·Smart Guidebook: Denver
City·Smart Guidebook: Kansas City
City·Smart Guidebook: Minneapolis/
St. Paul
City·Smart Guidebook: Nashville
City·Smart Guidebook: Portland
City·Smart Guidebook: Tampa/St.
Petersburg

Unique Travel Series

All are $10.95 paperback, except as noted.
Unique Arizona
Unique California
Unique Colorado
Unique Florida
Unique Georgia ($11.95)
Unique New England
Unique New Mexico
Unique Oregon ($9.95)
Unique Texas
Unique Washington

Travel✦Smart™ Trip Planners

American Southwest Travel✦Smart Trip
Planner, $14.95
Colorado Travel✦Smart Trip Planner,
$14.95
Eastern Canada Travel✦Smart Trip
Planner, $15.95
Florida Gulf Coast Travel✦Smart Trip
Planner, $14.95
Hawaii Travel✦Smart Trip Planner,
$14.95
Kentucky/Tennessee Travel✦Smart Trip
Planner, $14.95
Michigan Travel✦Smart Trip Planner,
$14.95
Minnesota/Wisconsin Travel✦Smart
Trip Planner, $14.95
New England Travel✦Smart Trip
Planner, $14.95
Northern California Travel✦Smart Trip
Planner, $15.95
Pacific Northwest Travel✦Smart Trip
Planner, $14.95

A Natural Destination Series

Belize: A Natural Destination, $16.95
Costa Rica: A Natural Destination,
$18.95
Guatemala: A Natural Destination,
$16.95

Other Terrific Travel Titles

The 100 Best Small Art Towns in
America, $15.95
The Big Book of Adventure Travel,
$17.95
The Birder's Guide to Bed and
Breakfasts: U.S. and Canada, $17.95
Indian America, $18.95
The People's Guide to Mexico, $19.95
Ranch Vacations, $22.95
Understanding Europeans, $14.95
Watch It Made in the U.S.A., $16.95
The World Awaits, $16.95

Automotive Titles

The Greaseless Guide to Car Care,
$19.95
How to Keep Your Subaru Alive, $21.95
How to Keep Your Toyota Pick-Up Alive,
$21.95
How to Keep Your VW Alive, $25.00

ABOUT THE AUTHORS

Michael J. Flynn and **Linda Kephart Flynn** are a Kansas City–based writing and editing team whose work has appeared in publications such as *Hemispheres*, *Endless Vacation*, *Modern Bride*, and the *San Francisco Chronicle*. Both are contributing editors at *Ingram's*, a Kansas City business magazine, and have been co-editors of *Kansas City Bride & Groom* and *Vanguard Discoveries*, a Kansas City–based in-flight magazine. Michael was born and raised in the Kansas City area and met Linda, an Arizona native, when they were editors at *Discover Hawaii* magazine in Honolulu. They now live and work in a three-story, 85-year-old house just south of Country Club Plaza.

The Bluebird at City Garden

1700 Summit, Kansas City, MO 64108
816-221-7559

free dessert!

One free dessert with each lunch purchase.

CiTY·SMART GUIDEBOOK **Kansas City**

Anthony's Restaurant

701 Grand Avenue, Kansas City, MO 64106
816-221-4088

$5.00 value!

Present this coupon for $5.00 off dinner.

CiTY·SMART GUIDEBOOK **Kansas City**

Club 427

427 Main Street, Kansas City, MO 64105
816-421-2582

$9.00 value!

One free appetizer with any dinner entree ($9.00 value)

CiTY·SMART GUIDEBOOK **Kansas City**

Winslow's City Market Smokehouse

20 E. 5th Street, Kansas City, MO 64106
816-471-7427

two FOR THE PRICE OF **one!**

Buy one entree, get a second entree free. (Not including ribs.)

CiTY·SMART GUIDEBOOK **Kansas City**

CiTY·SMART™
GUIDEBOOK
Kansas City

John Muir Publications • Santa Fe, New Mexico

CiTY·SMART™
GUIDEBOOK
Kansas City

John Muir Publications • Santa Fe, New Mexico

CiTY·SMART™
GUIDEBOOK
Kansas City

John Muir Publications • Santa Fe, New Mexico

CiTY·SMART™
GUIDEBOOK
Kansas City

John Muir Publications • Santa Fe, New Mexico